2001 Revised Edition
2001 年修订本

经贸中级汉语口语
BUSINESS CHINESE（INTERMEDIATE）

上　册
BOOK ONE

黄为之　编著

华语教学出版社
SINOLINGUA

First Edition 2001

ISBN 7-80052-538-4
Copyright 2001 by Sinolingua
Published by Sinolingua
24 Baiwanzhuang Road, Beijing 100037, China
Tel: 86-10-68326333/68996153
Fax:86-10-68994599
E-mail: sinolingua@ihw. com. cn

Printed by Beijing Foreign Languages Printing House
Distributed by China International
Book Trading Corporation
35 Chegongzhuang Xilu, P. O. Box 399
Beijing 100044, China

Printed in the People's Republic of China

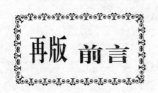

再版 前言

《经贸中级汉语口语》1992 年出版后,受到社会各界的热烈欢迎,被各院校和自学者广泛采用。出版至今,中国的经济贸易形势发生了很大变化,有许多新的内容、新的语言需要学习;在教学实践中,我们也积累了经验,听取了各方面的意见,觉得对这本口语教材,现在进行修订、再版,是适时的。

2001 年新版《经贸中级汉语口语》,在保持初版体例和优点的基础上,作了全面修改。全书从原来的 20 课增加到 40 课,由一册分为上、下册,原有的内容作了调整,增加了经贸领域出现的新话题、新词语。上册以货物贸易为主要内容,以贸易洽谈为中心,增加了"信用管理"、"网上贸易"等新的国际贸易运作方式;下册以"大经贸"为主要内容,从"全方位开放格局"的角度,展现经济贸易的各个领域,专业内容和专业语言,更加适应当代中国和国际经济贸易实务。我们相信,这个新版本,会在更高的水准上满足教师和学习者的需要。

2001 年新版《经贸中级汉语口语》的英语翻译是黄震华教授。

对外经济贸易大学
黄为之
2000 年 2 月

Preface
to the 2001 Edition

Since its publication in 1992, *Business Chinese* (Intermediate) has been well received by people from all walks of life and adopted by many universities, schools and self-taught learners. Since its publication, China's situation of economy and trade has undergone great changes, providing many new contents and expressions worth learning. We have also accumulated experiences in our teaching practice and listened to comments from different sources. We feel now it is the right time to revise the book and publish the revised edition.

While maintaining the format and the merits of the first edition, the revised 2001 edition of *Business Chinese* (Intermediate) is the outcome of a comprehensive revision. The book has been extended from 20 lessons to 40 lessons, and is now divided into two books. The original contents have been adjusted, with new topics and new expressions in the realm of economy and trade added. Book One mainly deals with trade in goods, with business negotiation at its center, with new modes of business operation such as "credit management" and "business on the net" added. Book Two takes "broadly based economy and trade" as the main content. From the angle of "the setup of all-round opening", it unfolds the various fields of economy and trade and their specific substance and language, thus being better suited to the contemporary economic and trade practice in China and all over the world. We believe that this new edition will, at a higher level, meet the needs of teachers and learners.

The English translation of *Business Chinese* (Intermediate) is done by Professor Huang Zhenhua.

Huang Weizhi
University of International
Business and Economics
February, 2000

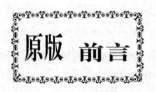

原版 前言

　　伴随中国对外开放的进程，外国人同中国的经济合作与贸易往来，出现了空前未有的高涨热潮。这种高涨的"经贸热"，使大有燎原之势的"世界汉语热"变得更加红火炽热。世界各国的贸易客商，想在华做生意，恨不能三日、五日，十天、半月就学好汉语。为了适应这种"经贸热"，满足外国朋友学习经贸汉语的要求，我编写了这本教材。

　　这本《经贸中级汉语口语》，是供具有初级汉语水平的外国朋友使用的专业汉语教材，共 20 课，1016 个生词。内容涉及到外国人在中国做生意的各个方面，从建立联系渠道，到洽谈的各个环节，乃至近十年来，在中国大地上兴起的"三资"企业、经济特区、开放城市、乡镇企业、农贸集市以及中国的改革开放政策等等。这些内容，反映了中国实行改革开放以来，对外经济贸易方面的新形势，新课题，新词语。每一课由课文、生词、练习三部分组成。课文都用对话体，是标准的普通话；生词有汉语拼音和英文注释；练习分 A、B 两大组。A 组是重点词语的例解和练习；B 组以灵活运用新课文的语言知识为主，适当重现旧课文的语言知识。在 B 组还有一篇短文，内容风趣，语言生动，为学员提供了当今中国广泛的风俗民情；外国友人在中国做生意，稔熟这些风俗民情也是必不可少的。考虑到经贸中级汉语专业性强,语言难度大,我们特别把 20 课课文全部译成英文,附在全书之后,这样可减少学习中的困难,帮助外国朋友更准确地理解和运用汉语。书后附有生词总表。

现在常用的对外汉语教材,每一课都由包括"注释"或"词语例释"在内的四部分组成,本书没有完全采用这种体例,省去了"注释"或"例释"部分。我是这样考虑的:凡是需要学生掌握的,就不仅要让学生弄懂,更要让学生会用;所以在"注释"或"例释"之后,应该紧紧伴随适量而有效的练习;如果不要学生掌握,只为理解生词或课文,则只需查查字典或课上点明即可,不需有详尽繁琐的"注释"、"例释",这样,学生可省去许多精力。

本书由对外经济贸易大学对外贸易理论教授孙玉宗先生审阅全部课文,保证了本书经贸专业知识的科学性;由对外经济贸易大学外贸英语系主任黄震华教授负责全书的英文注释和翻译,黄教授在英译过程中,还对本书的内容提过许多宝贵的修改意见;英籍专家 Angela O′Connell 女士校阅过全部英文译文;对外经济贸易大学校长孙维炎教授最后审定了全书。国家对外汉语教学领导小组办公室诸位领导同志,给本书的编写、出版给予了指导和帮助;我校校领导、出版社和外事处的同志们,都给这本书的出版以大力支持。在此,一并表示由衷的感谢。

黄为之
1991 年 5 月

Preface
to the First Edition

Along with China's opening to the rest of the world, there has emerged an unprecedented upsurge among foreigners in developing economic cooperation and trade relations with China. This growing "heat in economic relations and trade" has added to the "world's desire to learn Chinese", which has spread like wild fire. In order to do business in China, many businessmen from all over the world wish that they could learn Chinese in three, five, ten or fifteen days. Faced with this "heat in economic relations and trade", we have compiled this textbook so as to meet the desire of foreign friends to learn business Chinese.

This book, *Business Chinese* (Intermediate), is a textbook of Chinese for specific purposes, which is meant for those who have already acquired elementary Chinese. It consists of 20 texts, with 1016 new words and expressions in all. Its contents cover all aspects that concern a foreigner doing business in China, from the channels of establishing relations to all the links in the chain of business negotiations. It also introduces such phenomena as the foreign-funded enterprises, special economic zones, open cities, town and township enterprises, markets for farm and sideline products, and China's reform and open policy, which have emerged in China during the past 10 years and more. These contents reflect the new situations, new topics and new expressions used in foreign economic relations and trade since the adoption of the policy of reform and opening to the rest of the world. Each lesson comprises a text, new words and exercises, three parts in all. All the texts are in dialogue form, read with standard Chinese pronunciation. The new words are introduced with *pinyin* and English explanations. Exercises fall into Sections A and B. Section A consists of exemplifications and exercises on key words and expressions, while Section B is mainly for the purpose of flexible utilization of the linguistic knowledge learned from the new lesson, and also for the recycling of what was learned in previous lessons. Also included in Section B is a short article which is lively and humourous. These short articles provide the learners with broad knowledge about present customs and conditions of the Chinese people. Getting familiar with these customs and conditions is also indispensable for foreign friends to do business in China. Considering that a textbook of business Chinese at the intermediate level is rather specialized with a fair amount of difficult language, we have translated all the 20 texts into English and attached them at the back of the book as an appendix. We hope that this will help to reduce the difficulties in learning, and to develop a more accurate understanding of, and a higher level of proficiency in, the Chinese language. A vocabulary list is provided at the back of the book.

The usual format of a Chinese textbook for foreign learners is that each lesson consists of four parts including a part called notes or

7

exemplifications. We have not exactly followed this format, but have omitted the notes and examples. Our reasons are as follows: For the points that the learners should have a good command of, a mere understanding on their part is inadequate. We must ensure that they can use them competently. Therefore, the notes or exemplifications must be followed by the right amount of effective exercises. However, for those points that the learners do not have to master, the learners only need to look them up in the dictionary for the sake of understanding the text or the new words, or else a brief mention in the classroom teaching will be sufficient. There is no need to include detailed notes and exemplifications for these points, and thus a large amount of the learners' energy can be saved.

Professor Sun Yuzong, a professor of foreign trade theories at our University, went over the manuscript so as to ensure that the knowledge embodied in this book about foreign economic relations and trade is correct. Professor Huang Zhenhua, Dean of the Faculty of International Business Communications of our University, did the English translation for all the texts and explanations. In the course of translation, he also suggested many valuable amendments to the contents of the book. Ms Angela O' Connell, a British expert working at our University, went over the English translation. And finally Professor Sun Weiyan, President of our University, went over the manuscript of the whole book. Leading members from the office of the Leading Group for the Teaching of Chinese to Foreign Learners have provided concrete guidance and financial support for the compilation and publication of the present book. Leading members from our University, and comrades from our University Press and Foreign Affairs Office have also given substantial support to this book. I hereby extend my heartfelt thanks to all those who have made contributions to the compilation and publication of the present book.

Huang Weizhi

May, 1991

目录
Contents

第一课　建立联系
Lesson 1　Establishing Relationship

一、初次见面

李　宁：请问，哪位是从美国纽约来的罗斯先生？

罗　斯：我就是。您是——

李　宁：我是中国纺织品进出口总公司的代表，我姓李，叫李宁，公司派我来接待贵团。

罗　斯：认识您非常高兴。

李　宁：我也是。罗斯先生一路顺利吗？

罗　斯：很幸运，一路顺风。

李　宁：太好了。公司汽车在外面，请跟我来。

罗　斯：好，您先请。我第一次来中国，请李先生多多关照。

李　宁：不客气，您是我们的客人，希望您在华期间工作顺利，生活愉快。

罗　斯：谢谢，再次谢谢。

李　宁：罗斯先生，请允许我向您介绍，这位是中国纺织品进出口总公司的业务员，公司委派他跟你们具体洽谈业务。

王　安：罗斯先生您好，我姓王，叫王安，见到您我很高兴。欢迎您来中国，希望我们合作愉快。

罗　斯：您好，王先生，这是我的名片。请允许我向您介绍代表团成员：这位是我的助手杰克逊先生，这位是秘书布朗小姐，其他几位都是工作人员。布朗小姐将同你们保持密切联系。我相信，我们的合作将不仅是愉快的，而且是成功的。

二、询问如何建立商业联系

罗　斯：张总经理，请问外国公司如何与中国建立商业联系？

张　祥：罗斯先生，您是怎么开始的？

罗　斯：通过一个朋友介绍，结识了一位访美的中国经贸部负责人，经他推荐，我写了一封信并附上我需要订购的商品目录，寄给天津市外贸局，天津外贸局给我发来邀请信，我就这样来中国了。

张　祥：罗斯先生投石问路，做对了。不过，可以用更简便的办法。你只要到中国驻外商务机构，比如官方的商务处，民间的各大公司、子公司，海外代理处等，要一份中国各专业公司的介绍，按您的需要，给某公司写信，他们就会与您联系的。

罗　斯：我应该向贵方提供哪些资料呢？

张　祥：介绍一下贵公司的经营范围，附上希望订购或推销的产品目录。

罗　斯：噢，我明白了。这样建立联系，是简便多了。

三、建立商业联系的渠道

罗　斯：张总经理,同中方建立商业联系都有哪些渠道?

张　祥：啊,很多。除了上次给你介绍的以外,还有我们在国外举办的各种展销会、博览会,在国内举办的广交会和各省、市的地方交易会。

罗　斯：广交会? 我听说过,是在广州吗?

张　祥：是。那是一个综合性的大型交易会,全国各外贸公司都积极参展,国外的客商也纷纷前来参观和洽谈业务。

杰克逊：有了广交会,各省、市为什么还要举办交易会呢?

李　宁：各地经济都有自己的优势,举办地方或区域性交易会,也很有特色。

杰克逊：是这样。

张　祥：近几年,我们还常在国内外举行大型招商洽谈会,这是一个新的渠道。

罗　斯：这个渠道很好,我们怎么才能参加这样的招商洽谈会呢?

张　祥：我们可以为你们牵线搭桥。

罗　斯：那太好了! 真是条条道路通北京,谢谢张总的介绍。

张　祥：不必客气,很高兴为你们介绍中国的情况,欢迎你们来中国做生意。

生词

1. 纺织品　　fǎngzhīpǐn　　textile(s)
2. 总公司　　zǒnggōngsī　　head office (of a corpora-

tion)

3.	顺风	shùnfēng	favorable wind, pleasant journey
4.	关照	guānzhào	look after, help
5.	希望	xīwàng	hope
6.	期间	qījiān	time, period
7.	允许	yǔnxǔ	allow
8.	委派	wěipài	entrust, designate
9.	具体	jùtǐ	concrete
10.	代表团	dàibiǎotuán	delegation
11.	成员	chéngyuán	member
12.	助手	zhùshǒu	assistant
13.	保持	bǎochí	keep, maintain
14.	密切	mìqiè	close, intimate
15.	询问	xúnwèn	inquire
16.	结识	jiéshí	get to know
17.	推荐	tuījiàn	recommend; recommendation
18.	附上	fùshàng	enclose
19.	需要	xūyào	need, require
20.	订购	dìnggòu	order, place an order
21.	目录	mùlù	catalog, list
22.	局	jú	bureau
23.	投石问路	tóushíwènlù	(throw a stone) to explore the way
24.	简便	jiǎnbiàn	simple and convenient, handy
25.	驻	zhù	be stationed
26.	商务	shāngwù	commercial (affairs)

27.	机构	jīgòu	setup, organization
28.	官方	guānfāng	official
29.	处	chù	department, office
30.	民间	mínjiān	non-governmental
31.	子公司	zǐgōngsī	subsidiary
32.	专业	zhuānyè	specialized
33.	资料	zīliào	data, material
34.	范围	fànwéi	scope
35.	渠道	qúdào	channel
36.	举办	jǔbàn	hold
37.	博览会	bólǎnhuì	fair, exposition
38.	省	shěng	province
39.	市	shì	municipality, city
40.	地方	dìfāng	place, local
41.	综合性	zōnghéxìng	comprehensive
42.	交易会	jiāoyìhuì	trade fair
43.	大型	dàxíng	large-scale
44.	积极	jījí	active
45.	参加	cānjiā	attend, participate in
46.	纷纷	fēnfēn	in large numbers, one after another
47.	区域	qūyù	region
48.	招商	zhāoshāng	invite outside investment
49.	牵线搭桥	qiānxiàndāqiáo	pull strings and build bridges; bring…into contact with…
50.	道路	dàolù	road

专名

纽约	Niǔyuē	New York
罗斯	Luósī	Ross
杰克逊	Jiékèxùn	Jackson
布朗	Bùlǎng	Brown
经贸部（对外贸易经济合作部）	Jīngmào Bù (Duìwài Màoyì Jīngjì Hézuò Bù)	Ministry of Foreign Trade and Economic Cooperation
天津	Tiānjīn	Tianjin
广交会（中国广州出口商品交易会）	Guǎngjiāohuì (Zhōngguó Guǎngzhōu Chūkǒu Shāngpǐn Jiāoyì Huì)	Guangzhou Fair (The Chinese Export Commodities Fair held in Guangzhou)

练习

A

一路：

有多种含义：①在整个的行程中，沿路；②同一类；③一起（来、去、走）。

It has many meanings: 1) throughout the journey; all the way; 2) of the same kind; 3) go the same way; take the same route.

一、熟读下列各句,体会"一路"的意义和用法:

1. 祝你一路平安。
2. 这次我来中国,和张先生一路。
3. 张先生喜欢静,张太太喜欢动,俩人不一路,玩不到一块。
4. 这次我和你一路同来,买的又是一路货,互相关照,真幸运。

二、请用"一路"扩展句子:

1. 由张总经理推荐,我＿＿＿＿＿＿＿＿＿＿＿＿＿＿＿＿＿＿。
2. 我第一次来中国,希望＿＿＿＿＿＿＿＿＿＿＿＿＿＿＿＿＿。
3. 真没想到＿＿＿＿＿＿＿＿＿＿＿＿＿＿＿＿＿＿＿＿＿＿。
4. 今天开车真顺利,＿＿＿＿＿＿＿＿＿＿＿＿＿＿＿＿＿＿。

一下:

① 表示某动作发生、完成得迅速,或某种现象出现得突然,有"很快"和时间短的意思;② 用在动词后,表示做一次或试着做。

1) In a short while; all at once; all of a sudden. It is used to indicate the speed, suddenness or short duration of an action or a happening. 2) One time; once. It is to be used after a verb to show that it is done once or to refer to an attempt.

一、熟读下列各句,体会"一下"的意义和用法:

1. 我介绍一下,这位是张总经理。
2. 这份商品目录我看一下可以吗?
3. 我去一下就来。
4. 我走下飞机,一下就认出了他。
5. 贵公司的经营范围很广,我一下还不能都了解。

二、请用下列词语与"一下"组词,说一个句子:

1. 联系　　2. 询问　　3. 关照　　4. 接待
5. 参观　　6. 安排　　7. 洽谈　　8. 结识

三、用"一下"改说下列句子:

1. 你不知怎么与中国建立商业联系,不能问一问吗?
2. 有没有更简便的办法与中国建立商业联系,你应该打听打听。
3. 你需要什么资料就对秘书说说,她会帮助你的。
4. 我去去就来,你不要走。
5. 我第一次来中国推销产品,请你为我推荐推荐。

其他:

指示代词,指示一范围以外的人或物。跟在它后面表示人或物的名词如果是单音节词,则常常带"的",如"其他的人"、"其他的事";如果是双音节词,则常常不带"的",如"其他成员"、"其他机构"。也可直接作代词用,代替一定范围以外的人或物。

It is a demonstrative pronoun, indicating the persons or things outside a certain scope. It usually takes 的 when it is followed by a monosyllabic noun, but it does not take 的 when followed by a disyllabic noun. It can also be used as a pronoun to stand for other persons or things outside a certain scope.

一、熟读下列各句,仔细体会"其他"的意义和用法:

1. 先回旅馆休息,其他的事明天再谈。
2. 团长的其他助手已于昨天到达北京。
3. 除了公司老板,其他的人都回家了。
4. 这个问题解决了,其他都不难解决。

5. 我们先投石问路看看,再说其他。

二、用下面的词与"**其他**"组词造句:

1. 成员
2. 资料
3. 渠道
4. 目录
5. 专业

不仅……而且……:

表示前后意思之间有递进关系。"不仅"常与"而且"搭配使用,也可与"也、还、更"等副词搭配。"不仅"有时候也可以说成"不仅仅",它的作用是更加强调、突出后一层意思。

It indicates a progressive relationship between the two parts of the sentence. 不仅(not only)is often used together with 而且(but also). It can also collocate with such adverbs as 也(also),还(in addition),or 更(furthermore). 不仅 can sometimes be expressed as 不仅仅 to give extra emphasis to the latter part of the sentence.

一、熟读下列句子,体会"**不仅……而且……**"的用法:

1. 他不仅为我介绍朋友,而且推荐我到他公司工作。
2. 他不仅是我公司邀请的客人,而且是我公司的合作者。
3. 贵公司不仅这样说了,而且这样做了,谢谢你们的友好合作。
4. 经理跟我不仅见了面,而且具体洽谈了业务,真是荣幸啊。

二、请用"**不仅……而且……**"改说下列各句:

1. 他接待了我,还请我吃了饭。
2. 我们公司业务员多,经营范围大,建立联系的渠道也多。

3. 总经理来参观了商品展览会,总经理的夫人也来参观了商
   品展览会。
4. 外商可以在参观展览会时看样、洽谈、订货。

B

一、用下列词语组词：

例:举办展览　商务机构

关照	允许	看样	推荐	经营	业务	举办
渠道	商务	系统	具体	密切	附上	展览
顺利	洽谈	询问	需要	订购	目录	参观
简便	资料	机构	商品	范围	推销	订货

二、用上列词语,接着下面的句子,说一段话：

1. 我这是第一次来中国＿＿＿＿＿＿＿＿＿＿＿＿＿＿＿＿。

2. 在商品展览会上,可以＿＿＿＿＿＿＿＿＿＿＿＿＿＿＿。

3. 这次被邀请来贵国参观＿＿＿＿＿＿＿＿＿＿＿＿＿＿。

4. 谢谢你们的接待,希望你们能提供＿＿＿＿＿＿＿＿＿。

5. 我公司与贵公司的合作刚开始,＿＿＿＿＿＿＿＿＿＿。

6. 请问具体洽谈＿＿＿＿＿＿＿＿＿＿＿＿＿＿＿＿＿＿。

7. 我们需要＿＿＿＿＿＿＿＿＿＿＿＿＿＿＿＿＿＿＿＿。

8. 中国各外贸进出口公司驻外的机构,负责为本公司＿＿＿
   ＿＿＿＿＿＿＿＿＿＿＿＿＿＿＿＿＿＿＿＿＿＿＿＿＿。

9. 地方省、市外贸局也可以＿＿＿＿＿＿＿＿＿＿＿＿＿＿。

10. 我们很高兴跟贵公司建立＿＿＿＿＿＿＿＿＿＿＿＿＿。

三、选词填空:

贯彻	相信	委派	洽谈	顺利
允许	保持	经营	举办	渠道
成功	详细	结识	建立	提供

1. _____开放政策后,_____经济特区、开放城市自营出口,直接与外商建立联系。

2. 我公司与外国许多公司_____密切联系,相信不久将有更多的合作者。

3. 公司_____业务员来跟你们具体_____。

4. _____这次商品展览会一定举办得很_____。

5. 中国各外贸进出口公司驻国外的机构都与国内_____密切联系,同时也为本公司_____业务。

6. 我希望我们的业务_____是愉快的、成功的。

7. 我们非常_____地建立起了业务联系。

8. 在北京访问期间,我很高兴_____了中国国际贸易促进委员会(贸促会)的负责人。

9. 我们为贵公司_____的产品目录,_____介绍了本公司经营的各种商品。

10. 同中国_____商业联系的_____越来越多,真是条条道路通北京啊!

四、想一想,谈一谈:

1. 请谈谈你是怎样与中国或你的中国朋友建立联系的?

2. 请谈谈你或你的朋友来中国的第一次旅行。

3. 你或你的朋友在与中国交往中有什么趣事?

五、阅读下面的短文,并回答问题:

他会说汉语吗?

罗斯先生从旧金山乘飞机去中国,在飞机上,有许多中国人。罗斯先生用英语向身边的一个中国人打招呼,那个中国人只是笑着点了点头。罗斯先生又用英语说了一些什么,中国人也只是笑笑,没有说话。罗斯先生想,他一定是不懂英语,我先试试说汉语吧。罗斯先生就问:"先生,你去北京吗?"那个中国人好像听懂了一点什么,就回答说:"阿拉不是去贝肯(Peking)。阿拉是去北京(Běijīng)!"罗斯先生好像也听懂了一点,就又问:"我是做生意的,第一次来中国,我给中国的纺织品进出口公司发了电传,公司会派代表来接我吗?"那个中国人奇怪地看着罗斯,没有回答。罗斯说:"对不起,我的汉语说得不好!"中国人说:"对不起,我的英语也说得不好!"

1. 罗斯先生会说汉语吗?
2. 中国人为什么听不懂罗斯先生说的汉语?
3. 罗斯先生想向中国人打听什么?
4. 罗斯先生来北京顺利吗?

第二课 宴 请

Lesson 2 Entertaining Guests

一、下柬

王　安：罗斯先生，我们公司张总经理打算明天晚上在北京烤鸭店设宴，为贵代表团接风洗尘，不知你们方便不？

罗　斯：谢谢，客随主便，听从张总经理安排。

王　安：那好，就这么定了！这是请帖，敬请各位届时光临。

罗　斯：谢谢你们的盛情邀请，我们感到十分荣幸。

王　安：您能赏光，我们也很荣幸。那么，明天晚上六点半，我们开车到宾馆来接你们，可以吗？

罗　斯：可以，那就太麻烦你们了。

王　安：不必客气，这是应该的。好，明天见。

罗　斯：明天见。

二、宴会上

张　祥：罗斯先生，欢迎，欢迎！请入席吧！

罗　斯：张总经理费心了，请接受我和我的朋友们的真诚
　　　　感谢，谢谢你们为我们举行这个宴会。

张　祥：希望我们能一起度过一个愉快的夜晚。

罗　斯：一定，一定。我们一踏上中国的土地，就受到你
　　　　们热情周到的接待，我们代表团全体成员都非常
　　　　感动。

李　宁：中国有句俗话叫宾至如归，你们是客人，来了就
　　　　如同到了家，希望你们能像在自己家里一样。

杰克逊：说得太好了。中国人从来都是热情好客的。我
　　　　也知道一句中国话叫：主贤客来勤，是说主人好
　　　　客，所以引来八方客人。

张　祥：谢谢，我们希望能结交世界各国的朋友。哦，烤
　　　　鸭来了，大家趁热吃吧！来，首先请允许我举杯，
　　　　对罗斯先生一行表示热烈欢迎，为我们即将开始
　　　　的友好合作，干杯！

罗　斯：干杯！

三、宴会后

张　祥：罗斯先生，今晚的宴会如有不周的地方，请原谅。

罗　斯：哪里，哪里！我和我的朋友们都非常满意。我们
　　　　度过了一个愉快而难忘的夜晚，我认为我吃到了
　　　　最好的北京烤鸭。

张　祥：听到您这样说，我们十分高兴。

罗　斯：我们也十分高兴。我听说中国有这么一句话："不到长城非好汉。"那么我要说，不吃烤鸭不算到北京。我虽然到北京两天了，今晚张总经理下柬，我才得到了"入京（境）证"，我吃了北京烤鸭，才算真正到了北京。

李　宁：罗斯先生真幽默。不过，您还没去长城，还不能算是好汉！

罗　斯：好，好，我一定去长城，非当好汉不可！

李　宁：好极了。嗯，罗斯先生，这是为贵代表团安排的日程，请过目。有什么意见，请告诉我。

罗　斯：好。（看日程表）日程安排能不能稍作调整？我们想先参观有关工厂，看了产品生产过程后再进行谈判。这样，好心里有数。

王　安：这个不难办到。

罗　斯：如果时间允许的话，能否组织我们访问一些个体户，我很想知道他们在改革开放后的一些具体做法，尤其是他们的经营思想。

王　安：这也可以满足。大多数个体户经营第三产业，也就是服务行业。他们经营的主要有饮食店、服装店、理发店等。你们不妨先做他们的顾客，然后再进行采访。

罗　斯：好主意。"不入虎穴，焉得虎子"嘛！张总经理，这个成语用在这儿对吗？

张　祥：罗斯先生不愧是中国通。我希望罗斯先生不要被我国个体户这只新生的小老虎吃掉。

罗　斯:不会,不会! 那么,日程就这样定了。
王　安:好的,再次感谢罗斯先生光临,祝您成功! 再见。

生词

1.	设宴	shèyàn	give a dinner (a banquet)
2.	烤鸭	kǎoyā	roast duck
3.	接风	jiēfēng	welcome the wind (give a dinner for a visitor from afar)
4.	洗尘	xǐchén	wash the dust (give a dinner of welcome)
5.	客随主便	kèsuízhǔbiàn	the guest is at the host's disposal
6.	听从	tīngcóng	listen to, follow
7.	请帖(柬)	qǐngtiě(jiǎn)	invitation
8.	届时	jièshí	at the appointed time
9.	盛情	shèngqíng	boundless hospitality
10.	赏光	shǎngguāng	grant light [cliché: (request) the pleasure of your company; your coming]
11.	费心	fèixīn	take a lot of trouble
12.	感动	gǎndòng	be moved
13.	丰盛	fēngshèng	rich, sumptuous
14.	度过	dùguò	spend
15.	难忘	nánwàng	unforgettable
16.	夜晚	yèwǎn	evening
17.	踏上	tàshàng	set foot on
18.	土地	tǔdì	soil

19.	全体	quántǐ	all, whole, entire
20.	俗话	súhuà	common saying, folk adage
21.	好客	hàokè	hospitable
22.	结交	jiéjiāo	make friends with
23.	主贤客来	zhǔ xián kè lái	a worthy host attracts many
	勤	qín	guests
24.	趁	chèn	take this opportunity; while
25.	表示	biǎoshì	express
26.	即将	jíjiāng	be about to; soon
27.	好汉	hǎohàn	a fine man
28.	入境	rùjìng	enter a country
29.	日程	rìchéng	program, schedule, itinerary
30.	稍	shāo	a little, slightly
31.	调整	tiáozhěng	adjust, revise
32.	产品	chǎnpǐn	product
33.	生产	shēngchǎn	produce; production
34.	过程	guòchéng	process
35.	心里有数	xīnlǐyǒushù	know the score, have a pretty good idea of how things stand
36.	组织	zǔzhī	organize
37.	访问	fǎngwèn	visit
38.	个体户	gètǐhù	privately owned small enterprise or self-employed worker
39.	满足	mǎnzú	satisfy
40.	思想	sīxiǎng	thought, idea
41.	第三产业	dìsān chǎnyè	the tertiary industry
42.	行业	hángyè	trade, industry

43.	饮食	yǐnshí	food and drink
44.	服装	fúzhuāng	garments
45.	采访	cǎifǎng	interview
46.	不妨	bùfáng	there is no harm in…; might as well
47.	不入虎穴,焉得虎子	bùrùhǔxué, yāndéhǔzǐ	how can one catch tiger cubs without entering the tiger's lair
48.	成语	chéngyǔ	set phrase, idiom
49.	不愧	bùkuì	be worthy of; prove oneself to be; deserve to be called
50.	中国通	Zhōngguótōng	China hand

专名

长城　　　　Chángchéng　　　the Great Wall

练习

A

不知……不：

表示询问、商量或征求对方意见等,语气委婉。常见格式:
"不知+动词(或形容词)不?"

Not know whether…. It is a tactful expression used to make an enquiry or a consultation, or to solicit opinions. The pattern is: 不知 + verb (or adjective) + 不

一、熟读下列各句,体会"不知……不"的用法:

1. 代表团日程这么安排不知行不?
2. 今天晚上参加宴会,穿这套衣服不知合适不?
3. 五天前发出的邀请书,不知收到了不?
4. 商品展览会上展出的商品不知卖不?

二、请把下列各句改用"不知……不"来说:

1. 张总经理打算明天晚上在北京烤鸭店请客,代表团能来吗?
2. 烤鸭好吃吗?你喜欢吗?
3. 主人好客吗?
4. 你还记得那个愉快而难忘的夜晚吗?

感到:

动词,① 通过人的感觉器官感受到,一般不单独作谓语,它后边常带有宾语;不带宾语时,必带"了、过"。

② 表示有某种想法,同"认为"的意思差不多,但语意较轻,多用小句作宾语。

Verb: 1) Feel or sense through sense organs. As a predicate, normally it is not used alone, but takes an object. When it does not take an object, it is always followed by 了 or 过. 2) Have a certain idea. It has a meaning similar to that of 认为(think), but to a lesser extent. It usually takes a clause as its object.

一、熟读下列各句,指出"感到"表示的不同意思和用法:

1. 大家都感到很高兴。
2. 主人的热情,我们一下飞机就已经感到了。
3. 我从来没有感到过这么满足。
4. 你要是感到不舒服,就好好休息。

5. 我感到,这个日程安排得太紧了点儿。

6. 他说的话,我感到有些不对头。

二、用"感到"完成下列各句:

1. 今天我_____有点不舒服。

2. 从宴会上他对你的态度看,我_____事情有点不妙。

3. 他_____了成功的喜悦。

4. 今天走了那么多路,我_____累了。

5. 我_____这个个体户很有头脑。

趁(着):

利用时间或机会做某事。

Take advantage of; avail oneself of; while. It means to avail oneself of this chance or opportunity to do something.

一、熟读下列各句,仔细体会用法:

1. 烤鸭来了,趁热吃吧。

2. 趁这次来中国参观访问,我要采访一两个个体户。

3. 趁来北京学习汉语的机会,我要学做几个中国菜。

4. 趁下请柬的时候,问问代表团对日程安排有什么意见。

二、用"趁"改说下列各句:

1. 你去商店买东西,请为我买几个本子。

2. 参观工厂,买了几件这个工厂生产的产品。

3. 去中国南方旅行,我品尝了南方的风味小吃。

4. 天快下雨了,接我们的车子还没来,我回屋去拿件雨衣。

5. 这次来中国洽谈生意,我要多多了解中国经济改革的情况。

稍:

副词,表示数量不多或程度不深或时间短暂,也作"稍微、稍稍"。

Adverb: It means "a little", indicating a small quantity, a low degree, or a short duration. It can also be expressed as 稍微 or 稍稍.

一、熟读下列各句,仔细体会用法:

1. 你稍等一下,我就来。
2. 你能不能稍稍愉快一点儿!
3. 这几天,他稍微忙了点儿,就累病了。
4. 请稍安勿躁。

二、用"稍/稍稍"改写下列各句:

1. 他马上就回来,请坐下等一会儿。
2. 这茶太烫,凉凉我再喝。
3. 这件衣服有点儿大,再小一点儿就好了。
4. 接到女儿来信,知道她平安到达,母亲才放心了一些。

不妨:

表示可以这样做,没有什么妨碍。实际意思是这样做有好处或比较妥当。"不妨"也可说"无妨"。

Might as well; there is no harm in. The actual implication is that doing it this way will do you good or is more appropriate. It can also be said as 无妨.

一、熟读下列各句,体会用法:

1. 你虽然已经吃过北京烤鸭,不妨再尝一次。
2. 虽然没有用过筷子,你不妨试试。
3. 你既然第一次来中国,不妨在北京多住几天。
4. 不妨谈谈你们的具体做法,尤其是你们的经营思想。

二、把"不妨"用在下列各句中适当的地方：

1. 中国有句俗话叫"不到长城非好汉"，是什么意思，请你解释一下。
2. 王先生还没来，我们趁热边吃边等吧。
3. 这是一个愉快而又难忘的夜晚，我们多聊一会儿。
4. 这既然是新产品，价钱又不贵，你少买点试试。
5. 你们安排的日程太紧了，我建议你们调整调整。

B

一、熟读下列词语，并用每个词语说一句话：

宾至如归	主贤客来勤
客随主便	不入虎穴焉得虎子

二、用下列词语组词：

盛情	邀请	满意	感到	谈判	做法	采访
荣幸	安排	周到	接待	组织	进行	行业
真诚	表示	调整	服务	访问	意见	生产
费心	友好	日程	过程			

三、用上列词语完成下列各句子：

1. 这次来贵国＿＿＿＿＿＿＿＿＿＿＿＿＿＿＿＿＿＿＿＿。

2. 代表团参观贵厂＿＿＿＿＿＿＿＿＿＿＿＿＿＿＿＿＿＿＿。

3. 为了给代表团接风洗尘，我们＿＿＿＿＿＿＿＿＿＿＿

＿＿＿＿＿＿＿＿＿＿＿＿＿＿＿＿＿＿＿＿＿＿＿＿＿。

4. 中国人是＿＿＿＿＿＿＿＿＿＿＿＿＿＿＿＿＿＿＿＿＿。

5. 这次代表团＿＿＿＿＿＿＿＿＿＿＿＿＿＿＿＿＿＿＿＿。

四、想一想、谈一谈：

　　1．你或你的朋友参加过中国人的宴会吗？
　　2．你们听到中国人在宴请时常常说些什么？
　　3．你们参加中国人的宴会，发生过什么有趣的事吗？
　　4．你对中国人宴请朋友有什么看法？

五、阅读下面的短文，并回答问题：

我该怎么办

　　我去张总经理家做客，张总经理的夫人早早儿就站在家门口等我了。我一到，她就热情地握(wò)着我的手说："欢迎，欢迎，罗斯先生！快请进！"没多久，她就请我入席。嗬，满桌子菜，真丰盛。张总经理还拿出一瓶酒，边倒酒边说："这是中国名酒——茅台，罗斯先生多喝几杯！"我说："一定，一定，酒逢(féng)知己千杯少嘛，我要一醉(zuì)方休！"张总经理的夫人连连给我夹(jiā)菜。我不停地说："谢谢！谢谢！"不一会儿，我的碗里，放了满满一碗菜，鸡呀、鱼呀、土豆呀、青菜呀；有甜(tián)的，有咸(xián)的、有辣(là)的、有酸(suān)的。开始，我又喝酒，又吃菜，可我碗里的菜越吃越多，张总经理的夫人还一个劲(jìn)儿给我夹菜，连声说："没有什么好菜，罗斯先生不要客气，多吃点！"我碗里的菜快放不下了，我该怎么办？

　　1．张总经理怎样款待(kuǎndài)罗斯先生？
　　2．你觉得张总经理的夫人是怎样一个人？
　　3．罗斯先生见自己碗里的菜越吃越多，发愁了，说："我该
　　　怎么办？"你想，他该怎么办？

第三课　初次接触
Lesson 3　First Contact

一、交际序曲

张　祥：罗斯先生，很高兴我们又见面了，快请坐！

罗　斯：谢谢！很高兴再次见到张总经理和诸位同行们！

张　祥：这两天的参观、访问怎么样？

罗　斯：印象太深刻了！中国真是一个美丽的国家！

杰克逊：没想到中国市场上的商品这么丰富，真可以说是应有尽有。

罗　斯：尤其让我吃惊的是纺织品和服装市场，大小商场、大街小巷，到处都是卖服装的，我就好像走进了服装王国！

李　宁：罗斯先生说得一点儿没错。事实上，中国已经成为世界上最大的服装出口国。

罗　斯：我们这次来中国，就是为了洽谈纺织品和服装进出口业务，看来我们是来对了。

杰克逊：我们希望能得到贵公司的大力协助。

张　祥：只要我们能办到的，我们一定尽力办。我

们虽然是头一次打交道,但我相信,我们会成为
真正的朋友的。

罗　斯:真正的朋友,这太好了! 那就让我们互相信任、
互相帮助、互相支持吧!

张　祥:这正是我们国家对外贸易的一贯方针,广交朋
友,互通有无,平等互利嘛!

二、询问各自的经营范围

张　祥:坦率地说,罗斯先生,我们对贵公司还不是特别
了解。

罗　斯:这不奇怪,我们公司不大,知名度还不高。

杰克逊:不过,我们公司在国内的经营状况很好,我们会
成为你们感兴趣的合作伙伴。

张　祥:那么,你们主要经营什么商品呢?

杰克逊:主要经营各类纺织产品,包括棉、麻、毛、蚕丝、化
纤、各种纱、布及其制品。

李　宁:这些正是我们公司的主营产品。

罗　斯:我们希望从贵国进口纺织品,也希望我们国家的
纺织品能出口到贵国来。

张　祥:有来有往,互通有无嘛!

罗　斯:是这样。不过,我们第一次来中国,还需要对中
国市场做些调查,进出口货物才会做到心中有
数。

张　祥:怪不得你们对日程安排要做那样的调整了,原来
你们的主要目的是为了做市场调查!

杰克逊:是这样。我们必须知道,什么商品是适销对路的
商品。

李　宁:这的确很重要。商品没有销路,商店还不关门?

罗　斯:即使经过调查,最好也还是先订一批货试销试销。所以,我们这一次也准备订一批货。

张　祥:看得出来,你们做事很严肃、很认真,让人感到你们是可以信赖的。

罗　斯:谢谢你们能有这样的印象!

张　祥:我们一向认为,没有信任就不可能有真诚合作。

罗　斯:你说得很对,我们有了一个很好的开头。

杰克逊:还有一件事想麻烦你们一下。

张　祥:请讲。

杰克逊:受朋友委托,我们还想了解一下工艺品、小五金和中成药方面的情况。

李　宁:你知道,这不是我们公司的经营范围,不过我们可以为你们牵线搭桥。

杰克逊:那太谢谢你们了!

张　祥:不用客气。我们现在是不是休息一下?

罗　斯:那太好了!我们一起喝杯咖啡吧!

三、初涉双方感兴趣的项目

张　祥:现在,我们可以坐下来继续谈了。

杰克逊:咖啡真是好东西,让人兴奋。

罗　斯:啊,更让人心情愉快的是我们的中国朋友。

张　祥:谢谢。我想,你们来中国的时候,一定带有一份订货单,这一两天,你们又在中国市场转了转,现在有什么打算了吗?

罗　斯:是的。我想我们已经找到适销对路的产品。

杰克逊:我们对贵国的纯棉针织品和丝绸制品特别感兴

趣。

张　祥：你们很有眼光。事实上，我国的纯棉制品和高档
　　　　丝绸制品在世界各地都很畅销。

罗　斯：我们知道。不过，恕我直言，在工艺水平和花色
　　　　品种方面，与我国消费者的要求还有一定差距。

李　宁：我们清楚这一点。我们正在努力提高产品的科
　　　　技含量和附加值。

罗　斯：在这方面，我们可以合作。我们可以在中国投资
　　　　建工厂。

杰克逊：我们有先进的设备、生产工艺和技术。

张　祥：你们的这个想法很好。我们可以进行这方面的
　　　　可行性研究。

罗　斯：那太好了。我相信，我们之间会有广泛的合作前
　　　　景。

生词

1.	初次	chūcì	first time
2.	接触	jiēchù	contact
3.	交际	jiāojì	communication
4.	序曲	xùqǔ	prelude
5.	同行	tóngháng	people of the same occupation
6.	大街小巷	dàjiēxiǎoxiàng	wide streets and narrow lanes
7.	王国	wángguó	kingdom
8.	成为	chéngwéi	become
9.	协助	xiézhù	assistance

10.	尽力	jìnlì	do all one can
11.	信任	xìnrèn	trust, confidence
12.	支持	zhīchí	support
13.	一贯	yīguàn	consistent
14.	方针	fāngzhēn	guiding principle
15.	互通有无	hùtōngyǒuwú	supply each other's needs
16.	平等互利	píngděnghùlì	equality and mutual benefit
17.	坦率	tǎnshuài	frank
18.	了解	liǎojiě	understand
19.	状况	zhuàngkuàng	situation
20.	主要	zhǔyào	main, principal
21.	棉	mián	cotton
22.	麻	má	linen
23.	毛	máo	wool
24.	化纤	huàxiān	chemical fabrics
25.	纱	shā	yarn
26.	布	bù	cloth
27.	制品	zhìpǐn	products
28.	有来有往	yǒuláiyǒuwǎng	reciprocity
29.	调查	diàochá	investigate
30.	怪不得	guàibude	it is not surprising that ...
31.	高档	gāodàng	high-grade
32.	适销对路	shìxiāoduìlù	needed goods that suit the market
33.	的确	díquè	indeed
34.	即使	jíshǐ	even if
35.	试销	shìxiāo	trial sale
36.	准备	zhǔnbèi	be prepared to
37.	信赖	xìnlài	trust

38. 一向	yīxiàng	always
39. 开头	kāitóu	beginning
40. 委托	wěituō	entrust
41. 工艺品	gōngyìpǐn	handicrafts
42. 小五金	xiǎowǔjīn	hardware
43. 中成药	zhōngchéngyào	ready-made Chinese medicine
44. 涉及	shèjí	involve
45. 项目	xiàngmù	item
46. 继续	jìxù	continue
47. 兴奋	xīngfèn	excited
48. 心情	xīnqíng	mood, state of mind
49. 订货单	dìnghuòdān	order list
50. 恕	shù	excuse
51. 直言	zhíyán	straight forwardness
52. 工艺	gōngyì	technology, craftsmanship
53. 差距	chājù	gap
54. 科技	kējì	science and technology
55. 含量	hánliàng	content
56. 附加值	fùjiāzhí	value addcd
57. 投资	tóuzī	invest; investment
58. 先进	xiānjìn	advanced
59. 设备	shèbèi	equipment
60. 技术	jìshù	technique, technology
61. 可行性	kěxíngxìng	feasibility
62. 广泛	guǎngfàn	wide, broad, extensive
63. 前景	qiánjǐng	prospect

练习

A

怪不得:

① 表示明白原因,对某种情况就不觉得奇怪。常常可以与"原来"搭配使用。② 不能责备,别见怪。

1) No wonder; that explains why. It indicates that the reason is known and therefore one has no need to wonder about it. It often collocates with 原来(indicating that the truth is found out). 2) Not to blame.

一、熟读下列各句,指出"怪不得"表示的不同意思:

1. 怪不得他那么高兴,原来是他做生意赚了大钱。
2. 合同没写好,怪不得他。
3. 怪不得她生气,她又没买到满意的衣服。
4. 货卖不出去,怪不得我。

二、用"怪不得"完成下列各句:

1. ＿＿＿＿＿＿＿＿＿＿,老板喜欢他,他＿＿＿＿＿＿＿＿。

2. 怪不得他花钱那么大方,＿＿＿＿＿＿＿＿＿＿＿＿。

3. ＿＿＿＿＿＿＿＿房间里那么闷,＿＿＿＿＿＿＿＿＿。

4. 你信誉不好,＿＿＿＿＿＿＿＿＿＿＿＿＿＿＿。

5. 你们改善了投资环境,＿＿＿＿＿＿＿＿＿＿＿＿＿。

6. 简化了手续,＿＿＿＿＿＿＿＿＿＿＿＿效率高。

7. 价格那么优惠,＿＿＿＿＿＿＿＿＿＿＿＿＿＿。

8. 中国政府依法保护外商的合法权益，_____。

9. _____，原来你是第一次来中国。

10. 同中国发展贸易，前程似锦，_____。

的确：

完全确实；实在。用来表示肯定或强调语气。

Indeed; really. It is used to express certainty or emphasis.

一、熟读下面的句子，体会"的确"的意义和用法：

1. 这价格的确太贵了。

2. 中国的对外贸易的确采取了灵活的做法。

3. 他的的确确这么说了，怪不得你生气。

4. 中国愿意在平等互利、互通有无的原则基础上，同世界各国发展对外贸易。中国对外贸易的基本方针政策，的确是始终一贯的。

二、请用"的确"完成下面的对话：

1. 这次来中国洽谈贸易，你觉得中国对外贸易的具体做法灵活多了吗？

   _____。

2. 外商在中国投资的范围怎么样？

   _____。

3. 改革开放以来，中国政府不断采取措施，改善投资环境；为外商提供了许多优惠与方便吗？

   _____。

一向：

表示某种行为、状态或情况从过去到说话的时候一贯保持不变。

Consistently; all along. It says that a certain behaviour, manner or situation remains the same all the time and never changes.

一、熟读下列句子,体会"一向"的意义和用法:

1. 他身体一向不太好。
2. 我公司一向重信誉。
3. 中国人民一向好客。
4. 中国一向坚持独立自主、自力更生的原则。

二、用"一向"改说下列句子:

1. 你对中国哪一种商品感兴趣?
2. 你在忙些什么?
3. 中国丝绸销售情况怎么样?
4. 中国是我们最好的贸易伙伴。
5. 中国政府保护外商在中国经商的合法权益。

即使:

连词,连接两个分句。前后两部分,可以分指有关的两件事,前面表示一种假设情况,后面表示结果或结论不受这种假设情况的影响;前后两部分也可以指同一件事,后一部分表示退一步的估计。"即使"常与"也、还、都、总、仍然"等配搭使用。

Conjunction: Even though. It connects two clauses. The two parts connected may refer to two related things, the former of which indicates a supposition, and the latter indicates that the result or conclusion is not affected by the supposition. The two parts may also refer to the same thing, with the latter part expressing an estimation with some leeway. 即使 often collocates with 也,还,都,总 or 仍然.

一、熟读下列句子,体会"即使"的意义和用法:

1. 你即使发了邀请信,他也不一定来。
2. 即使是初次见面,我们也喜欢上她了。

3．工作即使做出了很大成绩，仍然不应该骄傲。

4．我即使不买这些衣服，看看总可以吧。

5．即使有钱也不应该浪费。

二、用"即使"改写下列各句：

1．你不去，我也要去。

2．对日程安排作了调整，时间仍然很紧。

3．不是我们公司经营的商品，我们也感兴趣。

4．他不同意，我们总会同意的。

5．市场上的商品十分丰富，也不能保证买到满意的商品。

B

一、用下列词语组词：

例：继续接触　尽力协助

接触	支持	先进	继续	差距	试销
协助	状况	设备	委托	前景	信任
尽力	调查	广泛	涉及		

二、说说下面短语的意思：

1．互通有无　　3．有来有往　　5．心中有数

2．平等互利　　4．应有尽有　　6．适销对路

三、用上面的短语完成下列各句：

1．朋友之间少不了互相帮助，只要我有的，你_____嘛。

2．一个国家要发展经济，不能没有外援，但是_____。

3．国家不分大小，在发展双边贸易时，都应该_____。

4．我们一向提倡_____，在当今高科技发展的时代，地
　　球变得越来越小，更应该_____。

5．作市场调查为的是产品_____，只有做到_____

才能使产品有市场。

四、回答下列问题：

1. 中国经济改革开放后,对外贸易采取了哪些灵活做法?
2. 为什么说外商同中国贸易天地广阔,大有作为?
3. 中国在外贸活动中奉行的是什么原则?
4. 你认为中国目前开展对外贸易的环境如何?

五、阅读下面的短文,并回答问题：

老王的惊喜

老王去上海出差,单位的一位女同志请他代买一件纯羊毛衫。他走了很多家商店,毛衣颜色鲜(xiān),式样新,又便宜,他看来看去,眼都看花了,不知道该买哪件好。最后,他终于满意而归。回到旅馆,老王高兴地拿出新买的毛衣向别人展示,说:"你们看,这件羊毛衫多漂亮!"女服务员小李,拿起来仔细看了看,说:"这不是纯羊毛衫,里面有兔(tù)毛。""这可糟了,人家一再说,她只要纯羊毛衫,不要有兔毛的,这怎么办呢?"小李说:"别着急,你拿去退换吧!""退换? 我们那儿可不行!""这里以前也不能退换,现在可以了。"老王第二天找到那家商店,说明了情况,商店经理说:"这件毛衣,不是纯羊毛的,含有 10%兔毛,售货员没有讲清楚,麻烦你又跑一趟,实在对不起,应该给你退换。"老王感动得不行,连声说:"现在的商店,怎么会有这么大的变化呢?"

1. 老王买毛衣碰到什么麻烦了?
2. 商店经理为什么同意退换?
3. 老王退换了毛衣后为什么感动得不行?
4. 你认为现在的商店发生了什么变化? 为什么会有那样的变化?

第四课　购销意向
Lesson 4　Intention of Buying and Selling

一、谈产品

罗　斯：张总经理，我们这次想订购一批纺织品回国试销，不知你们都有哪些型号，能给我介绍一下吗？

杰克逊：最好能给我们一些产品样品和目录。

李　宁：噢，这是产品目录。会后我们可以一起去样品室看样品。

罗　斯：你知道，我们最关心的是产品质量。

张　祥：近几年，我国纺织工业朝着精加工、深加工方向发展，开发了大批新型产品，产品质量也有了明显提高。

罗　斯：这是个好消息。

李　宁：比如高级纯棉针织品，高档真丝制品，高密防羽绒布、高支薄型苎麻织物等等。此外，我们还生产能阻燃、遮光、隔热、保暖、防污、防静电的系列高级装饰布。

罗　斯：花色品种确实很丰富。这几天，我们在市场上也看到一些，但质量还是不够理想。

杰克逊：据我所知，贵国产品因为加工水平低，产品质量不高，只能低价出售，在国际市场上缺少竞争力。

罗　斯：我这里有一个数字，同是 127 公分的宽幅丝绸，贵国一米只能卖 5.62 美元，而西班牙的售价是 65 美元，比利时的是 37.13 美元，法国的是 23.75 美元，意大利的售价最低，也卖到 11.37 美元。贵国实在太吃亏了！

张　祥：这种情况，我们也注意到了，所以我们采用高科技、新技术，对我国的纺织工艺进行了大力改造，产品质量已经发生了根本变化。

罗　斯：我相信中国人的决心和能力。我们是不是去看看样品？

张　祥：好，请吧！

二、谈价格

罗　斯：张总经理，我太吃惊了，这些样品的质量确实非常好！

张　祥：那么，你们有什么打算呢？

罗　斯：我已经向张总表明过我们的意向，我们想订购一批高级真丝制品和纯棉制品，只是看了产品说明书，觉得价格太高了，我们很难接受。

杰克逊：可不可以优惠些呢？

张　祥：我们公司的这两类产品，质量上乘，花色新颖，一投放市场，就十分走俏，已经成为我们公司的名优产品。

罗　斯：可是价格这么高，不怕吓跑我们这些新顾客？

张　祥：价格虽然不低，但一直是畅销的抢手货，可见价格还是公道、合理的。我相信,你们不会跑!

杰克逊:报价单上的价格都是实盘吗?

李　宁:不是。许多问题我们还没有谈判,价格要以我方
　　　　最后确认的为准。

杰克逊:请问贵方根据什么最后确认价格呢?

张　祥:主要取决于你们的订货量。如果你们的订货量
　　　　大,价格可以优惠些。

罗　斯:这恐怕很难,你知道,纺织品进出口要受配额的
　　　　严格限制。

张　祥:我们当然知道。但是,你们可以努力争取嘛!

罗　斯:就是争取,无论主动配额还是被动配额,都是有
　　　　限的。

张　祥:为了便于报价,还是请罗斯先生先报一个你方订
　　　　货的大概数量吧。

罗　斯:请你们先报一个 C.I.F.旧金山的最低价,只要
　　　　价格确实优惠,我们的订货量是不会太小的。

张　祥:啊,这好比下棋,总得有人先走一步,如果都等待
　　　　对方先走,就要成一盘死棋了。

罗　斯:我很欣赏张总经理的这个比喻。棋逢对手,将遇
　　　　良才,希望我们能下成平局!

三、代理与自主经营

罗　斯:张总经理,请原谅,我们还想到别的公司看一看。

张　祥:没关系,可以理解。

罗　斯:那么,你们能给我们介绍一两家吗?

张　祥:可以。过去,是国家专业外贸公司垄断经营进出
　　　　口业务,全国纺织行业只有我们一家专业外贸公

司。

杰克逊:那我们只能同你们打交道了。

张　祥:是的。现在情况不同了,我国对外贸易推行了代
　　　理制,一些生产企业委托我们代理经营进出口业
　　　务,而更多的生产企业和外贸公司现在有了外贸
　　　自主经营权。

罗　斯:这就是说,我们可以同更多的企业和公司直接打
　　　交道了。

张　祥:是这样。

杰克逊:那就请你多介绍几家,好吗?

罗　斯:特别是自主经营进出口的生产企业,说不定他们
　　　可以在花色品种和质量方面满足我们的一些特
　　　殊要求。

张　祥:好的,我跟他们联系一下吧!

生词

1. 型号　　　xínghào　　　model
2. 样品　　　yàngpǐn　　　sample
3. 关心　　　guānxīn　　　concern
4. 新型　　　xīnxíng　　　new type
5. 朝着　　　cháozhe　　　towards
6. 精加工　　jīngjiāgōng　　fine processing
7. 深加工　　shēnjiāgōng　　deep processing
8. 明显　　　míngxiǎn　　　obvious
9. 消息　　　xiāo xi　　　news
10. 高密防羽　gāomìfáng　　highly-dense down-proof
　　绒布　　　yǔróngbù　　cloth

11. 高支薄型 苎麻织物	gāozhī báoxíng zhùmá zhīwù	fine count thin ramie fabrics
12. 阻燃	zǔrán	flame-proof
13. 遮光	zhēguāng	light-proof
14. 隔热	gérè	heat-proof
15. 保暖	bǎonuǎn	thermally insulated
16. 防污	fángwū	dirt-proof
17. 静电	jìngdiàn	static electricity
18. 系列	xìliè	series
19. 装饰	zhuāngshì	decoration
20. 出售	chūshòu	sell
21. 缺少	quēshǎo	lack
22. 竞争力	jìngzhēnglì	competitiveness
23. 宽幅	kuānfú	extended width
24. 根本	gēnběn	fundamental
25. 决心	juéxīn	determination
26. 说明书	shuōmíngshū	catalog, manual
27. 表明	biǎomíng	indicate, disclose
28. 意向	yìxiàng	intention
29. 多功能	duōgōngnéng	multi-functional
30. 采用	cǎiyòng	adopt
31. 改造	gǎizào	remold, transform
32. 发生	fāshēng	take place
33. 上乘	shàngchéng	superior; top quality
34. 新颖	xīnyǐng	original, novel
35. 走俏	zǒuqiào	well-received
36. 抢手货	qiǎngshǒuhuò	goods people scramble to buy
37. 公道	gōngdào	fair
38. 合理	hélǐ	reasonable

39. 报价单	bàojiàdān	quotation list
40. 实盘	shípán	firm offer
41. 确认	quèrèn	confirmation
42. 取决于	qǔjuéyú	depend on
43. 订货量	dìnghuòliàng	amount of order
44. 配额	pèi'é	quota
45. 被动	bèidòng	passive
46. 限制	xiànzhì	restrict
47. 棋	qí	chess
48. 等待	děngdài	wait
49. 一盘	yīpán	a game
50. 比喻	bǐyù	metaphor
51. 棋逢对手,将遇良才	qíféngduìshǒu, jiàngyùliángcái	meet one's match; be well-matched in a contest
52. 平局	píngjú	a draw
53. 原谅	yuánliàng	excuse
54. 推行	tuīxíng	push, carry out, pursue
55. 自主	zìzhǔ	autonomous; decide for one-self
56. 垄断	lǒngduàn	monopoly
57. 直接	zhíjiē	direct

练习

A

一直:

表示在一定时间里某种行为、动作连续进行,没有间断;或者某种事物、状态始终没有发生变化。

Continuously; all along; all the way. This means that during a certain period of time something continues to happen or exist without stopping, or that something remains unchanged.

一、熟读下面的句子,体会"一直"的意义和用法:

1. 博览会从明天开始,一直举办到这个月底。
2. 从天安门沿长安街一直往东,就可以到北京友谊商店。
3. 他来北京以前,一直在 IBM 公司工作。
4. 近几年来,我们双方的合作,一直是顺利的,成功的。

二、用"一直"完成下面的句子:

1. 我们双方往来的渠道_____。

2. 这次贸易洽谈,从昨天上午开始,_____

_____。

3. 贵国的真丝绸质量好,价格便宜,_____。

4. 开发高科技_____。

5. 我虽得到了贵公司的产品目录,_____。

实在:

① 形容词,表示事物和情况真实,不虚假;②副词,强调某种情况的真实性。

1) Adj:True; real; dependable. This means that something is real and not false. 2) Adv:Indeed; as a matter of fact. It emphasizes the truthfulness or authenticity of something.

一、熟读下面的句子,体会"实在"的意义和用法:

1. 坦率地说,贵国这批纯棉制品加工水平低,质量不好,实在不好销售。

2. 这次实在无法满足你的要求,非常抱歉。

3. 这个人很实在,他的报价一般都很公道。

4. 他实在是位难得的贸易伙伴。

二、用"实在"回答下面的问题:

1. 你是行家,你看这批货怎么样?

2. 这批多功能新颖装饰布你是否能再早些装船。

3. 我想,这个消息对你订货很重要,是吗?

4. 你的话句句当真?

5. 最后报价,十天内有效,你看行吗?

取决于:

一件事由某方面或某种情况决定。"于",是介词,后面引出起决定作用的方面或情况。

Depend on; hinge on. It shows that something is dependent on something else. 于 is a preposition, to be followed by the situation or the thing that plays the decisive role.

一、熟读下面的句子,体会"取决于"的意义和用法:

1. 实盘价格,取决于订货量的大小。

2. 一种新产品投放市场,是否畅销,取决于这种新产品是否让顾客满意。

3. 新产品的开发,往往取决于科学技术的不断发展。

4. 我们的洽谈能否成功,取决于我们双方的诚意与合作。

二、用"取决于"改写下面的句子:

1. 最后确认的价格,要看你们的订货量来决定。

2. 只要你们的价格优惠,我们的订货量就会大一些。

3. 我们能否按时装船,要看你们是否及时派船来受载。

4．经济的发展，往往同国家政局的稳定有密切关系。

5．双边贸易的发展，要看我们双方是否都遵守平等互利、互通有无的原则。

确实：

① 形容词，表示事物或情况真实可靠；② 副词，对客观情况的真实性表示肯定。

"确实"和"实在"意义和用法都相近，但仍有某些区别。"实在"不只肯定真实性，而且在程度上更加强调。"确实"可用在问句里；"实在"则不能。

1）Adjective: True; reliable. It shows the truthfulness and reliability of something. 2）Adverb: Really; indeed. It is used to confirm the truthfulness of something.

确实 and 实在 are similar in meaning and use, but with some differences. Apart from confirming the truthfulness, 实在 also expresses emphasis. 确实 can be used in an interrogative sentence, whereas 实在 can't.

一、熟读下面的句子，体会"确实"的意义和用法：

1．目前国际市场上纯棉制品确实走俏。

2．你给我提供的确实是优惠价吗？

3．这个价格确实不会变了。

4．贵国的对外贸易政策确实是灵活多了。

二、用"确实"回答下面的问题。

1．你再打听一下，他是不是及时派船来接货？

2．我们采用了高科技、新技术，产品质量发生了根本变化，你看了样品后觉得怎么样？

3．你这次来中国洽谈贸易，参观访问，还满意吗？

4．这些名优产品在市场上的销售情况怎么样？有竞争力吗？

5. 你看,我们这次洽谈,是不是像下象棋,终于下成了平局?

B

一、用下列词语组词:

采用	销售	价格	等待	新颖	花色
转移	缺少	表明	装运	说明	竞争
科技	投放	担保	完成	明确	优惠
合同	合理	有效	市场	意向	消息

二、用括号中指定的词语完成会话:

1. 你别看这种商品价格高,可很畅销。

　　　　　　　　　　　　　　　　　　　　　。(竞相)

2. 质量上等,花色新颖的真丝织品,市场销售量大吗?

　　　　　　　　　　　　　　　　　　　　　。(走俏)

3. 你认为报价单上的价格有竞争力吗?

　　　　　　　　　　　　　　　　　　　　　。(公道)

4. 你们的报价包括保险费吗?

　　　　　　　　　　　　　　　　　　　　　。(包括)

5. 对这批货物的装运,我还有些不放心。

　　　　　　　　　　　　　　　　　　　　　。(担保)

6. 我们的贸易合同书什么时候可以生效?

　　　　　　　　　　　　　　　　　　　　　。(确认)

7. 你们对这种多功能装饰布感兴趣吗?

　　　　　　　　　　　　　　　　　　　　　。(意向)

8. 这是种新产品,我们怕不好销售。

　　_____。(风险)

9. 现在北京的高级饭店已经过剩,外商好像不愿在这方面投
　 资了。

　　_____。(转移)

10. 你们的价格太高了,我们无利可图。

　　_____。(吃亏)

三、根据课文回答问题:

1. 为什么中国的纯棉织品和真丝织品一直比较畅销?
2. 改革开放后中国的纺织品发生了什么变化?
3. 你认为价格应该根据什么决定?
4. 对方发出装船通知后,我方需做些什么?
5. 在风险担保问题上,贵国比较习惯的做法是什么?

四、阅读下面的短文,并回答问题:

聪明的商人

　　一天,一个服装公司的经理同一位订货商洽谈生意。订货
商看了样品,觉得服装加工精细,质量上等,确实是这个公司的
名优产品,投放市场后一定走俏,但他想大大压低价格,就对服
装公司的经理说:"你开的价太高了,我本想做成一笔大买卖,
看来只好算了。"说完,站起来就要走。经理眼看生意就要告
吹,忽然灵机(língjī)一动,满脸堆(duī)笑地说:"你穿的这双鞋
子真漂亮。"订货商一听,就站住了,高兴地问:"真的?""真的。
你买的东西还能不好?"订货商更高兴了,就把他脚上的鞋子足
足夸(kuā)了五分钟。订货商正说得高兴。服装公司的经理突

然反问:"你为什么要买这双鞋子,而不到旧货商店去另外买一双呢?"订货商听了,先一愣(lèng),接着哈哈大笑,于是双方握手成交。

1. 服装公司经理与订货商的洽谈顺利吗?

2. 订货商是否真的想向这家服装公司订货?

3. 服装公司经理怎么改变了洽谈形势?

4. 短文最后关于鞋子的谈话,究竟是什么意思? 为什么双方因此成交?

第五课　价格洽谈
Lesson 5　Talking About Price

一、询价与发盘

史密斯:陈先生,我们想洽购贵公司 50 吨花生米,
　　　　请你介绍一下商品和价格。

陈其然:好的。花生米是凭样品买卖,史密斯先
　　　　生,可以先看看样品和价格表。

史密斯:嗯,花生米颗粒饱满,均匀,成色新鲜,口
　　　　味香甜,质量不错。你们能保证供货品质
　　　　与样品完全一样吗?

陈其然:请史密斯先生放心,我们一贯讲信誉、守
　　　　合同。

史密斯:这我们相信。不过,每吨 485 美元,价格
　　　　太高了,我们无法接受。

陈其然:这是 C.I.F. 价,是成本加保险费、运费价
　　　　格。如果成交,我们可在明年五月底以前
　　　　在洛杉矶港交货。

玛　丽:但是价格太高,我们很难销售。

陈其然:我们的花生米多年来畅销世界各地,就是
　　　　价格再高一点,销售也不成问题。

玛　丽：可是,陈先生你知道,市场竞争很激烈,印度的花生米,价格就比贵公司的低得多。

陈其然：这,我不否认。但中国有句俗话,"不怕不识货,就怕货比货"。史密斯先生在这方面是行家,不难看出好坏。

史密斯：那好吧,我们考虑考虑。

二、还盘与反还盘

陈其然：史密斯先生,我们昨天的报盘,你们考虑得怎么样?

史密斯：陈先生,我们经过慎重研究,仍然觉得你们的报价太高了。如果贵公司不肯降价,我们只好放弃这笔生意。

陈其然：这样做恐怕不明智吧? 我们还可以再协商嘛。你是不是出一个价?

史密斯：我们认为每吨 405 美元比较合适。

陈其然：史密斯先生,你们还盘太低,与我们的报价差距太大了,看来我们的确很难成交。

史密斯：我相信我们双方都是有诚意的,我们能各自作些让步吗?

陈其然：这我赞成。如果你们再增加订货量,我们可以降价 5%。

史密斯：陈先生,这恐怕有困难,你知道,现在国际市场疲软,行情普遍看跌,花生米又容易霉烂,我们订货量太大,会有很大的风险,请你能理解这一点。

陈其然：是的,目前国际形势动荡不安,市场出现了某些不景气现象,但我们对前景是乐观的。

史密斯:那么,贵公司是否可以分批供货呢？如果可以,我们每吨加价5%。

陈其然:这还是太低了。就按每吨450美元吧,不能再比这个价低了。

史密斯:噢,我们之间仍然有很大差距,看来要做成这笔买卖,我们双方都需要更有耐心。

三、让步与成交

陈其然:史密斯先生,你看了我们的报价单,还有什么看法？

史密斯:陈先生,你们今年的报价,比去年提高了很多,这是为什么？

陈其然:这几年,化肥、水、电都不断涨价,农产品成本越来越高,我们不得不对价格作相应的调整。

史密斯:这点我们理解。但贵方应该想别的办法,降低产品成本,不能把化肥、水、电等价格上涨部分,都转嫁到客户身上。如果这样,贵方商品就没有销路了。

陈其然:请史密斯先生注意,在国际市场上,同类商品的价格,也都比去年上涨了,而且上涨幅度比我们还大,相对地说,我们的商品还是便宜的。此外,贵国货币的汇率持续下跌,我们也不能忽略。

史密斯:事实虽然如此,贵方的报价还是太苛刻,能不能再作些让步？

陈其然:史密斯先生的意思是——

史密斯:我们希望能再降价5%。

陈其然:要我们总共降价10%？不,这绝对不行。我们总不能做亏本买卖吧!

史密斯:那就8%。

陈其然:如果贵方订货量增加二成,我们可以再降价3%,
　　　　这是最低报价了。

史密斯:好吧,我们成交!

生词

1.	询价	xúnjià	inquiry
2.	发盘	fāpán	offer
3.	花生米	huāshēngmǐ	peanut kernel
4.	吨	dūn	ton
5.	凭	píng	base on, rely on, go by
6.	颗粒	kēlì	grain
7.	饱满	bǎomǎn	plump, full
8.	均匀	jūnyún	even, uniform
9.	成色	chéngsè	quality, percentage (of gold or silver)
10.	新鲜	xīnxiān	fresh
11.	口味	kǒuwèi	taste
12.	香甜	xiāngtián	fragrant and sweet, delicious
13.	供货	gōnghuò	supply
14.	品质	pǐnzhì	quality
15.	遵守	zūnshǒu	abide by
16.	合同	hétong	contract
17.	成本	chéngběn	cost
18.	保险	bǎoxiǎn	insurance
19.	运输	yùnshū	freight, transportation

20.	成交	chéngjiāo	conclude a transaction
21.	底	dǐ	end, bottom
22.	港口	gǎngkǒu	port
23.	销售	xiāoshòu	sale
24.	否认	fǒurèn	deny
25.	识货	shíhuò	know what's what; be able to judge
26.	行家	hángjia	expert
27.	明确	míngquè	clear and definite
28.	有效	yǒuxiào	effective
29.	交货	jiāohuò	delivery
30.	报盘	bàopán	quotation, offer
31.	慎重	shènzhòng	careful
32.	仍然	réngrán	still
33.	包括	bāokuò	include
34.	降价	jiàngjià	lower the price
35.	放弃	fàngqì	give up, abandon
36.	还盘	huánpán	counter-offer
37.	让步	ràngbù	concession
38.	诚意	chéngyì	sincerity
39.	赞成	zànchéng	agree
40.	疲软	píruǎn	slack
41.	跌	diē	fall
42.	霉烂	méilàn	deteriorate
43.	目前	mùqián	present
44.	形势	xíngshì	situation
45.	动荡不安	dòngdàngbù'ān	unstable
46.	景气	jǐngqì	boom, prosperity
47.	批	pī	batch, lot

48. 耐心	nàixīn	patience
49. 化肥	huàféi	chemical fertilizer
50. 不断	bùduàn	unceasingly，constantly
51. 涨价	zhǎngjià	rise in price
52. 相应	xiāngyìng	corresponding
53. 转嫁	zhuǎnjià	shift onto
54. 客户	kèhù	client
55. 幅度	fúdù	range, margin, scope
56. 相对	xiāngduì	relative
57. 货币	huòbì	currency
58. 持续	chíxù	continuously
59. 忽略	hūlüè	neglect
60. 事实	shìshí	fact
61. 苛刻	kēkè	harsh
62. 亏本	kuīběn	lose
63. 成	chéng	one tenth; ten percent

专名

| 洛杉矶 | Luòshānjī | Los Angeles |
| 印度 | Yìndù | India |

练习

A

凭：

　　① 介词，用来介绍出行为、动作所依据的或借助的事物、条件或理由；有时介绍出的是人物。② 连词，有"不管"、"无论"的意思。它后面必须跟疑问代词或词组。

1）Preposition:Relying on; based on; taking as the basis. It introduces the thing, condition or reason which forms the basis of something. Sometimes it may introduce a person or persons. 2）Conjunction:No matter (what, how, etc.). It says that something is true or happens in all circumstances and that it makes no difference what the particular circumstances are. It is followed by an interrogative word or expression.

一、熟读下面的句子,体会"凭"的意义和用法：

1. 凭票付款。
2. 汉堡包凭着它便宜、快速,走遍天下。
3. 你凭什么骂人?
4. 凭你磨破嘴皮子,他也不肯降价。
5. 凭你怎么劝,她都不听。

二、用"凭"完成下面的会话：

1. 你们看了样品,是好是坏,你们清楚,给个价吧。

   _____。

2. 一个商人的成功要靠什么?

   _____。

3. 这笔买卖可是能赚大钱的,你真愿意放弃?

   _____。

4. 服务行业在竞争中怎么取胜?

   _____。

5. 你说他以次充好,,有证据吗?

   _____。

只好：

不得不。表示由于种种条件的限制或情况的变化,只有这样,而没有别的办法去做某事。

Have to; be forced to. It says that, owing to the restrictions by various conditions or changes in circumstances, this is the only way of doing things, without any choice.

一、熟读下面的句子,体会"只好"的意义和用法:

1. 他自己不好意思说,只好我替他说。
2. 这次买卖没做成,只好下次做了。
3. 货卖不出去,只好降价处理。
4. 老板同意了,我只好去。

二、用"只好"改写下面的句子:

1. 价格太高,很难销售,我们不得不降价拍卖。

   _____。

2. 我们双方在价格上都不肯让步,看来这笔交易要吹了。

   _____。

3. 目前国际市场上同类商品的价格都上涨了,我们的商品涨价,也是不得已的。

   _____。

4. 现在国际市场疲软,我们不得不减少订货量。

   _____。

5. 成本越来越高,我们不能不提高商品价格。

   _____。

不得不:

有"必须"的意思,表示环境或情势迫使非如此不可。它的后面总是跟动词。这种"不 A 不"的格式,"A"还可以是"能、可、好",但意思有一些区别,例如:"不得不说"、"不能不吃"、"不可不听"、"不好不去"。

It has the meaning of "have to ", indicating that there is no choice because of the environment or situation. It is always followed by a verb. In this pattern of 不＋A＋不，"A" can also be 能，可，or 好，but with slightly different meanings.

一、熟读下面的句子,体会"不得不"的意义和用法。

1. 现在国际市场疲软,我们不得不减少订货量。
2. 现在市场竞争激烈,我们不得不做好售后服务。
3. 双方价格上差距太大,我们不得不取消订货。
4. 留学生在中国学习,有时不得不自己洗衣服。
5. 你们的报价太高,我们不得不放弃这笔生意。

二、选用"不能不"、"不可不"、"不好不"完成下面的句子,并仔细体会意思的区别。

1. 医生的话,病人＿＿＿＿＿＿听。

2. 我儿子要考研究生,＿＿＿＿＿＿加倍努力。

3. 供货品质与样品＿＿＿＿＿＿一样。

4. 经过慎重研究,我们＿＿＿＿＿＿降低报价。

5. 我跟朋友约好了,＿＿＿＿＿＿去。

6. 成本越来越高,我们＿＿＿＿＿＿提高商品价格。

仍然:

副词,表示某种情况维持不变;或虽有变化,但最后还是恢复了原样。"仍然"多用于书面,口语中多用"还是"、"仍旧"。

Adverb: It indicates that a certain state of affairs remains unchanged, or even if changed, it eventually returns to the original state. 仍然 is more often used in written Chinese. In spoken Chinese 还是 or 仍旧 is preferred.

一、熟读下面的句子,体会"仍然"的意义和用法:

1. 下班以后,他仍然在考虑工作中的问题。
2. 成本虽然高了,价格却仍然保持不变。
3. 谈判中我们虽然作了很大让步,但是他们仍然坚持最初的报价。
4. 这家商场,停业半年,现在重新营业,仍然是那么热闹。

二、把"仍然"放在下列各句中的适当位置:

1. 他们离婚了,但有来往。
2. 我们已经是爸爸妈妈了,可在自己的父母面前是孩子。
3. 今年国内的服装市场是买方市场。
4. 不知道为什么,电话打了几次,打不通。
5. 几年不见了,你一点没变,是老样子。

B

一、用下列词语组词:

竞争　　转嫁　　研究　　前景　　持续　　苛刻
市场　　激烈　　价格　　耐心　　协商　　疲软

二、用括号中指定的词语完成下列各句话:

1. 目前市场竞争激烈,你们的价格＿＿＿＿＿＿＿＿＿＿

＿＿＿＿＿＿＿＿＿＿＿＿＿＿＿＿＿。(相对地说)

2. 虽然目前国际市场疲软,行情普遍看跌,但

＿＿＿＿＿＿＿＿＿＿＿＿＿＿＿＿＿。(乐观)

3. 根据市场行情＿＿＿＿＿＿＿＿＿＿＿＿＿。(调整)

4. 我们差距太大,贵方又不肯让步,＿＿＿＿＿＿＿＿＿

_____。（放弃）

5. 时间这么晚了，_____。（恐怕）

6. 不经过慎重研究，就_____

_____。（明智）

7. 你方条件_____。（苛刻）

8. 价格_____原因是多方面的。（持续）

9. 我赞成_____买卖不成情义在嘛！（理解）

10. 我们双方的条件虽然差距很大，但我们都有诚意，_____

_____。（协商）

三、熟读下列各句,体会"口味"、"新鲜"在各句中的不同含义,然后模仿着各说一句:

1. 口味

(1) 这个菜合你口味吗?

(2) 这么说话不合老人口味吧?

(3) 她这身打扮合她先生口味吗?

(4) 他口味太重,你吃得了吗?

2. 新鲜

(1) 改革开放后新鲜事就是多,你说是不?

(2) 农民出国旅游,乡镇企业产品远销海外,你头一次听说,新鲜吧?

(3) 这衣服颜色很新鲜,你买一件吧!

(4) 你刚来中国,看什么都新鲜,是不是?

(5) 新鲜,谈判吹了怪我,这跟我有什么关系?

四、想一想、谈一谈:

1. 目前国际市场竞争激烈,贵公司商品销路怎么样?

2．你对目前市场出现的不景气现象怎么理解？

3．农产品成本越来越高，又不能把上涨部分都转嫁到客户身上，贵公司有什么好办法吗？

4．你同对方洽谈价格时有耐心吗？双方差距很大时你肯首先作出较大的让步吗？

5．你觉得作为贸易伙伴，中国人是不是行家？

五、阅读下面的短文，并回答问题：

谁最会砍价

现在，大街边，胡同里，到处都可见摆地摊的。"快来买呀，出口转内销，一次性降价处理。"老陈在一家地摊边站住了。"先生，你买点什么？牛仔裤？长统丝袜？罗斯旅行鞋？"摊主说一件，拿一件给老陈看，货怎么好，价钱怎么便宜，没有比他这儿更物美价廉的了。老陈拿起一双袜子问："多少钱？""便宜，便宜，12元！""12元？你怎么漫(màn)天要价？""看你说的！那你就地还钱好了！""5元！""嘿，你也太会讨价还价了！一下就砍了我一多半。10元！""7元！""8元！不能再少了，不买，你就请走！"老陈终于买了一双。他一路上高高兴兴，一进家门就对太太说："太太，我给你买了一双长统丝袜。"老陈夫人拿过去一看，问"多少钱？"老陈说："他要我12元，我压了他4元。""8元，便宜！我刚才也买了一双，同你这双完全一样，可一分钱也没少给，12元！还是你会买东西。"说完，她撕(sī)开塑料袋(sùliào dài)包装，拿出袜子一看："呀，怎么只有一只袜子！"老陈大叫一声："我挨宰了！"

1．你懂什么叫"出口转内销"吗？

2．"漫天要价，就地还钱"是什么意思？

3．老陈买的袜子便宜还是他妻子买的袜子便宜？为什么？

58

第六课　品种与数量洽谈

Lesson 6　Discussion on Variety and Quantity

一、订货

史密斯：陈先生，我这里有一张小五金清单，请你
　　　　看一下，贵公司能不能保证供货？

陈其然：嗬，都是久享盛誉的名牌货嘛！

玛　丽：是的，像808牌抽屉锁，三角牌不锈钢餐
　　　　具，555指甲刀，矛牌剪刀，在我国都很畅
　　　　销，我们公司每年进货不少，但总是脱销，
　　　　所以希望贵公司这次能满足我们的需要。

陈其然：小五金虽是千家万户的日用必需品，却又
　　　　是薄利商品。近几年，我们开放了市场，
　　　　厂家纷纷把资金转向获利大的商品生产，
　　　　如电脑，高档录像机，组合音响之类，不愿
　　　　生产小五金。小五金货源空前短缺，供不
　　　　应求，恐怕很难让史密斯先生满意。

史密斯：陈先生，我们是老主顾了，你一定得照顾
　　　　我们，只要质量稳定，供货有保证，价格我
　　　　们可以从优。

陈其然：好吧，如果贵公司价格从优，我们可以去

组织厂家生产名优产品,保证质量是第一流的,款式品种,尽量多样配套,请史密斯先生谈谈具体优惠条件。

史密斯:这个……我想,我们一要参照国际市场行情,二要按质论价,这是不是看看样品再谈。不过,我们一定保证优质优价。

陈其然:这个意见很合理,我们同意。但我们还有一个要求,就是必须保证相当的起订量。各种规格的起订量过小,我们就难以组织货源了。

史密斯:好的,我们一定考虑。

二、订货量

陈其然:史密斯先生,很对不起,贵公司要的上等毛尖茶,由于今年歉收,我们只能供应600箱。

史密斯:陈先生,去年我们销售贵公司的上等毛尖茶叶情况良好。今年我们十分希望增加订货量。600箱无论如何不能满足需要,我们是老关系,老主顾,能不能优先照顾我们,再增加100箱。

陈其然:600箱上等毛尖,我们已做了最大努力。非常抱歉,史密斯先生,我们实在不能满足您的要求,希望下次能让您满意。

史密斯:不能增加100箱,50箱怎么样? 这是最低订货量了!

陈其然:好吧,就再增加50箱。史密斯先生,福建的乌龙茶今年丰收,建议您也订购一些。

玛　丽:不是滞销商品吧?

陈其然:笑话,乌龙茶也是中国的名茶,它不仅是饮料,还

是营养滋补品,有奇特疗效,经常饮用,对健康有
益,深受外国友人的欢迎。

史密斯:这么说,我可以接受您的建议,不知贵公司要求
多大的起订量?

陈其然:史密斯先生是我们的老客户,上等毛尖我方没有
满足要求,我们愿意在乌龙茶供货上尽量弥补。
这样,总成交额基本不变。

史密斯:谢谢陈先生的美意,我们就这样定了。

三、取消订货

史密斯:陈先生,由于市场行情变化,我们打算取消与贵
公司上周洽谈的订货。

陈其然:这不好吧,我们双方一向是重信誉,守合同的。

史密斯:是的,这次实在是不得已,请谅解。

陈其然:那么,是什么原因呢? 可以做个合理的说明吗?

史密斯:陈先生,你很清楚,长时间以来,世界食糖市场持
续萧条,需求锐减,这个星期,糖价跌到了一年来
的最低点,一周内每吨跌了 3.60 美元。如果我
们按上周洽谈的合同进货,我们将承担巨大损
失。好在我们还没有正式签约,可以提出调整。

陈其然:这个情况在上周洽谈时,我们已经充分考虑到
了,所以最后的定盘价格十分优惠。

史密斯:是的,对这一点,我们非常感谢。不过,最近一周
来,食糖市场形势变得更加严峻,我们不得不采
取相应的措施。

陈其然:市场形势,瞬息万变,我们相信,不久会出现转机
的。

史密斯：陈先生,我们是商人,有敢冒风险的精神,可也必须注重实际,请您能理解这一点。

陈其然：那好吧,我们同意你们的要求。为了保持我们之间的贸易额,我们还有几种商品,货源充足,你们是不是能订购一批?

史密斯：好的。礼尚往来,来而不往非礼嘛。你们理解我们,我们也理解你们。我们就洽谈另一笔生意吧。

生词

1.	清单	qīngdān	detailed list，inventory
2.	久享盛誉	jiǔxiǎngshèngyù	reputable
3.	抽屉	chōuti	drawer
4.	锁	suǒ	lock
5.	不锈钢	bùxiùgāng	stainless steel
6.	餐具	cānjù	tableware
7.	指甲刀	zhǐjiadāo	nail clipper
8.	矛	máo	spear
9.	牌(牌子)	pái(páizi)	brand
10.	剪刀	jiǎndāo	scissors
11.	脱销	tuōxiāo	sold out
12.	必需品	bìxūpǐn	necessities
13.	日用品	rìyòngpǐn	articles of everyday use
14.	薄利	bólì	small profit
15.	资金	zījīn	funds
16.	资源	zīyuán	resources
17.	空前	kōngqián	unprecedented

18. 短缺	duǎnquē	shortage
19. 供不应求	gōngbùyìngqiú	supply falling short of demand
20. 主顾	zhǔgù	customer, client
21. 照顾	zhàogù	give consideration to, make allowance for
22. 稳定	wěndìng	stable
23. 从优	cóngyōu	be as favorable as possible
24. 第一流	dìyīliú	first class
25. 尽量	jǐnliàng	as far as possible
26. 多样	duōyàng	many varieties
27. 配套	pèitào	form a complete set
28. 条件	tiáojiàn	conditions
29. 参照	cānzhào	consult, refer to, in the light of
30. 起订量	qǐdìngliàng	minimum quantity to start with
31. 毛尖茶	máojiānchá	*Maojian* tea
32. 规格	guīgé	specifications
33. 歉收	qiànshōu	crop failure, poor harvest
34. 箱	xiāng	case
35. 关系	guānxì	relation, relationship
36. 优先	yōuxiān	have priority
37. 乌龙茶	wūlóngchá	Oolong tea
38. 滞销	zhìxiāo	slow-selling; unsalable
39. 滋补品	zībǔpǐn	tonic
40. 经常	jīngcháng	frequently, constantly

41. 疗效	liáoxiào	curing effect
42. 弥补	míbǔ	make up
43. 美意	měiyì	kind consideration
44. 不得已	bùdéyǐ	have no choice but, be forced
45. 谅解	liàngjiě	understand
46. 食糖	shítáng	sugar
47. 萧条	xiāotiáo	depression, slump, slack
48. 锐减	ruìjiǎn	fall sharply
49. 承担	chéngdān	bear, undertake, assume
50. 巨大	jùdà	huge, enormous
51. 损失	sǔnshī	loss
52. 好在	hǎozài	fortunately, luckily
53. 签约	qiānyuē	sign the contract
54. 定盘	dìngpán	price at which business is concluded
55. 严峻	yánjùn	severe, grim
56. 采取	cǎiqǔ	adopt
57. 措施	cuòshī	measure
58. 瞬息万变	shùnxīwànbiàn	a myriad of changes in the twinkling of an eye
59. 转机	zhuǎnjī	a favorable turn, a turn for the better
60. 冒	mào	risk, brave
61. 风险	fēngxiǎn	risk, hazard
62. 注重	zhùzhòng	lay stress on, attach importance to
63. 实际	shíjì	reality, practice
64. 同意	tóngyì	agree

65. 充足	chōngzú	abundant, sufficient, ample
66. 礼尚往来	lǐshàngwǎnglái	courtesy demands reciprocity

练习

A

相当：

① 指数量、价值、条件、情形等两方面差不多；配得上或能够相抵。② 强调达到比较高但还不到"很"的程度。

1）Match; correspond to; be equal to; be commensurate with. It shows that two things are the same, similar or in proportion to each other in quantity, value, condition or circumstances. 2）Quite; fairly; considerably. It means to a fairly great extent or to a greater extent than average, but not to the extent expressed by 很（very）.

一、熟读下面的句子,仔细体会"相当"的意义和用法：

1. 她的穿着相当漂亮。
2. 这家公司信誉相当好。
3. 这批货的起订量相当可观。
4. 外汇兑换比价相当不稳定。
5. 两家工厂条件和规模都相当,但产品销售情况大不一样。

二、熟读下列词组,然后选择适当的词组完成下列五个句子：

相当快	相当熟悉	条件相当	规模相当
相当高	相当有益	价格相当	地位相当

相当累　　相当麻烦　　技术相当　　相当激烈

相当大　　相当硬　　相当充分

1. 我公司每年购进的小五金＿＿＿＿＿＿＿＿＿＿＿＿＿＿。

2. 这种高档录像机价格＿＿＿＿＿＿＿＿＿＿＿＿＿＿＿。

3. 他在大学学的是国际贸易,他要找＿＿＿＿＿＿＿＿

＿＿＿＿＿＿＿＿＿＿＿＿＿＿＿＿＿＿＿＿＿＿＿。

4. 现在,国际市场＿＿＿＿＿＿＿＿＿＿,所以我们只好取消

订货。

5. 我们已经考虑＿＿＿＿＿＿＿＿＿,所以才作出这样的调

整。

不得已:

受客观情况或条件影响,不得不这样。

Have no alternative but to; act against one's will. Under certain conditions or in certain situations, you are forced to do something, without any choice.

一、熟读下面的句子,体会"不得已"的意义和用法:

1. 货卖不出去,不得已降价。

2. 各种规格的起订量过小,我们不得已放弃。

3. 万不得已,就把投资转向获利大的商品。

4. 商品滞销,工厂不得已停产整顿。

5. 人们都说商人敢冒风险,其实常常是不得已的事。

二、用"不得已"完成下列各句:

1. 他学的专业现在找不到工作,＿＿＿＿＿＿＿＿＿改行。

2. 名优产品供不应求,＿＿＿＿＿＿＿＿＿＿＿＿＿＿。

3. 市场持续疲软,我们_____。

4. 毛尖茶歉收,_____。

5. 市场行情瞬息万变,_____。

无论如何:

是一个固定格式,意思是"不管怎样",表示不管条件怎样变化,其结果始终不变。

In any case; at all events; whatever happens. It is a set expression, meaning that in spite of anything that has happened or may happen, the result remains unchanged.

一、熟读下面的句子,体会"无论如何"的意义与用法:

1. 定盘价格无论如何不能再降低了。

2. 这个产品意向书,你无论如何要转交给厂方。

3. 做生意自然要赚钱,但无论如何也不能坑害顾客。

4. 非常抱歉,5点以前我无论如何赶不到了。

5. 我们是多年的老主顾了,无论如何得满足我们的要求。

二、用"无论如何"和括号里的词完成下面的句子:

1. 合同上写明的_____。(履行)

2. 按质论价_____。(公平合理)

3. 你到了北京,_____。(取消)

4. 请你_____。(信誉)

5. 我们这次取消订货实在是不得已的,_____

_____。(谅解)

B

一、熟读下列词语,解释其意义,然后用每个词语说一句话:

1. 瞬息万变　　4. 誉满全球　　6. 久享盛誉
2. 礼尚往来　　5. 大名远扬　　7. 千家万户
3. 驰名中外

二、用下列词语组词:

必需品	货源	脱销	空前	需求	设计
第一流	短缺	满足	款式	取消	特色
日用品	品种	多样	陈旧	尽量	变化
成交额	稳定	配套	要求	锐减	保持

三、从上面选择适当的词语,完成下面的句子:

1. 目前行情稳定,我建议你＿＿＿＿＿＿＿＿＿＿＿

   ＿＿＿＿＿＿＿＿＿＿＿。

2. 不能参照去年的成交额,因为＿＿＿＿＿＿＿＿＿＿

   ＿＿＿＿＿＿＿＿＿＿＿。

3. 这次无论如何不能满足你的要求,＿＿＿＿＿＿＿＿

   ＿＿＿＿＿＿＿＿＿＿＿。

4. 希望新产品能＿＿＿＿＿＿＿＿＿＿＿＿＿＿＿＿＿

   ＿＿＿＿＿＿＿＿＿＿＿。

5. 你们的产品真如广告上说的＿＿＿＿＿＿＿＿＿＿＿

   ＿＿＿＿＿＿＿＿＿＿＿。

四、想一想,谈一谈:

1. 请用所学的词语,自己设计一个"订货洽谈"。
2. 贵国日用必需品中哪些是名牌?你喜欢用名牌货吗?为什么?

3．请介绍贵国二三种深受欢迎的薄利畅销商品。

4．你买东西时首先考虑价格还是质量？

5．你在中国买到过价廉物美的东西吗？请谈一件你购货中的趣事。

五、阅读下面的短文，并回答问题：

一次性消费雨伞

一天，一个美国商人来到了一家雨伞厂，找到厂长说："你这里有既便宜，质量又次的雨伞吗？有多少我要多少。"厂长以为这个外国人不是疯子就是故意开玩笑，要次伞做什么？厂长拿给他一把伞，说："你看看怎么样？"这个美国客商看了一眼就说："这太好了，太牢固（láogù）了，价格肯定也不便宜，我不知贵厂能不能专为我生产一种雨伞，伞把和骨架都不要金属的，全用不结实的塑料，伞面颜色要漂亮，但质地不要好，可以遮雨就行。"厂长说："这种伞，用一次两次不就坏了？这可要倒我们厂的牌子！"美国客商笑着说："我们为了实现'温馨（wēnxīn）服务'，就要一次性消费的雨伞，我们可以定牌订货嘛，这不会倒贵厂的牌子。"经过他的反复说明，厂长终于明白了，接受了这位客商 10 万把次伞订货。

1．什么是"一次性"消费？你能举出这种消费的例子吗？

2．什么是"温馨服务"？在贵国的商店有这类服务吗？

3．生产和销售次货，符合什么样的市场供求原则？

第七课 折扣与佣金
Lesson 7　Discount and Commission

一、要求折扣

罗　丹:关于折扣问题,请问李先生是怎么考虑的?

李　宁:原则上我们不给折扣。

罗　丹:这不合惯例吧,我们这次订货总额很大,按照惯例,我们至少可得到 10％的折扣。

李　宁:你们这次订货数量虽然不算小,但都是热门货,售销快,利润大,再说我们在价格方面已经优惠了,实际上等于给了折扣,所以不能再给折扣了。

罗　丹:真太遗憾了,这样做对我们太不公道了。

李　宁:如果你们能再增加一些订货量,我们可以考虑给一定折扣。

罗　丹:那好吧,我们再增加一成订货。

二、折扣争议

罗　丹:李先生,我们订购了 10 万台石英钟,准备给多少折扣?

李　宁:可以按净价给 2% 的折扣。

罗　丹:这是不是太低了？我们从别的国家进口同类产
　　　品可以得到 10% 的折扣。

李　宁:罗丹先生不会忘记,我方给的报价是最优惠的,
　　　我们已经把折扣考虑进去了。如果贵方能按合
　　　同提前付清货款,我们可以按净价再减收 2%。

罗　丹:李先生,我们订的这批货是新产品,又是试销,风
　　　险较大,为了打开市场,是不是可以再多给一点
　　　折扣？

李　宁:这个要求可以考虑,我们破例再给 2% 的折扣吧。
　　　这样,总折扣已超过 5%。说实在的,这真是特殊
　　　的照顾了。

三、要求佣金

琼　斯:张先生,这次我给你们介绍生意,你们考虑给多
　　　少佣金？

张　祥:很遗憾,琼斯先生,按我们的规定,原则上是不给
　　　佣金的。

琼　斯:张先生,我要提请您注意,不给佣金不符合国际
　　　贸易惯例。

张　祥:琼斯先生,我们只对中间商、代理商付给一定酬
　　　劳。

琼　斯:事情正是这样,您很清楚,我们只是代理商。

张　祥:那好吧,我们可以根据成交额和商品的性质,支
　　　付琼斯先生一定的劳务费。

琼　斯:不,我愿意名正言顺地得到佣金。张先生,要知
　　　道本公司是通过取得合理的佣金来进行商业活

动的。

四、佣金争议

琼　斯：张先生,作为你们产品的代理商,我们很关心佣金问题。

张　祥：我们很理解。我们在价格上已经给了你们较大的优惠,佣金就要相应地少一些,给1%,怎么样?

琼　斯：1%?开什么玩笑!我们通常从每笔交易中得到3%的佣金,这次成交额如此大,我们理应得到比3%更高的佣金,你们却只给1%,是不是太不合情理了?

张　祥：我们都知道,佣金是按成交额的一定比例来计算的,成交额越大,你们提取的佣金就越多嘛。

琼　斯：话不能这么说。为了扩大贵公司产品的销路,争夺市场,我们要雇更多的推销员,花更多的广告费。我们订货量越大,付出的代价也越大。我们理应得到相应的补偿。

张　祥：你们从按比例提取的佣金中已经得到了补偿。

琼　斯：但这远远不够,不足以补偿我们付出的代价!

张　祥：这样吧,如果你们能再增加订货量,我们可以考虑再多给1%的佣金。

琼　斯：我们不能接受这样的附加条件。1%的佣金,在国际贸易中恐怕没有先例。

张　祥：我们的报价如此低廉,在国际市场上你们恐怕也找不出第二家了。如果你们坚持要提高佣金,我们就不能不适当调整价格。琼斯先生,你看怎么办更合理?

琼　斯:看来,我们彼此想问题的思路不同,方法不一样,
　　　　是很难沟通了,真遗憾!

生词

1.	折扣	zhékòu	discount
2.	佣金	yòngjīn	commission
3.	原则	yuánzé	principle
4.	惯例	guànlì	convention, usual practice
5.	等于	děngyú	be equal to
6.	热门货	rèménhuò	fast-selling goods
7.	利润	lìrùn	profit
8.	争议	zhēngyì	dispute
9.	石英钟	shíyīngzhōng	quartz clock
10.	净价	jìngjià	net price
11.	同类	tónglèi	same kind
12.	付清	fùqīng	pay in full, pay off
13.	货款	huòkuǎn	payment for goods
14.	减收	jiǎnshōu	reduce (money received)
15.	守约	shǒuyuē	abide by the contract
16.	破例	pòlì	break a rule, make an exception
17.	符合	fúhé	conform to
18.	中间商	zhōngjiānshāng	middleman
19.	代理商	dàilǐshāng	agent
20.	酬劳	chóuláo	remuneration, reward
21.	性质	xìngzhì	nature
22.	支付	zhīfù	pay
23.	劳务费	láowùfèi	fee for one's service

24.	名正言顺	míngzhèngyán shùn	be perfectly justifiable
25.	作为	zuòwéi	as; regard as
26.	通常	tōngcháng	usually, normally, generally
27.	却	què	but, yet
28.	情理	qínglǐ	reason, sense
29.	比例	bǐlì	proportion, ratio
30.	计算	jìsuàn	calculate
31.	提取	tíqǔ	draw, pick up
32.	扩大	kuòdà	enlarge, expand
33.	争夺	zhēngduó	contend for, scramble for
34.	雇用	gùyòng	employ, hire
35.	推销员	tuīxiāoyuán	salesman
36.	代价	dàijià	cost
37.	补偿	bǔcháng	compensate
38.	先例	xiānlì	precedent
39.	低廉	dīlián	low price; cheap
40.	坚持	jiānchí	insist
41.	适当	shìdàng	proper, suitable
42.	思路	sīlù	way of thinking, train of thought
43.	沟通	gōutōng	link, connect, bridge

练习

A

按,按照:

    ① 提出行为、动作所遵循的准则或依据;② 提出一种标准,

用于比较两种事物;③ 表示行为、动作依照时间顺序进行;④ "按……说","按……说来","按……来说"格式,都是先举出所根据的事理,再由此作出结论。"按照"没有第三项意义和用法。

According to; in accordance with; in the light of; on the basis of. 1) It says that something is done or arranged according to a particular principle or criterion. 2) It introduces a criterion according to which two things are being compared. 3) It expresses a time sequence according to which some events or actions take place. 4) In such expressions as 按…说,按…说来,按…来说, the principle or criterion is first mentioned, to be followed by the result. 按 can be used in all these four ways, while 按照 does not have the meaning and usage expressed in 3).

一、熟读下列句子,体会"按"、"按照"的意义和用法:

1. 按照惯例,中间商都要提取佣金。
2. 按时发货,是合同明确规定的条款。
3. 按照商品质量的优劣,决定出售价格。
4. 按理说,我们不能再增加折扣了。
5. 按工厂的生产规模和能力来说,我们接受这批货是不会有问题的。

二、用"按"、"按照"和括号里的词语完成下列句子:

1. _____,我们决定付给你方相应的佣金。
   （销售量）
2. _____,我们随时调整商品价格。
   （订货量）
3. 折扣的多少,_____。
   （惯例）
4. 这些都是热门货,_____,

你们应该获得较大的利润。(道理)

5. 你们的商品质量不合要求,_____,
   我们可以取消订货。(合同)

门:

① 房屋、车船等的出入口;② 门路和途径;③ 事物的分类。

1) Entrance, door, gate (to a building, a vehicle, a ship, etc.) 2) Way to do something; social connections. 3) Class; category.

一、熟读下列各句,并指出句中带"门"的词含有上面的哪一项意义:

1. 中国政府欢迎来华外商合法经商,但不准搞邪门歪道。
2. 今天的天气真邪门,怎么这么冷?
3. 这是种热门货,刚投放市场,就一抢而空。
4. 在今天的中国,改革开放成了最热门的话题。
5. 他开始学做生意的时候,一点儿也摸不着门儿,现在却成了几家大公司的代理商了。

二、用下列词语,各说一句话:

1. 没门儿:
2. 热门儿:
3. 邪门儿:
4. 抠门儿:

通常:

副词,是"在一般情况下"的意思。它与"经常"、"常常"义近,但有区别。"经常"、"常常"表示某种情况屡次发生。

Adverb: Generally, usually, as a rule. Its meaning is near to that of 经常 or 常常, but with some difference. 经常 and 常常 indicate that something occurs repeatedly.

一、熟读下面各句,体会不同词义:

1. 他通常在晚上 12 点睡觉。
   (没特殊情况,差不多都这样)
2. 他常常在晚上 12 点睡觉。
   (这种情况发生的次数比较多)
3. 我们通常给中间商 5% 的佣金。
4. 我们常常给中间商 5% 的佣金。
5. 总经理通常是周末带着全家参加健身活动。
6. 总经理常常一边吃早饭,一边看报。

二、选用"通常"、"经常"、"常常"填空:

1. 我方给你们的报价＿＿＿＿是最优惠的。
2. 我＿＿＿＿给你们介绍生意,你们是否考虑可以多给佣金。
3. 佣金＿＿＿＿是按成交额的一定比例来计算的。
4. 在北京,每一个家庭＿＿＿＿有 1 辆~2 辆自行车。
5. 北京人＿＿＿＿喝花茶,上海＿＿＿＿喝绿茶,广东人＿＿＿＿喝红茶。
6. 你＿＿＿＿参加朋友的聚会吗?

足以:

"足",是"足够"、"完成"、"全部"的意思。"以"是介词,这后面省略了一个介词宾语。课文中的句子"不足以补偿我们付出的代价","以"字后省略了"你们付的佣金"。

足 means enough, sufficiently, totally. 以 is a preposition with its prepositional object omitted. The sentence in the text:"It is insufficient to compensate for our cost" can be understood as having omitted "your commission".

一、熟读下面各句,体会"足以"的意义和用法:

1. 吸食过量的毒品足以致人死命。
2. 你这点汉语足以应付在中国的日常生活交流了。
3. 产品质量不好,价格优惠也不足以吸引顾客。
4. 放心吧,这笔财产足以保证你幸福的晚年生活了。
5. 我这么做还不足以表明我对你的感情吗?

二、用"足以"和括号里的词语完成下列句子:

1. 考虑到贵方为推销我们的新产品做出了很大的努力,我们 破例给贵方5%的折扣_____。(补偿)
2. 这么优惠的报价_____。(竞争)
3. 我们提供低廉的劳动力_____。(争夺)
4. 总经理每年都要提出新的改革办法_____。(思路)
5. 每月开一次公司职工代表会_____。(沟通)

B

一、用括号里的词语完成下列各句:

1. 按惯例,我们应该得到的折扣_____ _____。(3%)
2. 虽然_____,但是我们彼此是有 诚意的,态度是友好的。(争议)
3. 这是一种新产品,_____,因 此还只是小批量生产。(试销)
4. 这笔交易做得很成功,因为_____ _____。(利润)
5. 我们这次签订的合同,_____

_____。(符合)

6. 我们提供了劳务,_____

_____。(酬劳)

7. 你付出了多大的努力_____

_____。(补偿)

8. 我们一贯奉公守法,_____

_____。(名正言顺)

9. 考虑到目前市场行情的变化,_____

_____。(破例)

10. 中间商从事商业活动的目的是_____

_____。(佣金)

二、想一想、谈一谈:

1. 按惯例,中间商或代理商做成一笔交易应该得多少折扣或佣金?

2. 折扣和佣金应根据什么原则计算比较公道?

3. 劳务费和佣金有实质上的差别吗?

4. 请你谈一次要求折扣或佣金的见闻。

三、阅读下面的短文,并回答问题:

价格俱乐部

有个美国人叫索尔·普赖斯(Sol Price),开了一个商店俱乐部,因为 price 是价格的意思,所以又叫"价格俱乐部"。人们只要加入俱乐部,凭会员卡,就可到"价格俱乐部"去买任何东西。这里的东西特别便宜,比如 1 台金星牌彩色电视机,在普通商店零售价是 500 美元,进价(批发价)仅 300 美元,除掉税收,可净赚约 130 美元。而在"价格俱乐部"每台可打 20％的折扣,零售只卖 399 美元。除掉税收,只净赚 30 美元左右。有人问他:

"你这不是太吃亏了吗?"索尔回答说:"一般人对买便宜货非常兴奋,买得越多似乎越显得自己比别人聪明,又有会员优惠卡,不买白不买,一进商店,见什么买什么,一个人每次进商店平均要花去100美元。就说彩电吧,普通商店,一天可能只卖出1台,我这里可能卖出8台~10台,你说谁赚得多呢?"

1.“价格俱乐部”经商遵循的是什么原则?

2.索尔·普赖斯是怎样理解顾客的消费心理的?

3.普通商店与索尔的商店,谁的营业额大? 获取的利润大?

第八课　支付方式
Lesson 8　Modes of Payment

一、选择支付货币

李　宁：罗斯先生，这笔进口交易的货款，我们希望能用人民币支付。

罗　斯：对不起，我们通常都用美元作计价货币，这也比较方便。

李　宁：其实用人民币付款也没什么不方便，欧洲的许多银行和北京的中国银行有账户往来。

罗　斯：但我们不熟悉这方面的情况，还是用美元支付简便些。

李　宁：噢，手续很简单。你方只要到贵国与中国银行有账户往来的银行议付就可以了。

罗　斯：坦率地说，我们担心用人民币付款，会因国际汇率波动蒙受经济损失。

李　宁：关于这一点，罗斯先生尽可放心，人民币的汇率十分稳定，我们还可以给保值汇率，这下就万无一失了。

罗　斯：好吧，我们不妨做一次尝试。

二、采用哪种付款方式

罗　斯:李先生,你们一般采用什么付款方式?

李　宁:我们一般只接受不可撤销信用证的付款方式,你
　　　　方可以在收到装运单据后,凭单据付款。

杰克逊:你们能不能接受承兑交单(D/A)?

李　宁:实在报歉,我们无法接受你们的建议。

杰克逊:我们公司一向是讲信誉的。我们一旦收到承兑
　　　　交单,即予承兑,汇票到期时,我们一定付款。

李　宁:我们相信这一点,但我们要承担很大风险,用不
　　　　可撤销信用证方式,对我们安全收汇较有保障,
　　　　请罗斯先生理解。

罗　斯:李先生,这么大笔的货款在银行开立信用证所需
　　　　费用太大,不但要付手续费,还得付数目可观的
　　　　押金,这必然提高进口商品价格,影响销售。请
　　　　贵方能考虑到这些。

李　宁:很对不起,正因为货款金额大,而目前国际金融
　　　　市场又极不稳定,为了保险起见,我们不得不坚
　　　　持采用信用证付款方式。

杰克逊:那么,能不能采用付款交单(D/P)方式呢?

李　宁:这同承兑交单一样,仍然不能提供可靠的银行担
　　　　保,只是我们承担的风险小一点。因此,很遗憾,
　　　　我们也不能采用付款交单的方式。

罗　斯:好吧,但你们也务必履行不可撤销信用证规定的
　　　　条款。

李　宁:这是自然的。我们一定如期交货,并尽可能提前
　　　　交货。请贵方一定要在交货期前 30 天把信用证

开达我方。这样便于我方作必要的安排。

罗　斯：这点我们可以做到。

李　宁：我们还有一个要求，开出的信用证有效期应为 15 天，在货物装船后，自提单签发之日算起，并请在信用证上注明到期地点和"在中国有效"的字样。

罗　斯：好的，我们照办。

三、分期付款

王　进：格林先生，这次进口项目，货款金额大，我们将采用分期付款方式，希望能得到贵方的合作。

格　林：王先生，考虑到贵方具体困难，为了今后的贸易往来，这次我们同意接受分期付款方式。但长期垫付这笔巨款，对我们公司资金周转压力太大，希望贵方在支付第一笔货款时，数额大一些。

王　进：这可以考虑。我们在合同正式签订后，可以先付一半货款定金，余款分两次付清，你看好不好？

格　林：这很好。明天，我就可以准备好一张远期汇票，请你承兑，并请北京中国银行附签，以证明贵公司的承兑是有效的。然后，再还给我。

王　进：好的。只要贵方按期交货，货的质量、规格与合同条款相符，我们保证，银行会在我们承兑的期票到期时支付货款的。

格　林：为了确认双方的合同权利和责任，我们希望在合同上清楚地写明各批货的装船数量、日期和付款细节。

王　进：请放心，我们公司一向严格履行与外商签订的合同条款。

四、补偿贸易

王　进：格林先生,这次进口的露天煤矿设备,我们准备用补偿贸易的方式,你们看可以吗?

格　林：我们这次洽谈的设备用来开发的露天煤矿,煤种为低磷、低硫,中灰长焰煤,是品位很高的优质动力用煤,我们很乐意将这种产品返销到我国去。因此,这笔生意,用补偿贸易方式成交,原则上我们没有意见。

王　进：很好。那么,请问格林先生,是直接补偿贸易呢?还是综合补偿贸易?

格　林：我们更喜欢直接补偿贸易。因为能源危机始终是困扰我国经济的一个重要因素,这样好的优质煤,十分难得,我们希望用这批设备投产的优质煤偿付全部货款。

王　进：格林先生,您说得很对,我们也十分需要这个矿山的优质煤,所以,我们更倾向于采取综合补偿贸易。

格　林：贵公司是不是准备向别的客商提供这种优质煤?如果是这样,我们理应优先!

王　进：即使是多边贸易,也是正常的。不过,目前我们还没有同其他客商洽谈这种产品的出口问题。我再重申一下,首先是我们也很需要这种原煤,请格林先生相信。

格　林：好吧,我们就用综合补偿贸易方式吧。不过,希望用直接产品偿还的部分尽量大一些,用间接商品偿还的部分小些。

王　进:这个原则,我们也同意。

生词

1. 计价　　　jìjià　　　　　calculate the price
2. 账户　　　zhànghù　　　　account
3. 开立　　　kāilì　　　　　open
4. 信用证　　xìnyòngzhèng　letter of credit
5. 议付　　　yìfù　　　　　negotiate payment
6. 波动　　　bōdòng　　　　fluctuate
7. 蒙受　　　méngshòu　　　suffer
8. 保值　　　bǎozhí　　　　guarantee the value
9. 万无一失　wànwúyīshī　　perfectly safe, absolutely
　　　　　　　　　　　　　certain
10. 一般　　　yībān　　　　　generally, normally
11. 尝试　　　chángshì　　　try, attempt
12. 方式　　　fāngshì　　　　mode, manner
13. 撤消　　　chèxiāo　　　　revoke, cancel
14. 单据　　　dānjù　　　　　document
15. 承兑　　　chéngduì　　　acceptance
16. 交单　　　jiāodān　　　　hand over the documents,
　　　　　　　　　　　　　delivery
17. 到期　　　dàoqī　　　　　mature, expire
18. 保障　　　bǎozhàng　　　ensure, guarantee
19. 数目　　　shùmù　　　　　number, amount
20. 可观　　　kěguān　　　　considerable, sizable
21. 押金　　　yājīn　　　　　cash pledge, deposit
22. 必然　　　bìrán　　　　　inevitable, necessary
23. 影响　　　yǐngxiǎng　　　affect, influence

24. 金融	jīnróng	finance
25. 付款	fùkuǎn	payment
26. 可靠	kěkào	reliable, trustworthy
27. 担保	dānbǎo	guarantee
28. 务必	wùbì	must, be sure to
29. 履行	lǚxíng	perform, fulfill, carry out
30. 条款	tiáokuǎn	terms
31. 如期	rúqī	as scheduled
32. 提前	tíqián	ahead of schedule, move up, advance
33. 必要	bìyào	necessary
34. 货物	huòwù	goods
35. 注明	zhùmíng	give clear indication of
36. 照办	zhàobàn	act accordingly
37. 垫付	diànfù	give somebody an advance
38. 周转	zhōuzhuǎn	turnover
39. 压力	yālì	pressure
40. 签订	qiāndìng	conclude and sign
41. 定金	dìngjīn	down payment, deposit put down on sth. for future purchase
42. 远期	yuǎnqī	for future purchase; at a specified future date
43. 汇票	huìpiào	draft
44. 附签	fùqiān	countersign
45. 按期	ànqī	on schedule, on time, in time
46. 期票	qīpiào	promissory note, time draft
47. 证明	zhèngmíng	prove, testify, certify

48. 责任	zérèn	responsibilities
49. 细节	xìjié	detail
50. 露天	lùtiān	open-cut, in the open
51. 煤矿	méikuàng	coal-mine
52. 磷	lín	phosphorus
53. 硫	liú	sulfur
54. 长焰煤	chángyànméi	coal with long flames
55. 品位	pǐnwèi	grade
56. 动力	dònglì	power
57. 乐意	lèyì	be willing to; pleased
58. 返销	fǎnxiāo	resell (to where it is produced)
59. 能源	néngyuán	energy resources
60. 危机	wēijī	crisis
61. 困扰	kùnrǎo	be hard pressed, perplex
62. 因素	yīnsù	factor
63. 投产	tóuchǎn	go into operation, put into production
64. 倾向	qīngxiàng	be inclined to, prefer
65. 多边	duōbiān	multilateral
66. 重申	chóngshēn	reiterate
67. 间接	jiànjiē	indirect

练习

A

其实:

副词,用在动词前或主语前,表示所说的情况是真实的,承接上文而含转折的意思,或是引出与上文相反的意思,或是修改、补充上文。

Adveb: Actually; as a matter of fact. It is placed before the verb or the subject to indicate that the state of affairs being referred to is a fact. It continues from what has been said before, indicating a transition. It either introduces something which is opposite to what was said previously, or amends or supplements it.

一、熟读下列各句,体会"其实"的意义和用法:

1. 他说熟悉市场行情,其实他并不熟悉。
2. 他担心开立人民币信用证手续麻烦,其实很简单。
3. 他说他们是老朋友,其实他们认识的时间并不长。
4. 他以为商品价格越高越能赚钱,其实薄利多销才是最有效的。

二、请用"其实"完成下列各句:

1. 他说保证提前交货,_____。

2. 别看他开高级车,住高级宾馆,_____

   _____。

3. 你把这些商品都当成滞销商品_____

   _____。

4. 他说得很好听,_____。

5. 你认为合同正式签字后就不会有问题了,_____

   _____。

为……起见:
是一个固定格式,用来介绍动作或行为的目的。

A set expression: For the sake of. It expresses the purpose of an action or event.

一、熟读下列各句,体会"为……起见"的用法:

1. 为保险起见,我们不得不坚持用信用证付款方式。
2. 为避免麻烦起见,我们应尽力把合同写得清楚准确一点。
3. 为说明问题起见,我简单回顾一下我公司的发展过程。
4. 为简单快速起见,你就直接找总经理谈吧。

二、熟读下列词语,并完成句子:

1. 为完全起见,_____。

2. 为方便起见,_____。

3. 为可靠起见,_____。

4. 为熟悉起见,_____。

5. 为保值起见,_____。

6. 为保险起见,_____。

于:

介词,同名词、代词或词组构成介词结构,表示范围、时间、处所、对象等,意义有多种:在、向、给、自、从等,还可表示比较、被动。

Preposition: It is used together with a noun, a pronoun or an expression to form a prepositional phrase, indicating scope, time, location, and object. It has various meanings, including 在(in),向(towards),给(for),自(from), and 从(since), etc. It also expresses comparison and passiveness.

一、熟读下列各句,指出"于"在各句中的不同含义:

1. 倾向于采用综合补偿贸易。
2. 不能把成本涨价转嫁于顾客。

3．请你方尽早通知我们船名、船期,便于我方作必要的安排。

4．交货时间不会早于本月 28 日。

5．今年春季广交会于 4 月 15 日开幕。

二、请把下列各句,改用"于"来表达:

1．这是一家老字号商店,在 1940 年开业。

2．佣金不能比 2% 少。

3．这次洽谈的设备,我们将用来开发露天煤矿。

4．为了安全收汇,我们坚持用不可撤销信用证付款方式。

5．同世界各国友好往来,互通有无,能帮助我国经济发展。

一旦:

相当于"有一天",时间短或时间不确定。常见格式:"一旦
……就……",表示有了某种条件,结果就随之发生。

Once; in case; now that. It corresponds to "some day", indicating a short or indefinite period of time. The usual pattern is 一旦
…就, which shows that with certain conditions, something would
happen immediately afterwards.

一、熟读下列各句,体会"一旦"的意义和用法:

1．一旦收到承兑交单,我方即予承兑。

2．我们担心用贵国货币付款,一旦国际汇率波动,我方蒙受
经济损失。

3．交货期一旦有变动,请及时(电话)通知我方。

4．我们两国的银行一旦建立账户往来,进出口贸易就方便多
了。

二、请用"一旦"改写下列各句:

1．资金周转不灵,我们就无法按期付款。

2. 合同正式签订后,可以先付一半定金。

_____

3. 能源危机解决了,我国经济会有一个大发展。

_____

4. 这种产品返销到贵国去,我们相信可以在贵国打开市场。

_____

5. 贵国如果能履行各项合同条款,我们保证,银行会在我们
承兑的期票到期时支付货款。

_____

B

一、用下列词语组词:

选择	帐户	稳定	履行	信用证	严格
计价	担心	撤销	条款	确认书	保障
货币	汇率	押金	相符	付(交)款单	权利
开立	波动	可观	按期	偿(还)付	签发(订)

二、用括号中的词语完成下列句子:

1. 我们同意分期付款方式,但_____

_____。(垫付)

2. 目前国际金融市场_____

_____。(汇率)

3. 我们希望承担的风险小一点,_____

_____。(不可撤销信用证)

4. 我们担心用贵国货币付款_____

_____。(蒙受)

5. 一般来说,开立信用证所需费用大,_____
_____。(不但……而且……)

6. 货物装船后,买方应该立即_____
_____。(单据、汇票)

7. 请务必严格履行_____。(条款)

8. 我们很乐意采用补偿贸易方式,全部货款_____
_____。(偿付)

9. 中国银行_____
_____。(账户)

10. 为证明你方汇票承兑有效,_____
_____。(附签)

三、想一想、谈一谈:

1. 谈谈你在付款问题上最担心的问题是什么?
2. 你认为哪一种是最好最方便的付款方式?哪一种是风险最大、最麻烦的付款方式?
3. 买方开立的信用证怎样才是有效的?
4. 分期付款一般怎么做?第一笔货款金额是多少?分几批付清?
5. 补偿贸易是双方都乐于接受的方式吗?为什么?

四、阅读下面的短文,并回答问题:

圣诞卡交易

外商 N,在个体户小李的商店买了 500 张音乐圣诞卡,每张 3 元,又漂亮又便宜,他非常满意,当即付了款,然后提出,他还要订购 3500 张,但要求圣诞卡的图案和颜色都适合他们国家顾客的口味。双方经过一番讨价还价,终于以每张 2.8 元成交,两个星期后全部交货,客商 N 先付定金 1000 元。小李按时备齐了货,客商 N 也如期到来,却要退货,不仅拒绝付款,还要求退还定金。双方争执(zhēngzhí)起来。小李说 N 不守信誉,N 说质量不合要求;小李说可以退货,但 N 必须赔偿经济损失;N 说我们成交时没有这样的协议。双方各说各的理,谁也不肯让步。

1. 双方两次的成交总额是多少?
2. N 如果拒不付款,小李将蒙受多大损失?
3. N 不付款对不对?责任究竟在哪一方?
4. 双方的争执如何解决?

第九课　交货与装船
Lesson 9　Delivery and Shipment

一、交货日期

罗　　斯：李先生，一般来说，贵方需要多少时间才能交货？

李　　宁：通常在收到信用证以后 30 天内可以交货装船。

杰克逊：季节性商品能不能提前交货呢？

李　　宁：这要看具体情况，如果厂家生产任务重，安排不开，就很难提前交货。

罗　　斯：时间对季节性商品至关重要，如果赶不上销售季节，畅销货就变成滞销品，只有降价处理，我们就要蒙受很大损失。

李　　宁：这点我们很理解，一定保证按期交货。能否提前交货要与厂家磋商，估计有一定困难。

杰克逊：希望李先生对我们的要求给予特殊照顾。

李　　宁：我们一定尽最大努力。但不管怎样，这批货的交货时间不会早于 9 月 15 日，再早确实有困难。

二、装运日期

李　宁：罗斯先生，我们今天讨论货物装运问题。

罗　斯：好的，请贵公司先谈谈意见。

李　宁：我们这笔生意，是按 F.O.B. 价格条款成交的，不言而喻，交货装船的港口，应是中国港口，你方只有及时派船来接货，我们才能严格履行合同。如果你方没有如期履行派船义务，你方应承担对我公司造成的经济损失。

罗　斯：关于这个问题，我们没有异议。我们合同规定的交货日期是明年 5 月 30 日以前，那么，你们什么时候交货呢？

李　宁：我们在收到信用证以后 30 天内可以交货。

杰克逊：不能再提前一点吗？

李　宁：恐怕很困难。我们需要有足够的时间备货，制单，办理出口海关手续等。

罗　斯：那好吧，我们回去就立即开立信用证。希望贵公司收到信用证后，用传真及时通知我们装船的具体时间，以便我们派船受载。

李　宁：我们会办到的。我们也希望你方接到通知后，能及时电告你们的船舶到港受载日期，以便我们安排货物出运和装船工作。

罗　斯：一定，一定，希望我们双方能通力合作。

三、提单

李　宁：罗斯先生，关于提单，我们是不是也应该约定一下。

罗　斯：这也正是我们要提出的问题。我们希望在信用
　　　　证中写明,卖方应将三份正本提单中的一份直接
　　　　寄给买方。

李　宁：很遗憾,我们不能接受这种三分之一正本提单的
　　　　要求。

罗　斯：为什么?

李　宁：按国际惯例,三份正本提单具有同等效力,你们
　　　　可以不向银行付款赎单就可提走全部货物,而我
　　　　们则可能收不到货款,造成财货两空的重大损
　　　　失。

罗　斯：你对我们没有最基本的信任!

李　宁：请不要见怪,罗斯先生。我们是为了避免不必要
　　　　的提单纠纷。

罗　斯：好吧,我们放弃这个要求。那么,关于滞期费和
　　　　速遣费条款呢?

李　宁：我想,我们应该首先在合同的附加条款中明确每
　　　　天的装卸量。

杰克逊：装卸货时间,也应该有明确规定。按我们的习
　　　　惯,装卸港晴天每天连续工作 24 小时,节假日除
　　　　外。

李　宁：我看,最好是在合同中注明,节假日不用不算,用
　　　　了则要算,这样可能更灵活些,以后在计算速遣
　　　　费和滞期费时也可以避免发生争议。

罗　斯：好的,这些原则,我都同意。我们就来进一步讨
　　　　论细节吧!

四、分批与转船

李　宁:罗斯先生,我们这次洽谈的是一笔大宗生意,成
　　　交数量大,我们希望能分批装运。

罗　斯:这恐怕不行,因为这批货,都是季节性很强的商
　　　品,我们希望同时到货,以便趁销售旺季脱手。

李　宁:我们可以保证按合同如期交货。只是这批货不
　　　是一个厂家的产品,我们只能把货物集中在几个
　　　中国港口装船。

杰克逊:那么,贵公司打算分几批装运呢?

李　宁:这是不是就不要限制了,只在合同上写明"准许
　　　分运"就可以了。

罗　斯:好吧。不过,希望分批越少越好,并且保证按时
　　　全部交货。

李　宁:谢谢罗斯先生的合作。还有一个问题,我们这笔
　　　生意是按 C.I.F. 价格成交的,我国没有海船直
　　　达贵公司指定的目的港,必须在中途换装其他船
　　　舶。

杰克逊:李先生,中途转船,必然延长海运时间,增加转船
　　　费用,而且造成转船破损,请李先生充分考虑到
　　　这些不利因素。

李　宁:我们考虑过,但只有转船才能到达你方指定的目
　　　的港,除非另外选择对我们双方都合适的目的
　　　港。

罗　斯:好,我们现在就研究李先生的这个建议。

生词

1. 至关重要	zhìguānzhòngyào	most important
2. 处理	chǔlǐ	handle, deal with, settle
3. 估计	gūjì	estimate
4. 磋商	cuōshāng	consult, exchange views
5. 给予	jǐyǔ	give
6. 不言而喻	bùyán'éryù	it goes without saying
7. 及时	jíshí	in time, without delay
8. 义务	yìwù	duty, obligation
9. 造成	zàochéng	cause, create, give rise to
10. 异议	yìyì	objection, dissent
11. 足够	zúgòu	enough, sufficient
12. 备货	bèihuò	get the goods ready
13. 制单	zhìdān	make out the documents
14. 办理	bànlǐ	manage, handle
15. 海关	hǎiguān	customs
16. 传真	chuánzhēn	fax
17. 以便	yǐbiàn	so that, in order to, so as to
18. 受载	shòuzài	be loaded
19. 船舶	chuánbó	vessel
20. 通力合作	tōnglìhézuò	full cooperation
21. 约定	yuēdìng	arrange, fix, agree upon
22. 正本	zhèngběn	original
23. 具有	jùyǒu	have, possess
24. 同等	tóngděng	equal
25. 效力	xiàolì	force, effect
26. 赎单	shúdān	redeem (the documents)

27.	提走	tízǒu	take delivery of
28.	财货两空	cáihuòliǎngkōng	lose both the money and the goods
29.	重大	zhòngdà	significant, great
30.	见怪	jiànguài	take offense, feel offended
31.	避免	bìmiǎn	avoid
32.	纠纷	jiūfēn	dispute
33.	滞期费	zhìqīfèi	demurrage
34.	速遣费	sùqiǎnfèi	dispatch
35.	装卸	zhuāngxiè	loading and unloading
36.	连续	liánxù	continuous, in succession
37.	节假日	jiéjiàrì	holidays
38.	宗	zōng	(a measure word expressing quantity)
39.	脱手	tuōshǒu	dispose of, sell
40.	集中	jízhōng	put together
41.	分批	fēnpī	in batches
42.	按时	ànshí	on schedule
43.	直达	zhídá	direct, through, non-stop
44.	指定	zhǐdìng	designate
45.	中途	zhōngtú	en route
46.	延长	yáncháng	prolong
47.	破损	pòsǔn	damage

练习

A

赶不上：

① 有一定距离，追不上，跟不上；② 时间来不及；③ 遇不着

1) Be a distance behind; fail to catch up with; fail to keep pace with. 2) Be not in time for; be late. 3) Miss.

一、熟读下列句子,体会每句中"赶不上"的不同意义：

1. 这批货怕赶不上圣诞节了。

2. 飞机就要起飞了,她到现在还没出门,要赶不上飞机了。

3. 我两次休假去中国南方旅行都没赶上好天气。

4. 季节性商品赶不上销售季节,我们就要蒙受重大经济损失。

二、请用"赶上"、"赶不上"、"赶得上"回答下列问题。

1. 这批货能保证按期装船吗?

2. 中途转船,必然延长海运时间,可能出现什么结果?

3. 时间这么紧,贵方能保证按时全部交货吗?

4. 这批设备我们希望年底运到,你看怎么样?

5. 他积压的一批商品,竟迅速脱手了,你知道什么原因吗?

除非：

连词,表示唯一的条件,相当于"只有"。常见格式"除非……

才(否则、不然)"

Only if; only when; unless. It is a conjunction indicating the sole condition, similar to 只有. The usual pattern is 除非…才(否则,不然)(otherwise)....

一、熟读下列各句,体会各句中"除非"的意义和用法:

1. 除非他有了更重要的事情,才没有来参加签字仪式。
2. 除非另外选择对我们双方都合适的目的港,否则只好转船装运。
3. 除非厂家任务重,安排不开,不然不会不照顾。
4. 估计资金周转有一定困难,除非银行增加贷款。

二、用"除非"完成下列各句:

1. 能否提前交货要与厂家磋商,＿＿＿＿＿＿＿＿＿
   ＿＿＿＿＿＿＿＿＿＿＿＿＿＿＿＿＿＿＿。

2. 贵方对我们的要求一向给予特殊照顾,＿＿＿＿＿＿＿
   ＿＿＿＿＿＿＿＿＿＿＿＿＿＿＿＿＿＿＿。

3. 这批货的交货时间不会晚于本月中旬,＿＿＿＿＿＿
   ＿＿＿＿＿＿＿＿＿＿＿＿＿＿＿＿＿＿＿。

4. 我回去立即开立信用证,＿＿＿＿＿＿＿＿＿＿＿
   ＿＿＿＿＿＿＿＿＿＿＿＿＿＿＿＿＿＿＿。

5. ＿＿＿＿＿＿＿＿＿＿＿＿＿＿＿＿＿＿＿＿,
   我们一定严格履行合同。

以便:

用在下半句话的开头,表示使下文所说的目的容易实现。

So that; in order to; so as to. It is used at the beginning of the second half of the sentence showing that the result or consequence mentioned there is facilitated by what is mentioned in the first half of the sentence.

一、熟读下列各句,体会"以便"的意义和用法:

1. 我说慢点,以便你听明白。
2. 贵公司收到信用证后,请用电传及时通知我们装船的具体时间,以便我们派船受载。
3. 我们一定尽最大努力,保证季节性商品按期交货,以便赶上销售旺季。

二、请用"以便"完成下列句子:

1. 请你们谈谈具体意见,_____。
2. 请你方及时派船来接货,_____。
3. 我们希望合同写得具体明确,_____。
4. 新产品要有使用说明,_____。
5. 我们在洽谈中应该考虑到各种因素,_____。

不过:

① 用在形容词性的词组后或双音节形容词后,表示程度最高;② 副词,表示范围,有往轻处、小处说的意思,跟"只"、"仅仅"差不多;③ 连词,连接分句或句子,表示转折,跟"只是"、"但是"用法与含义相近似。

1) Used after an adjectival phrase or a dissyllabic adjective to indicate the highest degree. 2) Adverb: Only; merely; no more than. It is used to indicate scope, emphasizing that someone or something is no more important, useful or valuable than you say they are, similarto 只,仅仅. 3) Conjunction: But; however; only. It is used to indicate a turn in tone, similar to 只是,但是, etc.

一、熟读下列各句,仔细辨别"不过"的不同意义与用法:

1. 他心里明白,不过嘴里不说罢了。
2. 可以分批交货,不过希望分批越少越好。
3. 如果你们能提前交货,那是最好不过了。
4. 我们在交货与装船的主要问题上都是一致的,只不过一些细节还须进一步磋商。

二、熟读下列短语,并各造一个句子:

通不过	最好不过	不过二批	跑不过
信不过	最巧不过	不过三片	最漂亮不过
说不过	最快不过	不过十七岁	不过十万元

B

一、写出下列词语的反义词和近义词:

延长	降低	赞成	按时	安全	集中
滞销	增加	疲软	灵活	优质	热门
获得	下跌	稳定	接受	远期	担心
合法	短缺	保留	遵守	破损	吃亏

二、从上面至少选择十个词,说一段话:

三、熟读下列词语,并选择适当的词填空:

至关重要　　磋商　　准许　　延长　　不言而喻
通力合作　　选择　　脱手　　按时　　备货　　估计

1. 季节性商品能否＿＿＿＿＿＿＿＿交货＿＿＿＿＿＿＿＿

希望＿＿＿＿＿＿＿＿＿＿＿＿＿＿＿＿＿＿＿＿＿。

2. 你方如不履行合同，_____

　　应承担对我公司造成的经济损失。

3. 这批大宗货_____需多长时间？

4. 因为我们没有班轮直达贵方指定的目的港，_____

　　_____交货还需进一步_____。

5. 中途转船，必然_____海运时间，赶不上

　　销售季节，商品_____会有一定困难。

四、想一想，谈一谈：

　　1. 贸易洽谈中，你在磋商交货的具体细节时有什么趣事和经验？

　　2. 货物装运中最大的麻烦是什么？你最担心什么？

五、阅读下面的短文，并回答问题：

上海外运公司

　　上海外运公司同世界 170 个国家和地区的 3.6 万家客商建立了贸易往来关系，承办了上海口岸 80% 的海运出口业务。在全世界设有 78 家货运代理，在欧洲、日本、澳大利亚、新加坡、香港地区和美国开展了集运分拨(bō)业务，拥有全国最大的集装箱货运站，采用先进的电脑管理。他们提出了"安全、迅速、准确、方便"的运输方针，以优质运输服务，赢得了国外客户的信任。一次，有一批黄铜(tóng)管要用集装箱运往国外，但铜管长短不一，每箱重达 300 多公斤，装箱难度极大。货主既怕影响交货期，又怕黄铜因磕碰(kēpèng)而损坏。外运公司"急客户所急，想客户所想"，终于把这批货物安全、完好地运抵目的地，货主和买主都非常满意。

1. 上海外运公司的主要业务是什么？
2. 上海外运公司都同哪些国家、地区建立了业务往来？
3. 上海外运公司的服务方针是什么？
4. 找出短文中的生词和词组练习造句。

第十课　包　　装
Lesson 10　Packing

一、包装与装潢

陈其然：史密斯先生，今天我们谈谈包装。

史密斯：好。这个问题很重要，我们应该好好谈谈。

陈其然：我们知道，包装作为商品的重要组成部分，至少有三大作用，即保护商品，便于储运，传达信息。

史密斯：无论是内包装，还是外包装，起码应该具有这三个功能。我们就按这个原则来谈吧！

陈其然：那么，我们是先谈内包装呢，还是先谈外包装？

史密斯：我们就先谈内包装吧，也就是销售包装，你看怎么样？

陈其然：好的。史密斯先生已经看了样品，对我们的销售包装有什么印象？

史密斯：在当今国际市场上，同类商品竞争激烈，包装和装潢往往是成败的关键。我希望贵公司的产品包装能重视这一条市场规律。

陈其然：佛要金装，人要衣装嘛，商品当然也要有好的包装喽！怎么，史密斯先生对我们的包装不满意？

史密斯：恕我直言，如果商品是一流质量、二流包装、三流价格，在市场上就没有竞争力了！

陈其然：我们有过忽视包装的深刻教训。包装傻、大、粗，不美观漂亮，不便仓储运输，每年都因商品包装不善造成很大的经济损失。

玛　丽：包装也是提高商品附加值的重要手段，一流质量、二流包装，就只能卖三流价格，这个潜在的经济损失恐怕更大。

陈其然：是的。所以我们现在非常重视这个问题。

玛　丽：这是一个好消息。

陈其然：这几年，我们的包装和装潢都有了很大改进。仅以出口茶叶为例，从粗糙的大包装改为方便精致的小包装，中国茶叶在国际市场上的售价就提高了 10% ～ 50%。

史密斯：是的，我们注意到，近几年来中国商品包装变得轻巧、精致多了。像可口可乐易拉罐、雀巢咖啡筒装和一些国外名牌软饮料包装，都是在中国制造的，而且都已经达到国外同类产品的包装质量水平。

陈其然：看来，史密斯先生对我国的包装业了如指掌！

史密斯：哦，不了解不行嘛！

二、包装与运输

陈其然：史密斯先生，关于包装问题，我们已经谈得很多了,你还有什么具体意见吗?

史密斯:我们这次订购的一批袋泡茶,采用了上等无毒、
　　　无味过滤纸,冲泡方便,清洁卫生,我很满意。

陈其然:罐装茶呢?

玛　丽:罐装茶的罐盒加工精细,密封度好,开合很省力,
　　　很容易。

陈其然:那么,装潢呢?

史密斯:总的来说,装潢设计不错,既有中国民族特色,又
　　　符合我们国家消费者的心理;既古色古香,又现
　　　代味十足。

陈其然:听起来,史密斯先生好像还有不满意的地方。

史密斯:标签太简单了。从外观,只能看见商品名称和产
　　　地,缺少一些很重要的说明,比如成份含量,是否
　　　有人工颜料和添加剂、防腐剂,保质期,生产日
　　　期,使用方法等等。

陈其然:我们国内的商品标签和包装上说明都这样简单。

玛　丽:在我们那里,顾客对商品一无所知,是不会掏腰
　　　包的。你们放弃了用商品做广告的好机会。

陈其然:可惜生米已经煮成熟饭了。

玛　丽:那就再煮一锅新饭。包装材料、包装设计、包装
　　　印刷都要十分考究,一定要让顾客一见就爱,不
　　　买就舍不得走。

陈其然:我们尽量去说服厂家。我相信,让商品有一个漂
　　　亮包装,也是他们的心愿,何况还可以提高附加
　　　值呢!

史密斯:好,我们就这么说定了。现在,我们来谈谈外包

装、也就是运输包装问题。

陈其然：噢，史密斯先生可以放心。这批货，我们准备用优质牢固胶合板箱、内衬铝薄纸，箱外有两道加固带，远洋运输，万无一失。

史密斯：很好，再加上良好的内包装，就可以防水、防潮、防霉、防串味、防碰撞破损，海运我们也就放心了。

陈其然：你们这次订购的茶叶，不够装一个标准集装箱，恐怕得和别的货物拼箱装运。

史密斯：所以请你们注意大包板箱的内外径尺寸，尤其是瓦楞纸箱内外径尺寸相差很大，弄不好，拼箱时一个标准集装箱装不下，就要增加运费了。

陈其然：好的，我们一定注意。

生词

1.	包装	bāozhuāng	packing
2.	装潢	zhuānghuáng	packaging, decoration
3.	组成	zǔchéng	constitute, make up, compose
4.	保护	bǎohù	protect
5.	储存	chǔcún	storage
6.	传达	chuándá	transmit, communicate
7.	信息	xìnxī	information
8.	起码	qǐmǎ	minimum, at least
9.	当今	dāngjīn	nowadays, in our time
10.	重视	zhòngshì	attach importance to, lay stress on
11.	规律	guīlǜ	law, regular pattern

12.	佛	fó	Buddha
13.	忽视	hūshì	neglect
14.	教训	jiàoxun	lesson
15.	美观	měiguān	beautiful, pleasing to the eye
16.	仓库	cāngkù	warehouse
17.	不善	bùshàn	not good, bad
18.	潜在	qiánzài	potential
19.	改进	gǎijìn	improve
20.	精致	jīngzhì	fine, exquisite
21.	轻巧	qīngqiǎo	light and handy
22.	易拉罐	yìlāguàn	pull-to-open can
23.	筒装	tǒngzhuāng	canned
24.	软饮料	ruǎnyǐnliào	soft drink
25.	制造	zhìzào	make, manufacture
26.	了如指掌	liǎorúzhǐzhǎng	know something like the palm of one's hand
27.	毒	dú	toxin, poison
28.	过滤	guòlǜ	filter
29.	冲	chōng	pour boiling water on, rinse, flush
30.	罐装	guànzhuāng	packed in cans
31.	精细	jīngxì	meticulous, fine, careful
32.	密封	mìfēng	air tight, sealed
33.	省力	shěnglì	save effort
34.	设计	shèjì	design
35.	民族	mínzú	nationality
36.	古色古香	gǔsègǔxiāng	antique, quaint
37.	现代	xiàndài	modern
38.	标签	biāoqiān	label

39. 外观	wàiguān	exterior, outer appearance
40. 成分	chéngfèn	ingredient
41. 人工	réngōng	artificial
42. 颜料	yánliào	coloring, pigment
43. 添加剂	tiānjiājì	additive
44. 防腐剂	fángfǔjì	antiseptic
45. 一无所知	yīwúsuǒzhī	know nothing about
46. 腰包	yāobāo	purse, wallet
47. 生米已煮	shēng mǐ yǐ	the rice has been cooked
成熟饭	zhǔchéng shúfàn	
48. 印刷	yìnshuā	printing
49. 材料	cáiliào	material
50. 考究	kǎojiu	exquisite
51. 舍不得	shěbude	be unwilling to
52. 说服	shuōfú	persuade
53. 心愿	xīnyuàn	cherished desire, wish
54. 何况	hékuàng	much less, let alone
55. 牢固	láogù	firm, secure
56. 胶	jiāo	glue
57. 板箱	bǎnxiāng	wooden case
58. 衬	chèn	line, place something underneath
59. 铝	lǚ	aluminum
60. 加固带	jiāgùdài	strap for reinforcement
61. 防水	fángshuǐ	waterproof
62. 防潮	fángcháo	moisture proof
63. 防霉	fángméi	mildew inhibiting
64. 串味	chuànwèi	contaminated by external odor

65. 碰撞	pèngzhuàng	collision
66. 集装箱	jízhuāngxiāng	container
67. 拼箱装运	pīnxiāng zhuāngyùn	fit together (in one container)
68. 直径	zhíjìng	diameter
69. 尺寸	chǐcùn	measurement
70. 瓦楞纸	wǎléngzhǐ	corrugated paper

练习

A

往往：

　　表示某种情况一般是怎么样或可能会是怎么样。与"常常"相近，但有不同。"常常"表示行为经常反复，更强调没有例外。

Often; frequently; more often than not. It shows what something is or will be like generally. It is similar to 常常. The difference is that 常常 implies the frequent repetition of the event and emphasizes that there is no exception.

一、熟读下列各句,体会和比较"往往"、"常常"的用法：

　　1．他常常天一亮就起床。

　　2．一到冬天,他往往天一黑就睡觉了。

　　3．聪明的商人都知道,成功与失败往往只差一步。

　　4．包装不精巧,往往影响商品销售。

二、用"往往"和下面的词语造句：

　　1．竞争：

　　2．规律：

3．潮流：

4．考究：

何况：

连词,用反问的语气表示比较起来有更进一层的意思,用于后一小句句首。前一小句常用"尚且"、"都"、"连……都(也)……"等表示让步意义的连词相呼应。"何况"前面还可以加"更、又",后面可以加"又"。

Conjunction: Let alone; in addition. It uses a rhetorical question to express going a step further by comparison. It is placed at the beginning of the second clause. In concert with it, connectives expressing concession such as 尚且,都,连...都(也) are often used in the first clause. 何况 can also be preceded by 更 or 又, and can be followed by 又.

一、熟读下列各句,体会"何况"的意义和用法：

1．这么小的字,眼睛好的人看着都吃力,何况你是近视眼呢？

2．这么优质的产品都卖不出去,何况质量一般的产品呢？

3．他汉语听说尚且吃力,何况读写？

4．他忙得连睡觉都没有足够的时间,更何况与朋友交往？

5．这个标准他连自己都做不到,又何况别人？

二、用"何况"完成下列各句：

1．按时交货都有困难,＿＿＿＿＿＿＿＿＿＿＿＿＿＿＿。

2．连用不可撤销信用证付款老板都担心,＿＿＿＿＿＿＿＿

＿＿＿＿＿＿＿＿＿＿＿＿＿＿＿＿＿＿＿＿＿＿。

3．直达目的港我们还怕赶不上销售季节,＿＿＿＿＿＿＿

＿＿＿＿＿＿＿＿＿＿＿＿＿＿＿＿＿＿＿＿＿＿。

4. 长途运输注意包装尚且会出现碰撞破损，＿＿＿＿＿＿＿＿

＿＿＿＿＿＿＿＿＿＿＿＿＿＿＿＿＿＿＿＿＿＿＿。

5. 精巧的小包装尚且不受欢迎，＿＿＿＿＿＿＿＿＿＿＿

＿＿＿＿＿＿＿＿＿＿＿＿＿＿＿＿＿＿＿＿＿＿＿。

舍不得：

动词，意思是不忍分离、不忍抛弃、不忍使用，后面可带名词、动词词组作宾语。"舍不得"的肯定形式是"舍得"。"舍得"常用于问句和对比句中。

Verb: Hate to part with, abandon or use. It can take a noun or a verbal phrase as its object. Its corresponding positive form is 舍得, which is often used in an interrogative or a comparative sentence.

一、熟读下列各句，体会"舍不得"的意义和用法：

1. 中国的父母为了孩子花多少钱都舍得，为自己却舍不得了。
2. 先生舍不得时间陪太太逛商店。
3. 外出旅行他舍不得住高级宾馆。
4. 母亲就我这么一个女儿，她舍不得我离开她出国求学。
5. 中国有句俗话叫"舍不得孩子，套不了狼"意思是冒大风险才能有大收获。

二、用"舍不得"和指定的词语造句：

1. 降价处理
2. 陈旧设备
3. 提供资料
4. 科技投资
5. 放弃

弄：

动词,基本意思是"做",也可表示其他一些动词的意思。如说"弄饭(做饭)"、"弄鱼(杀鱼、洗鱼)"、"一定要弄(调查)个水落石出"等等。

Verb: Its basic meaning is "do". It can also be used to express the meaning of some other verbs such as 弄饭(做饭),弄鱼(杀鱼,洗鱼),一定要弄(调查)个水落石出,etc.

注意下面的两个用法：1.弄+得,意思是"使得",多用于不好的方面,如说"他讲得有理,弄得我无话可说"；"这件事弄得我进退两难"。2."弄"表示设法取得的意思,后面常带数量词语,例如"你去弄点吃的来","你想法去给我弄两张电影票来"。

Please pay attention to the following two uses: 1) 弄 + 得, with the meaning of "cause" or "render", is more often used with a negative sense. For instance:他讲得有理,弄得我无话可说;这件事弄得我进退两难. 2)弄 can mean "get" or "fetch". In this case it is often followed by a quantitative word, for instance:你去弄点吃的来;你想法去给我弄两张电影票来.

一、熟读下列各句,体会"弄"的意义和用法：

1. 真弄不懂市场行情变化怎么这么快！
2. 同类商品竞争这么激烈,及时弄到信息至关重要。
3. 我太太手巧,简单的几样菜可以弄得很好吃。
4. 这次教训是深刻的。我们必须弄清市场规律。
5. 饮料中放了那么多添加剂、防腐剂,弄得谁都不敢喝了！

二、用"弄"完成下列各句：

1. 这身衣服太考究,_____。
2. 外观粗糙的包装_____。
3. 外包装的加固带不牢固,_____。

4．茶叶包装密封度要好，_____。

5．下雪天路面太滑，_____。

B

一、用下面的词语完成下列各句：

1．一无所知：

（1）他对目前市场行情_____。

（2）他第一次来中国，对贵国消费者心理_____。

（3）请你详细介绍最近贵国所创的名牌商品，_____

_____。

（4）很难相信，推销员对所推销商品_____。

2．万无一失：

（1）这批货的海运问题我们已作好安排_____

_____。

（2）这批大宗货的交货日期_____。

（3）既然商品是第一流的，我们希望包装和装潢也是第一流

的，这样_____。

（4）这批高档商品，为安全起见，我们已保了特别险，_____

_____。

3．古色古香：

（1）这套家具从款式到颜色都_____。

（2）我太太既喜欢有现代味的，也喜欢_____

_____的中国瓷器。

（3）地毯的图案_____，很有民族特色。

（4）_____的手工艺品，刚投放市场就销售一空。

4．生米已煮成熟饭：

（1）你的建议提得很好，商品说明是太简单了，但_____

_____

（2）中国饮茶有这么多讲究，我第一次听说。这包名牌茶叶

我冲泡不当。_____,下次我一定按你说的去做。

(3) 他们已签合同,_____,_____你阻止也晚了。

(4) 货已装上船,无法追回,_____,_____你着急也没有用了。

5. 佛要金装,人要衣装:

(1) 在当今国际市场,吸引人的包装,对销售起很大作用,_____。

(2) 不但商品质量要好,包装也要讲究。要人见人爱,_____嘛。

(3) 贵国包装一改过去的傻、大、粗,看来经营思想有了改变,懂得了_____,这是一个不小的进步。

(4) 你看老板今天穿了设计新颖的服装,现代味十足,人也年轻、漂亮了,真是_____。

二、熟读下列词语,然后选择适当的词语填空:

符合	时代	轻巧	民族	名称	规律	潮流
广告	改进	忽视	独特	材料	放弃	装潢
产地	牢固	碰撞	串味	防潮	运输	远洋
粗细	特色	领导	设计			

1. 有的商品包装要求_____;有的商品包装要求_____,但顾客都喜欢_____包装。

2. 远洋运输的包装首先要求_____同时要求_____、_____、_____。

3. 好的包装和装潢讲究_____。

4. _____包装,一定影响销售,所以_____。

三、想一想、谈一谈：

1. 你喜欢什么样的包装？请举出贵国或中国有民族特色的二三种名牌商品包装。你觉得它好在哪儿？
2. 有特色的包装和装潢要注意些什么？你对中国商品的包装和装潢有什么看法？你认为哪些地方需要改造？

四、阅读下面的短文，并回答问题：

一个仓库收发员

我是一个外运仓库的收发员，有人说我的工作太简单，没意思。工作嘛，只要货单相符，照单收发货物呗。可我给自己立了三条规矩：有损仓库信誉的事不做！有损客户利益的事不做！违反外贸制度的事不做！有一次，食品进出口公司在我库提取 3000 箱马蹄（tí）丁运往美国，但在装货时，我突然发现有一个纸箱外有黄色斑迹（bānjì），有的地方已经发黑变霉（méi）。经验告诉我，这箱罐头发生"胖听"了。我当然扣下这箱检查，但已经装上车的近千箱里有没有"胖听"呢？是照样发箱装运还是停止运货，重新检查呢？要重新检查，就要把近千箱罐头全部倒腾（dǎoteng）一遍，这是多大的工作量啊！可我最后还是决定检查。我们从这 3000 箱中剔除瘪（biě）听、胖听，甚至生锈（xiù）、变质的罐头，一共 15 箱，使这批货按期、保质运往美国了。

1. 外运仓库收发员为自己立了哪三条规矩？
2. 这批食品罐头的内包装和外包装出现了什么问题？
3. 外运仓库收发员为什么决定把已经装上车的近千箱罐头全部倒腾一遍？
4. 外运仓库收发员的工作有什么结果？

第十一课　保　　险
Lesson 11　Insurance

一、险别与业务范围

史密斯：陈先生，请问，对外贸易货物运输保险应
　　　　向哪家公司投保？

陈其然：我国的保险业务由中国人民保险公司统
　　　　一经营，一切进出口货运保险都归他们办
　　　　理。如果被保险货物在运输途中发生保
　　　　险范围内的损失，保险公司负责赔偿。

史密斯：这与国际保险业务一样嘛。

陈其然：是这样的。投保人的故意行为，双方不履
　　　　行合同，货运中自然损耗等，保险公司概
　　　　不负责。

史密斯：这也是相同的。请问，贵国保险公司主要
　　　　有哪些保险业务？

陈其然：主要有平安险、水渍险和一切险三种。如
　　　　客户要求，可加保一般附加险和特殊附加
　　　　险。

史密斯：保险责任起讫期限多长？

陈其然：我国一般采用国际保险中惯用的"仓至

仓"责任条款。但如属于特殊附加险的战争险，就不采用"仓至仓"条款。如果中途转船，另有规定，细节就更复杂了。

史密斯：这么说，我还应该认真研究一下贵国的保险法。

二、具体险别的责任范围

史密斯：陈先生，你能介绍一下贵国"平安险"的责任范围吗？

陈其然：可以。顾名思义，"平安险"负责货物在海、陆运输中的平安到达。确切地说，是指投保货物在运输途中由于自然灾害和意外事故造成的全部损失，保险公司负责赔偿。

玛　丽：那么，也包括单独海损吗？

陈其然：你的意思是否指不在船、货共同危难中发生的损失？

玛　丽：是的。

陈其然："平安险"的英文原意就是单独海损不赔。

玛　丽：那么，贵国保险公司承担的"水渍险"，是否就负责赔偿单独海损呢？

陈其然：是的，"水渍险"的英文原意就是单独海损负责。因此，水渍险的责任范围，既包括平安险责任范围内的全部责任，也负责由于海上自然灾害所引起的货物的部分损失。

玛　丽：这就是说，水渍险的责任范围比平安险要宽啰！

陈其然：是的，所以保险费也高一些。

史密斯：陈先生，我们这一次订货是按 F.O.B. 价格成交的，我们应该怎么投保呢？

陈其然：我建议你投保水渍险。

史密斯：可以投保战争险和罢工险吗？

陈其然：可以。不过，那是属于特殊附加险业务了。

史密斯：好的，我明白贵国的保险业务了，现在我们可以来具体商谈合同中的保险条款了。

三、保险费的计算与赔偿

史密斯：陈先生，我们这批货是按 F.O.B 离岸价格条款成交的，我们双方的保险责任应该怎么划分？

陈其然：F.O.B 是装运港船上交货价。这就是说，货物越过船舷，我方就完成了交货，也就完成了风险转移。

史密斯：那么，货物越过船舷前的风险由你方承担，越过船舷后的风险则由我方承担？

陈其然：是这样。这一点已经明确写在合同中了。

史密斯：陈先生，我们这批货物容易破损，你们能为我们加保破碎险吗？

陈其然：破碎险属于一般附加险，我们可以代你们投保，但费用要由你们负担。

史密斯：这没问题。

陈其然：好吧，我们办理完毕，就把保险单交给你们。

玛　丽：谢谢。陈先生，还有一个问题，货物运到目的港后，一旦发现短缺或破损，我方应在哪儿提出索赔？

陈其然：中国人民保险公司在贵国设有理赔、检验代理人，你们可以凭合同、保险单和有关证件在当地申请索赔。

史密斯：话虽这么说，我们还是希望万事如意！

陈其然：但愿如此！

生词

1.	保险	bǎoxiǎn	insurance
2.	投保	tóubǎo	insure
3.	统一	tǒngyī	unify
4.	归	guī	put in somebody's charge
5.	一切	yīqiè	all, everything
6.	途中	túzhōng	in transit
7.	赔偿	péicháng	indemnify
8.	行为	xíngwéi	act
9.	损耗	sǔnhào	loss, wear and tear
10.	概不负责	gàibùfùzé	not liable for any of these
11.	平安险	píng'ānxiǎn	free from particular average (F.P.A.)
12.	水渍险	shuǐzìxiǎn	with particular average (W.P.A.)
13.	附加险	fùjiāxiǎn	additional risks
14.	起讫	qǐqì	commencement and termination
15.	期限	qīxiàn	time limit
16.	仓至仓	cāngzhìcāng	warehouse to warehouse
17.	战争险	zhànzhēngxiǎn	war risk
18.	复杂	fùzá	complex
19.	顾名思义	gùmíngsīyì	as the name suggests
20.	陆运	lùyùn	land transportation
21.	确切	quèqiè	exact

22.	灾害	zāihài	calamities
23.	意外	yìwài	unexpected
24.	事故	shìgù	accident
25.	程度	chéngdù	extent
26.	均	jūn	without exception, equal
27.	单独	dāndú	particular (average), alone
28.	海损	hǎisǔn	average
29.	危难	wēinàn	peril
30.	罢工	bàgōng	strike
31.	离岸价	lí'ànjià	FOB price
32.	划分	huàfēn	divide
33.	越过	yuèguò	cross, go over
34.	船舷	chuánxián	board, side of a ship, gunwale
35.	完成	wánchéng	complete
36.	转移	zhuǎnyí	shift, transfer
37.	破碎险	pòsuìxiǎn	breakage risk
38.	属于	shǔyú	belong to
39.	任何	rènhé	any
40.	负担	fùdān	bear (a burden), shoulder
41.	完毕	wánbì	finish
42.	一旦	yīdàn	as soon as
43.	缺损	quēsǔn	shortage and/or damage
44.	索赔	suǒpéi	lodge a claim
45.	理赔	lǐpéi	settle a claim
46.	检验	jiǎnyàn	inspection
47.	证件	zhèngjiàn	certificate
48.	当地	dāngdì	local
49.	申请	shēnqǐng	apply
50.	万事如意	wànshìrúyì	everything goes well as one

51. 但愿如此　dànyuànrúcǐ　wishes let's hope so

练习

A

要：

副词。① 表示动作、事件即将发生，前边有时有"就"、"快"等词；② 表示比较，常与"比"相搭配用；③ 表示希望、提醒或命令某人做某事。有"应该"、"必须"的意思。

Adverb: 1) Shall; will; be going to. It says that something will happen soon, and is often preceded by such words as 就(right away), 快(soon), etc. 2) Used to show comparison, often used together with 比(compare). 3) Must; should. It is used to express that you want, wish, or command someone to do something.

一、熟读下列各句，指出各句中的"要"属于上面的哪一种意义和用法：

1. 旅游旺季就要到了，我们急于购进一批旅游纪念品。
2. 请你们及时派船来受载，如果误期，你们要赔偿我方的经济损失。
3. 平安险的保险范围比水渍险的要窄。
4. 我们认为，还是加保偷窃险要好一些。
5. 保险起讫日期要在合同中写清楚。
6. 这批货的保险期限快要到了，再不提出索赔，公司就要蒙受巨大经济损失了。

二、用"要"和括号中指定的词语完成下列各句：

1. 这批货物装船以后，＿＿＿＿＿＿＿＿＿以便我们及时安

排。(通知)

2. 水渍险比平安险所负的责任宽,保险费_____。(高)

3. 这次出的事故不在保险范围以内,责任_____。(承担)

4. 投保虽然增加了费用,但_____

_____。(放心)

5. 对货物损坏程度,_____。(检验)

6. 中国人民保险公司在贵国设有理赔、检验代理人,_____

_____(方便)

概不:

"概"是副词,总括前边提到的事物、意义等。"概不"意思是一律不,后面多跟双音节动词或词组。

Do not...; without exception. Here 概(without exception) is an adverb, summing up what is mentioned above. 概不 is often followed by a disyllabic verb or expression.

一、熟读下列词组,体会"概不"的意义和用法:

概不退换	概不赔偿	概不接见	概不索赔
概不负责	概不接受	概不负担	概不理赔
概不投放(保)	概不装运	概不担保	概不办理
概不照顾	概不受理	概不补偿	概不试销
概不安排	概不签订(发)	概不垫付	概不保护

二、从上面选择十个词组各造一个句子:

由:

① 动词,意思是听任、听凭,后面必带名词宾语或兼语。

② 介词,引进施动者。代表受动者的名词或在它的前面作主语,或在它的后面作宾语。

注意:有时一个句子里的"由"字可能是作动词用,也可能是作介词用,怎么判断呢? 重音在"由"上,是动词;重音在后面的名词上,是介词。

1) Verb: allow; let (somebody do as he pleases). It takes a noun as its object. That noun may also function as the subject of the verbal group that follows. 2) Preposition: It introduces the agent of the verb. The noun in the affected case may be placed before it, functioning as the subject; or placed after it, functioning as the object.

Attention: Sometimes, 由 in a sentence may be understood either as a verb or as a preposition. How do we judge then? If the stress falls on 由, it is a verb. It the stress falls on the noun after if, it is a preposition.

一、熟读下列各句,指出各句中"由"属于哪一种意义和用法:

1. 我已经说过了,信不信由你。
2. 谁的话他都不听,只好由他去。
3. 我这儿的东西,只要你喜欢,由你挑。
4. 这事由你全权处理。
5. 这个委员会由三方七位代表组成。
6. 你们来北京以后,由我们公司负责接待。
7. 这事由你决定。

二、用"由"和下列词语造句:

1. 投保
2. 负担
3. 完成
4. 设计
5. 赔偿
6. 检验

B

一、用下列词语组词：

范围	办理	故意	期限	责任	危难	程度
险别	发生	履行	惯用	细节	破碎	缺损
投保	赔偿	损耗	条款	复杂	事故	造成
意外	完成	索赔	一般			

二、用下面常见的词组各造一个句子：

确切地说　　　　　据我的经验

一般说来　　　　　包括……在内

三、想一想、谈一谈：

1. 贵公司在进出口货物时，一般都投保吗？投保什么险别？
2. 贵国保险公司一般负责哪些赔偿？不负责哪些赔偿？
3. 贵公司与中国人民保险公司有业务往来吗？往来情况怎样？
4. 你有过保险索赔的经历吗？试谈一个案例。

四、阅读下面的短文，并回答问题：

被告变原告

一次，一艘外轮抵达青岛港，货物卸船后，发现严重残(cán)损，价值达33000多美元。按规定，只有货主才有权提出索赔，但这批货的货主众多，一时难以统一理赔，眼看一年的索赔期限就要过去了，外贸运输公司的王海决定以租船人的名义向卖方索赔。七次致函(zhìhán)，卖方都置之不理。原来，卖方用的是缓(huǎn)兵之计。一年后，卖方向仲裁(zhòngcái)部门提请仲裁,理由是外运公司不是货主,而且索赔期已过,王海根据《租约条款》中"不受一年时效限制"的条文,以租船人名义提出索陪,并替卖方向各货主——赔款,然后由中国保险公司出具了赔款证据,确认了追偿权。因此王海向卖方提出反诉,由被告变为原告,这场官司以卖方如数赔付全部损失而告终。

1. 货物残损,按规定应由谁提出索赔?
2. 外贸运输公司有资格提出索赔吗?
3. 卖方为什么要用缓兵之计?
4. 王海为什么能由被告转变为原告,而且胜诉?

第十二课　海关与商检
Lesson 12　Customs and Commodity Inspection

一、海关与商检实务

陈其然：史密斯先生,我们现在开始讨论合同中
　　　　的商检条款。

史密斯：陈先生能先介绍一下贵国的海关与商检
　　　　实务吗?

陈其然：可以。海关必须对进出口货物实行监管,
　　　　这是国际上通行的做法,中国也不例外。

玛　丽：不过,各国海关如何实施监管却不完全相
　　　　同。

陈其然：是这样。海关监管的目的,是为了维护国
　　　　家的利益和贸易关系人的利益,不同国家
　　　　就难免有不同的监管要求。

史密斯：正因为这样,特别是涉及安全、卫生、环保
　　　　和动植物检疫,各国的检验要求就有比较
　　　　大的区别了。那么,贵国有什么特别的法
　　　　规吗?

陈其然：这方面的有关法规比较复杂,我建议你仔
　　　　细看一看我们国家的《商检法》及其实施

细则。

史密斯：好的。关税，也是我十分关心的问题，陈先生能粗略介绍一点情况吗？

陈其然：啊，有一个好消息告诉你。从 1992 年以来，我国多次大幅度自主降低进口关税税率，关税总水平现在已经从原来的 43.3％降至 17％。

史密斯：这确实是一个令人振奋的消息。

陈其然：降税涉及 4874 个税号，占我国现行税则规定范围的 73％以上。

玛　丽：啊，我要为贵国如此大幅度削减关税壁垒，大声喝彩！

陈其然：谢谢！

玛　丽：陈先生，我还有一个问题。

陈其然：是关于海关申报手续吧？

玛　丽：是的。我听说贵国海关申报手续很复杂。

陈其然：噢，那是过去的事了。现在申报手续已经大大简化了，是又快捷、又简单。

玛　丽：可以说得详细一点吗？

陈其然：现在各海关都采用了自动化通关系统，报关、审单、征税、查验、放行，都实现了计算机联网。

玛　丽：啊，这是很先进的现代化管理嘛！

陈其然：是的，报关员只需把报关单交给接单官员，在出单窗口等候出单，再持提单或装货单到监管现场办理查验放行手续就行了。

玛　丽：好，我明白了，这样报关确实是快捷、简单！

二、合同条款磋商

陈其然：史密斯先生，关于商检条款，有许多问题，我们已
　　　　经达成一致意见了。

史密斯：是的。比如品质、规格、包装、数量等的检验标
　　　　准，我们都没有争议了。

陈其然：那么，你看还有什么问题呢？

史密斯：关于商检的出证机构和商检的时间、地点，我们
　　　　还需要进一步磋商。

陈其然：我同意。因为这涉及到议付、索赔和索赔期限。

史密斯：我们希望以到岸的品质、重量为依据。

陈其然：你是说，要由目的港的商检机构进行商检？

史密斯：是的。以他们出具的商检证明作为议付和索赔
　　　　的最后依据。

陈其然：史密斯先生，国际上现在很少有人采取这种做
　　　　法，你知道，这种做法明显对卖方不利。

史密斯：那么，陈先生有什么建议呢？

陈其然：以我国装运港商检机构出具的检验证书作依据。

史密斯：哈，哈，陈先生，你认为这对我们公平吗？

陈其然：货到目的港后，你们有复检权嘛！

史密斯：嗯，这还差不多，我们可以接受。

陈其然：不过，复检机构应该是我们也认可的。

史密斯：可以。

陈其然：货到目的港后，复检时间最多不能超过30天。

玛　丽：从哪天算起？

陈其然：当然从到港日算起。

玛　丽：这批货的目的港十分繁忙，30天内我们根本无法

完成卸货、拆箱、检验的任务。

陈其然：我们了解你们目的港的情况，30 天复检时间已经
很富裕了。

玛　丽：30 天包括节假日吗？

陈其然：啊，当然是工作日。

史密斯：那好吧，我们就这么定了。

陈其然：史密斯先生，我们在办理出口手续时，要填写出
口检验申请单，希望能得到你们的协助。

史密斯：你的意思是……

陈其然：你知道，我们需要提供合同、信用证、来往信函等
有关文件。

史密斯：噢，我明白了，陈先生是担心我们不按时开立信
用证，你们无法报关？

陈其然：信用证与合同不符，不仅不能顺利报关，以后议
付也有麻烦，你说是不是？

史密斯：合同、单证要相符，这是最起码的嘛，我们也希望
你们能严格履行这个义务。

陈其然：当然，我们会及时给你们寄去发票、运单、提单、
装箱清单等有关单证，保证准确无误。

史密斯：那太好了！希望我们能顺利、安全提货，你们也
能顺利、安全收回货款！

生词

1．商检　　shāngjiǎn　　commodity inspection
2．实务　　shíwù　　　　actual practice
3．监管　　jiānguǎn　　supervision and control

4. 通行	tōngxíng	general, current
5. 例外	lìwài	exception
6. 维护	wéihù	safeguard, maintain
7. 环保	huánbǎo	environmental protection
8. 动物	dòngwù	animal
9. 植物	zhíwù	plant
10. 检疫	jiǎnyì	quarantine
11. 法规	fǎguī	laws and regulations
12. 实施	shíshī	implementation
13. 细则	xìzé	detailed rules
14. 关税	guānshuì	customs duty, tariff
15. 粗略	cūlüè	brief, sketchy
16. 报告	bàogào	report
17. 降低	jiàngdī	reduce, lower
18. 税率	shuìlǜ	tariff rate
19. 振奋	zhènfèn	heartening
20. 税号	shuìhào	tariff number
21. 税则	shuìzé	tariff regulations
22. 削减	xuējiǎn	reduce
23. 壁垒	bìlěi	barrier
24. 喝彩	hècǎi	acclaim
25. 申报	shēnbào	declare
26. 简化	jiǎnhuà	simplify
27. 快捷	kuàijié	fast
28. 自动化	zìdònghuà	automation
29. 通关	tōngguān	clearance
30. 系统	xìtǒng	system
31. 报关	bàoguān	declaration
32. 审核	shěnhé	verify, check

33. 征收	zhēngshōu	collect
34. 查验	cháyàn	examine, check
35. 放行	fàngxíng	clearance
36. 联网	liánwǎng	networking
37. 官员	guānyuán	officer, official
38. 等候	děnghòu	wait
39. 提单	tídān	bill of lading
40. 现场	xiànchǎng	scene, site, spot
41. 一致	yīzhì	in conformity with
42. 标准	biāozhǔn	standard
43. 出证	chūzhèng	issue a certificate
44. 到岸	dào'àn	arrive at the port
45. 依据	yījù	according to, foundation, basis
46. 出具	chūjù	issue
47. 证书	zhèngshū	certificate
48. 复检权	fùjiǎnquán	right to re-inspect
49. 认可	rènkě	approve
50. 繁忙	fánmáng	busy
51. 卸货	xièhuò	unloading
52. 拆箱	chāixiāng	unpack
53. 信函	xìnhán	letters
54. 单证	dānzhèng	documents
55. 准确无误	zhǔnquèwúwù	accurate and with no mistakes
56. 提货	tíhuò	take delivery of goods

练习

A

正因为：

　　"正"，副词，有"恰好"的意思，起强调作用。例如："这笔资金正可以用来缴纳关税。"

　　"正"常与"如"、"像"、"因为"结合在一起，意思是"恰好如"、"恰好像"、"恰好因为"，也是起强调指明的作用。

　　正 is an adverb for emphasis, with the meaning of "just right". For instance，这笔资金正可以用来缴纳关税.

　　正 is often used together with 如，像，因为 for emphasis, with the meanings "just as"，"just like"，"just because".

一、熟读下列各句，体会"正"、"正因为"等的意义和用法：

1. 正如我们所希望的那样，一切顺利。
2. 正因为市场竞争激烈，我们才有危机感。
3. 正像人离不开空气一样，人也不能没有粮食。
4. 正因为是你的事，我才这么关心。

二、用"正因为"改写下列各句：

1. 为了维护国家的利益和贸易关系人的利益，不同国家就难免有不同的监管要求。
2. 现在实现了计算机联网，申报手续已经大大简化了。
3. 关于商检条款还有许多问题，我们要继续磋商。
4. 我们担心以后议付有麻烦，所以请你们为我们提供一切有关文件。
5. 我这次行李又多又重，希望出关时得到你的帮助。

及其：

"及其",是连词"及"加代词"其"组成的一个固定词组,意思相当于"和他的"。"及其"连接的后一项事物是从属于前一项的,或与前一项有关的。

This set expression is made up of the conjunction 及 and the pronoun 其, with the meaning being equivalent to "and his (its, etc.)". The matter placed after 及其 either belongs or is related to the one before it.

一、熟读下列各句,体会"及其"的意义和用法:

1. 总统及其随行人员同机到达。
2. 明天一定要准备好合同正本及其附件。
3. 谈判的进展及其结果,都没有出乎他的意料。
4. 对外开放政策的制订及其实施,使中国的经济发生了巨大变化。

二、用"及其"和它组成的短语造句:

1. 提供样品及其有关资料
2. 资源开发及其利用
3. 环境保护(环保)及其综合治理
4. 推销商品及其售后服务

那么:

①"那么"可作连词,用来承接上文的假设或前提,引出下文的判断或结果;②"那么"也可作副词,修饰形容词或动词成分,表示程度或方式。

1) It can be used as a conjunction to continue from the preceding supposition or assumption and lead to the judgment or result that follows. 2) It can also be used as an adverb, modifying an adjective or a verbal group, indicating its degree or manner.

一、熟读下列各句,体会"那么"的意义和用法:

1. 如果你们没有诚意,那么,我们只好放弃这笔生意。
2. 假如他们只是嘴上说得好听,实际做的却是另一回事,那么,我们就不应该同他们继续打交道了。
3. 他长得那么高,我总得仰着头同他说话。
4. 他做事那么精明,你还有什么不放心的。
5. 那么你说怎么修改合同吧。
6. 合同条款写得那么具体、明确,还要怎么修改?

二、用"那么"完成下列各句:

1. 现在贵国的申报手续真像你说的＿＿＿＿＿＿＿＿＿＿。

2. 时间对季节性商品至关重要,如果赶不上销售季节,＿＿＿

＿＿＿＿＿＿＿＿＿＿＿＿＿＿＿＿＿＿＿＿。

3. 既然贵公司每年都因商品包装不善造成很大的经济损失,

＿＿＿＿＿＿＿＿＿＿＿＿＿＿＿＿＿＿＿。

4. 我一定要学好汉语,我不相信＿＿＿＿＿＿＿＿＿＿＿。

5. 海关必须对进出口货物实行监管,这是国际上通行的做

法,＿＿＿＿＿＿＿＿＿＿＿＿＿＿＿＿＿＿＿。

B

一、用下列词语组词:

监管	依据	实施	出具	标准	关税
审核	维护	细则	削减	降低	法规

二、选用上面的词语完成下列各句:

1. 海关对进出口货物＿＿＿＿＿＿＿＿,但各国海关如何

$\underline{\hspace{10cm}}_{\circ}$

2. 买方希望以$\underline{\hspace{5cm}}$作为$\underline{\hspace{4cm}}_{\circ}$

3. 为什么进口国$\underline{\hspace{5cm}}$会令出口国喝彩？

4. 海关监管的目的是$\underline{\hspace{7cm}}_{\circ}$

5. 各国海关监管的要求不同,所以贸易伙伴必须了解对方国

家的$\underline{\hspace{7cm}}_{\circ}$

三、想一想、谈一谈：

1. 为什么各国海关实施监管时不完全相同？

2. 为什么以前海关申报手续比较复杂而现在极大地简化了？

3. 现在的报关员只需怎么做？

4. 你和你的朋友在进出海关时遇到过麻烦吗？为什么？请
讲讲具体过程。

5. 办理出口手续时要注意什么？

四、阅读下面的短文,并回答问题：

请君入瓮

唐朝武则天时,有两个掌刑法的官员叫来俊臣和周兴,在
审理案子时,爱用酷刑。一天,有人密告周兴犯法,武则天让来
俊臣去审理。来俊臣把周兴请来,一边吃饭喝酒,一边向周兴
请教,说:"有的罪犯不肯老实交代,有什么好办法让他认罪
呢?"周兴说:"这个好办。用一口大瓮,让犯人进瓮里,下面烧
大火,还怕他不招?"来俊臣说:"那就请你现在入瓮吧!"

现实生活中,常能看到这类故事。一个很有钱的商人,喜
欢收集古董。一天,他在逛古玩店时,看到一件几百年以前的
花瓶,用 100 万元买下。回家请专家鉴定,却是假的。过了两

天,他又去了那家古玩店,对老板说:"我上次花100万买的那只花瓶实在太好了,你还有吗?"老板一听,赚大钱的生意又来了,就满脸堆笑说:"有,有,我去给你拿。"他随即就拿来两个。富商说:"我要10个。"老板说:"啊,这么名贵的古董,小店哪有这么多。"富商说:"那我就到别的店去看看。"老板连忙拦住说:"别,别,我给你准备,三天以后取货。"老板用尽全部家产进了一批货,有真有假,想从中大赚一笔。三天后,富商同一个朋友一起来了。老板高高兴兴搬出10个花瓶。富商说:"我上次买的那个花瓶,经专家鉴定是假的,这10个花瓶,说不定也都是假的。现在我全部退货。"跟富商一起来的那个人说:"我是海关的。经调查,你走私文物,贩卖假货,店内商品现在全部封存,等待处理。""这下完了!"老板一屁股坐在了地上。

1. "请君入瓮"是一种什么方法?
2. 富商用了什么办法来对付古玩店老板?
3. 古玩店老板犯了什么错误? 结果如何?
4. 读了这个故事,你还有什么感想?

第十三课 信用风险与管理

Lesson 13 Credit Risk and Its Management

一、信用风险意识

张　祥：小王,我们同罗斯先生有了一些接触,你的印象如何?

王　安：印象良好。

张　祥：噢,具体说说。

王　安：据罗斯先生说,他们公司资金雄厚,买卖做得很大,商业信用很好,是一个大客户。

张　祥：还有呢?

王　安：还有……就是说话真诚坦率。

张　祥：那么,你认为我们可以放心大胆地同他打交道了?

王　安：啊,当然,这个大主意还得经理你来拿啰!

张　祥：你这个小滑头! 你去同迪陶商务信用管理公司联系一下,我们要同他们谈一下委托业务。

王　安：经理的意思是说,我们要请他们作资信调查? 这可要花不少咨询调查费,值吗?

张　祥:咨询调查费也不过几百美元,我们做的可是几百万美元的生意!

王　安:可是,罗斯先生说……

张　祥:啊,只听客户怎么说,或只凭自己的印象,都是不可靠的。

王　安:我也知道,国际贸易,是在没有得到支付的情况下,为外国客商提供产品或服务,这实质上是一种信贷,自然也就存在信用风险。但是……

张　祥:我们也不能无端怀疑客户,是不是?

王　安:是。

张　祥:可是,我们也必须有信用风险意识。国际贸易中的欺诈案件不少,世界各国都有这样的教训,所以都十分重视信用风险评估和管理。我这里有一些资料,你好好看看。

二、委托信用调查业务

大　卫:啊,欢迎! 请坐!

张　祥:大卫先生,我们是来请你们作一项资信调查的。

大　卫:秘书已经把你们的委托申请书交给我了。

张　祥:我们正在进行一笔国际货物贸易洽谈,对方是一位新客户,除了一些信函往来和初步接触外,我们对对方几乎不了解。

大　卫:信用管理通常包括信用调查、信用监控和逾期账款追收三个环节。信用调查应该是成交的前提。

张　祥:我明白。不只是新客户,就是老客户的情况,也不是一成不变的。

大　卫:是的。老客户也可能经营不善,资金周转不灵,甚至破产倒闭,或人事变动,企业经营策略发生重大变化。这些都可能带来信用风险。

张　祥:所以我们公司从一开始就建立了客户档案。但是,现在的业务发展很快,需要掌握的信息量很大,我们只能求助于专业信用咨询和管理公司。

大　卫:现在,全球的专业公司,已经实现资信调查国际网络化和标准化,有完备的数据库,可以及时满足客户的各种要求。

张　祥:那么,我们可以得到哪些信息呢?

大　卫:首先是公司存在的真实性,比如买方提供的公司名称、地址、电话、传真、网址是否真实,公司是否登记、注册。

张　祥:有过这样的案例,当你发现货款两失,准备起诉时,对方已是人去楼空。原来,跟你做生意的那家公司根本不存在。

大　卫:哈,这就是所谓的皮包公司。

张　祥:赚了钱,夹着皮包就溜了,你在哪儿找他去!

大　卫:当然,更重要的是,我们要详细了解买方的付款记录和公共记录。

张　祥:是的。作为卖方,最关心的自然是能不能及时、安全收回货款。

大　卫:有的公司,有足够的偿还能力,可以及时支付货款,而且确实及时支付了。有这样的记录,说明公司商业信誉好。

张　祥:跟这样的公司打交道,就可以比较放心。

大　卫:一般来说,这样的公司不会无故迟付或拒付货款。

张　祥:你说的公共记录,是不是指公司的法律记录和抵押记录?

大　卫:是。你通过这些记录,可以了解这家公司是否被起诉过,起诉的原因是什么,判决结果如何;公司的资产是否抵押,抵押给谁了。

张　祥:嗯,掌握这些情况很重要,可以预防潜在的风险。

大　卫:当然,正式的资信调查报告内容还包括公司的历史、股东和经营者情况、经营状况、资产和债务、往来银行及信用、财务状况等等。

张　祥:这太好了。那么,什么时候能给我们这个报告呢?

大　卫:你们这是办普通件,还是加急件?

张　祥:因为客人在中国逗留的时间不长,希望尽快签订合同,最好能在一个星期内把报告给我们。

大　卫:没问题。我们需要签一份《企业资信调查委托书》。

张　祥:费用呢?

大　卫:委托书上有这一项。

张　祥:好的。请把委托书给我!

生词

1. 信用	xìnyòng	credit
2. 意识	yìshí	awareness
3. 雄厚	xiónghòu	ample, abundant
4. 大胆	dàdǎn	bold

5.	滑头	huátóu	slicker
6.	资信	zīxìn	reputation
7.	咨询	zīxún	consult
8.	实质	shízhì	essence
9.	信贷	xìndài	credit
10.	存在	cúnzài	existence
11.	无端	wúduān	for no reason
12.	怀疑	huáiyí	suspect, doubt
13.	欺诈	qīzhà	fraud
14.	案件	ànjiàn	case
15.	评估	pínggū	assessment
16.	监控	jiānkòng	monitoring and control
17.	逾期	yùqī	overdue
18.	账款	zhàngkuǎn	credit
19.	追收	zhuīshōu	pursue, demand payment
20.	环节	huánjié	link
21.	前提	qiántí	prerequisite
22.	一成不变	yīchéngbùbiàn	invariable, unalterable
23.	破产	pòchǎn	go bankrupt
24.	人事	rénshì	personnel matters
25.	变动	biàndòng	change
26.	策略	cèlüè	tactics, strategy
27.	档案	dàng'àn	files, record
28.	掌握	zhǎngwò	grasp, master, know well
29.	求助	qiúzhù	turn to sb. for help
30.	实现	shíxiàn	realize
31.	网络	wǎngluò	network
32.	完备	wánbèi	complete, perfect
33.	数据库	shùjùkù	databank

34. 真实	zhēnshí	real, genuine
35. 名称	míngchēng	name
36. 传真	chuánzhēn	fax
37. 网址	wǎngzhǐ	web-site
38. 注册	zhùcè	register
39. 案例	ànlì	case
40. 起诉	qǐsù	prosecute, bring a suit against sb.
41. 皮包	píbāo	briefcase
42. 夹	jiā	place in between, place under the arm
43. 溜	liū	sneak off, slip away
44. 记录	jìlù	record
45. 偿还	chánghuán	pay back
46. 无故	wúgù	without reason
47. 法律	fǎlǜ	law
48. 抵押	dǐyā	pledge, mortgage
49. 判决	pànjué	sentence, verdict
50. 资产	zīchǎn	asset
51. 预防	yùfáng	guard against
52. 内容	nèiróng	content
53. 股东	gǔdōng	shareholder
54. 债务	zhàiwù	debt
55. 财务	cáiwù	financial affairs
56. 加急	jiājí	urgent
57. 逗留	dòuliú	stay

练习

A

可、可是：

"可"，副词，表示强调语气。用在一般陈述句中，有时含有出乎意料的意思；用在祈使句中，强调必须如此，有时有恳切劝导的意思。

"可是"，连词，表示转折，可用在主语前，也可用在主语后。

可 is an adverb for emphasis. When used in a declarative sentence, it sometimes has the meaning of "out of expectation". When used in an imperative sentence, it stresses that it is a must, sometimes with the meaning of "sincere advice".

可是 is a conjunction for transition. It can be placed either before or after the subject.

一、熟读下列各句，体会"可"、"可是"的意义和用法：

1. 500 万？这可不是一笔小数。
2. 你同皮包公司打交道，这个风险可就太大了！
3. 你可要加强风险管理意识！
4. 你说话可要算数！
5. 他平时说话的声音不高，可是大家都怕他。
6. 这笔生意利润不大，风险可是不小。
7. 他接受了我们的委托，可是不为我们干事。
8. 他费尽了心血，可是最终还是破产了。

二、用"可"、"可是"和指定词语造句：

1. 资信调查
2. 无端怀疑

3. 资金雄厚
4. 一成不变
5. 潜在风险

所谓：

形容词，意思是"通常所说的"，多用于提出需要解释的词语，接着加以解释。

"所谓"还常用于引述别人的话，所引的话大多加上"引号"，含有讽刺、不同意的意思。

It is an adjective with the meaning of "what is generally called (or known as)". It is often used together with a word or expression that needs explanation, to be followed by the explanation.

It is also often used when quoting others, with the quoted part placed in quotation marks. It has the implication of irony or disagreement.

一、熟读下列各句，体会"所谓"的意义和用法：

1. 所谓"卖方市场"，就是卖方起支配作用的市场。
2. 所谓"信用"，是指能够履行自己的承诺从而取得的信任。
3. 他所谓的"成功"，其实是很值得怀疑的。
4. 如今所谓的"时髦"东西，早在 20 年前就已经流行过了。
5. 难道这就是所谓的"亲密合作"？
6. 她所谓的"理想"，其实只是一种梦想。

二、用"所谓"和指定的词语造句：

1. 皮包公司
2. 加急件
3. 欺诈案件
4. 破产
5. 监控

尽快:

副词。"尽",修饰单音节形容词如"快"、"早"、"先"等,表示尽力达到某种状态。

Adverb (as soon as possible):尽(to the limit) modifies such monosyllabic adjectives as 快(soon),早(early), or 先(earlier), expressing the idea of "doing one's utmost to reach a certain state".

一、熟读下列各句,体会"尽快"的意义和用法:

1. 我们尽快办好这件事。
2. 我们应该尽快占领市场。
3. 请你尽快拿出一个方案来。
4. 请你们尽快找到债务人。

二、用"尽快"和指定的词语造句:

1. 逾期账款
2. 改进包装、装潢
3. 掌握信息
4. 简化手续
5. 取得详细资料

B

一、用下列词语组词:

存在	监控	信贷	支付	逾期
风险	调查	偿还	信用	货款
资信	咨询	债务	评估	抵押

二、用括号中的词语完成下列各句:

1. 据我们了解,贵公司资金雄厚_____

_____。（信用）

2. 信用调查是成交的前提。信用管理通常包括_____

_____。（环节）

3. 及时掌握变化的情况，_____。（预防）

4. 跟贸易伙伴打交道，不能仅凭对方的自我介绍和得到的印

象，_____。（资信）

5. 任何时候，作为卖方，最关心的是_____。（货款）

6. 现在全球专业信用咨询和管理公司，已经_____

_____。（完备）

7. 现在国际市场瞬息万变，为了掌握市场行情，及时制定经

营策略_____。（信息）

8. 在国际贸易中必须有信用风险意识，一来是市场变化快，

竞争激烈；二来是国际贸易中欺诈案件不少，所以都

_____（评估）

三、想一想、谈一谈：

1. 为什么在国际贸易中越来越重视信用风险评估和管理？
2. 全球化的专业信用咨询和管理公司有什么样的现代化服
   务？可以给客户提供哪些信息？
3. 什么样的公司是商业信誉好的公司？
4. 公共记录指什么？

四、阅读下面的短文，然后回答问题：

精心设计的"陷阱"

公司招聘人才，是件非常严肃的事，但考官们有时也会别出心裁，用一些幽默、机智的方法，让被考者原形毕露。

一天，某公司的人才招聘会正在进行。一个男青年走到考官面前。考官说："先生，您进门前是否已经把您的鞋底在小垫子上擦干净了？"青年说："那当然！我仔细地擦过了，先生！""您很肯定？""考官先生，这是一分钟以前的事，我会忘吗？""啊，对不起，看来是我忘了，门口根本就没有小垫子。"

一位小姐又走了进来。考官问了她许多问题，突然惊讶地叫起来："小姐，我在英国伦敦见过你，你那时在一个大型商务研讨会上作演讲，十分精彩，给我留下了很深的印象，怪不得一见到你就觉得有些面熟！你来我们公司工作，我们十分欢迎！"小姐迟疑了一下，说："先生，您认错人了。""不，绝对不会，我的记性一向很好。""先生，您确实认错人了，我至今还没有到过英国。"考官满意地笑笑，说："谢谢！"

招聘考试结束了，男青年落选，小姐被录用。

1. 男青年为什么没有被录用？
2. 小姐在回答考官的话以前，为什么"迟疑了一下"？她为什么被录用了？
3. 考官精心设置的"陷阱"，是为了考察应聘者哪方面的素质？
4. 你赞成考官精心设置"陷阱"的做法吗？为什么？

第十四课　签订合同
Lesson 14　Signing the Contract

一、磋商合同条款

陈其然：史密斯先生，我们经过几轮友好洽谈，已经达成一致协议。你看现在是不是可以来具体磋商合同文本了？

史密斯：可以。有前几轮谈判作基础，合同的书面文字好写，我们都不是生意场上的新手，对吧？

陈其然：我们已经领教了，史密斯先生确实是个精明、老练的行家，谈判高手！

史密斯：哦，谈判中我是不是有什么地方失礼或者冒犯先生了？

陈其然：哪里，哪里，我是真心敬佩史密斯先生！

史密斯：陈先生就过奖了！

陈其然：为了便于磋商，我们根据洽谈，草拟了一份合同文本，请史密斯先生仔细看看。

史密斯：很好。我想约首和约尾，都不会有什么问题，主要是合同正文和附件，需要仔细看看。

陈其然：当然,当然。合同是一种规定双方权利与义务的契约,我们谁都不会当作儿戏。

史密斯：你说得很对。我们双方都是真诚、坦率的,我们谁都不会有意忽略和遗漏什么,为以后不履行合同留下任何借口。

陈其然：我很欣赏史密斯先生的这个态度。

史密斯：那就让我带回去好好琢磨琢磨,我们明天再谈。

二、审核与修改合同

陈其然：史密斯先生,合同看得怎么样了？还有什么需要补充或进一步明确的吗？

史密斯：我逐项审核了合同条款,与我们的谈判内容完全相符,术语使用准确,表述简明,总体上我是满意的。

陈其然：这么说,事情就可能简单多了。

史密斯：是的。我完全同意关于装运和唛头的条款,对商品质量检验和罚款条件,也没有异议。

陈其然：其他条款呢？

史密斯：我想,在装运日期后面,是不是应该再强调一下,"卖方如不按期交货,买方有权提出索赔"？

陈其然：可以。不过,我们这批货是按 F.O.B. 价格成交的,是否也应该明确写上"买方未能如期派船受载,则买方须承担对卖方所造成的损失"？

史密斯：好,这样公平合理,都写上吧。嗯,关于商品品质这一条,合同上写的是 F.A.Q.,是否改为 G.M.Q. 呢？

陈其然：史密斯先生,我们认为用 F.A.Q. 比较好,这是良好平均质,合同书上已经写明了具体的规格要求,而 G.M.Q. 是"品质上好,适于商销",这种品质概念含糊不清,容易发生争执,我们建议不要采用这种品质条件。

史密斯:好,我们同意,那就不要修改了。将来,我们就按 F.A.Q. 品质条件交货与验收。

陈其然:史密斯先生,如果对合同及其附件没有什么异议和补充,我们就带回去修改一下,明天正式签字吧。

史密斯:没有了,明天签字时再见。

三、双方签字

陈其然:史密斯先生,合同及其附件一式二份,一份用中文书写,一份用英文书写,我们都准备好了,昨天会谈时提出的问题,也都一一作了修改、补充,请你们再看一看,如没问题,我们就可以签字了。

史密斯:好的。让我看看。嗯,这是一份非常具体、明确而又完善的合同,避免了任何含糊不清和令人费解的词句,我非常满意,这是我们顺利圆满执行合同的良好基础。

陈其然:这也是我们之间友好合作的良好开端。希望今后能继续合作。

史密斯:长期合作!

陈其然:好,我们签字吧。

生词

1.	轮	lún	round
2.	达成	dáchéng	reach
3.	协议	xiéyì	agreement
4.	文本	wénběn	text, version
5.	基础	jīchǔ	basis, foundation
6.	书面	shūmiàn	in writing
7.	文字	wénzì	wording
8.	新手	xīnshǒu	new hand
9.	领教	lǐngjiào	receive instructions
10.	老练	lǎoliàn	experienced
11.	高手	gāoshǒu	master-hand
12.	失礼	shīlǐ	commit a breach of etiquette
13.	冒犯	màofàn	offend
14.	敬佩	jìngpèi	admire, esteem
15.	过奖	guòjiǎng	overpraise
16.	草拟	cǎonǐ	draft, draw up
17.	约首	yuēshǒu	beginning part of the contract
18.	约尾	yuēwěi	ending part of the contract
19.	正文	zhèngwén	main body
20.	附件	fùjiàn	appendix
21.	契约	qìyuē	contract, deed
22.	儿戏	érxì	trifling matter
23.	遗漏	yílòu	omit, leave out
24.	借口	jièkǒu	excuse
25.	琢磨	zhuómó	ponder, turn over in one's

mind

26. 补充	bǔchōng	add, replenish
27. 逐项	zhúxiàng	item by item
28. 术语	shùyǔ	technical terms
29. 表述	biǎoshù	state, explain
30. 简明	jiǎnmíng	concise and clear
31. 强调	qiángdiào	emphasis
32. 复核	fùhé	re-check
33. 总体上	zǒngtǐshàng	on the whole
34. 唛头	màitóu	shipping mark
35. 罚款	fákuǎn	fine, penalty
36. 概念	gàiniàn	concept, idea
37. 含糊	hánhu	ambiguous
38. 争执	zhēngzhí	dispute
39. 修改	xiūgǎi	revise
40. 验收	yànshōu	check and accept
41. 正式	zhèngshì	formal
42. 书写	shūxiě	write
43. 完善	wánshàn	perfect
44. 费解	fèijiě	obscure, hard to understand
45. 圆满	yuánmǎn	satisfactory, complete
46. 执行	zhíxíng	execute
47. 开端	kāiduān	beginning
48. 签字	qiānzì	sign

练习

A

轮:

①动词,表示一个接替一个做某一动作。可带"着、了、过",还带动量词。②可作量词,多用来说循环的事物或动作。

1) Verb:Take turns to do something. It can take 着,了,过,or verbal measure words that go with a verb. 2) It can be used as a measure word (round),referring to cycling matters or actions.

一、熟读下列各句,体会"轮"的意义和用法:

1. 今天该轮到我值班了。
2. 现在大家都轮过几遍了。
3. 几轮下来,他已经输光了。
4. 这是本赛季第十二轮的一场比赛。
5. 这样的好事哪里轮得着我!
6. 下一轮谈判,可能很困难。
7. 我们同对手已经有了几轮较量,还没分出高下。
8. 下一次兴许就轮上你了。

二、用"轮"和下列词语造句:

1. 磋商
2. 补充
3. 罚款
4. 验收

令人:

常同动词、形容词或词组构成兼语式短语,充当句子的谓语。

Make one...; cause one.... It often forms a complex phrase

together with a verb, an adjective or a phrase and functions as the predicate of the sentence.

一、熟读下列词组,体会它们的意义和结构:

令人费解　　令人头疼　　令人吃惊　　令人扫兴
令人遗憾　　令人佩服　　令人兴奋　　令人困惑
令人烦恼　　令人起敬　　令人担心　　令人难忘

二、选择上面的词组填空:

1. 这次来华洽谈生意进行得如此顺利,真＿＿＿＿＿＿＿＿。
2. 贵公司如此合作,＿＿＿＿＿＿＿＿＿＿＿＿＿。
3. 目前国际市场动荡不安,公司不景气,＿＿＿＿＿＿＿＿。
4. 你方采取这样的态度,＿＿＿＿＿＿＿＿＿＿＿＿。
5. 贵国的服务＿＿＿＿＿＿＿＿＿,我们一定会常常谈起的。
6. 坦率地说,每个人都会做(有)＿＿＿＿＿＿＿＿,朋友们要互相照顾。
7. 合同迟迟不能签字,实在＿＿＿＿＿＿＿＿＿＿＿＿。
8. 改革开放后,贵公司的工作效率如此之高,＿＿＿＿＿＿
＿＿＿＿＿＿＿＿＿＿＿＿＿＿＿＿＿＿＿＿＿＿＿。
9. 贵公司一贯严格履行合同,＿＿＿＿＿＿＿＿＿＿＿＿。
10. 今年我们十分希望增加名牌产品的订货量,贵公司一再
拒绝,＿＿＿＿＿＿＿＿＿＿＿＿＿＿＿＿＿＿＿。

逐:

表示依次、挨个儿的意思。它总是与数词一或个、项、件、次等量词连用,表示动作依次进行,并含有细致谨慎的意思;“逐”还常与年、月、日连用,表示状态随着时间的推移而变化。

One by one. It means in proper order, or successively. It is always used together with the numeral 一 (one), or such measure words as 个, 项 (item), 件 (piece), 次 (time), to indicate that only one thing is dealt with or happens at a particular time. It also implies the meaning of being careful and cautious. 逐 is also often used together with 年(year), 月(month), or 日(day), to express that the circumstances change as the time passes.

一、熟读下列各句,体会"逐"的意义和用法:

1. 他逐个检验产品质量。
2. 双方对合同条款逐一进行磋商。
3. 公司的新职员逐字逐句阅读公司文件。
4. 本公司的营业额和利润都逐年增加。

二、熟读下列词语,然后各造一个句子:

逐一　逐个　逐条　逐字逐句　逐步　逐月　逐项

一一:

副词,是"逐一"、"逐个"的意思,表示动作挨个儿施于对象。

Adverb: One by one; one after another. It expresses that the action is performed in turn on the objects.

一、熟读下列各句,体会"一一"的意义和用法:

1. 推销员把商品一一送到顾客家里。
2. 保险法十分复杂,我不能一一给你解释。
3. 这些罐头的味道都很不错,我都一一尝过了。
4. 这份合同的条款,他都一一研究过了。

二、用"一一"改写下列句子:

1. 洽谈双方逐条逐款地对合同进行了磋商。
2. 推销员挨家挨户推销商品。
3. 我们无法一个罐头一个罐头地去检查这批货的质量。
4. 这个商品博览会实在太丰富了,我没法把所有展厅的商品都看过来。

5. 这条食品街有各地风味小吃,我几乎尝了个遍。

总体:

①若干个体所合成的事物;②整体。

Overall; total. 1) A thing that is formed by combining many individuals. 2) Entirely.

一、熟读下列词组,体会它们的意义和结构:

总体规划　　总体设计　　总体安排　　总体上考虑
总体上看　　总体上说　　总体上着眼

二、完成下列各句:

1. 这批合资项目的总体规划＿＿＿＿＿＿＿＿＿＿＿＿。

2. 从总体上来看,我们这次来中国洽谈生意＿＿＿＿＿＿

　　＿＿＿＿＿＿＿＿＿＿＿＿＿＿＿＿＿＿＿＿＿＿＿＿。

3. 贸易代表团在华访问的日程安排,总体上＿＿＿＿＿＿

　　＿＿＿＿＿＿＿＿＿＿＿＿＿＿＿＿＿＿＿＿＿＿＿＿。

4. 贵公司承包修建的这座贸易中心大楼,总体设计＿＿＿

　　＿＿＿＿＿＿＿＿＿＿＿＿＿＿＿＿＿＿＿＿＿＿＿＿。

5. 在洽谈和签订合同的过程中,不仅要从总体上＿＿＿＿,

　　而且＿＿＿＿＿＿＿＿＿＿＿＿＿＿＿＿＿＿＿＿＿＿。

B

一、用下列词语组词:

复核　　圆满　　合同　　内容　　验收
草拟　　争执　　基础　　异议　　正式

补充　　执行　　费解　　修改　　签字

二、用括号中的词语完成下列句子：

1. 我们草拟的这份合同，_____

_____。（完善）

2. 我方对合同草案的主要内容_____。（异议）

3. 合同的每一个细节都很重要,否则_____。（争执）

4. 对合同的附件,贵方有没有_____？（补充）

5. 合同与附件都要写得具体明确,_____。（避免）

6. 合同规定的义务和权利,对双方_____

_____。（公平合理）

7. _____

_____,另一方有权要求赔偿经济损失。（履行）

8. 如果双方对合同都没有异议,_____

_____。（签字）

9. 经过双方的共同努力,合同谈判_____。（圆满）

10. 合同的签订是_____（基础），也

是_____。（开端）

三、想一想、谈一谈：

1. 一份好的合同必须具备哪些条件？

2. 签订合同作为洽谈的最后阶段,还可能遇到什么麻烦？

3. 你签过合同吗？请谈谈你的经验和当时的心情。

四、阅读下面的短文,并回答问题:

不留后患

甲公司(某中国公司)和乙公司(某外国公司)洽谈一项价值几百万美元的机械进出口合同。合同文本是乙公司草拟的。合同中关于仲裁的条款是这样写的:"凡因执行本合同所发生的或与本合同有关的一切争议,如双方协商不能解决,或者提交中国对外经济贸易仲裁委员会仲裁,或者提交第三国国家仲裁院仲裁。"甲公司认为,这项条款内容含糊,容易引起争议,如果一方对仲裁地点和仲裁法有异议,就无法申请仲裁。所以,甲公司提出修改这一条款。经磋商,双方一致达成协议,最后这样规定:"凡因执行本合同所发生的与本合同有关的一切争议,如双方协商不能解决,应提交中国对外经济贸易仲裁委员会根据该会仲裁规则进行仲裁。仲裁裁决是终局的,对双方均有约束力。"这个修改具体、明确,甲乙双方都感到满意。这样,合同就顺利签字了。

1. 甲、乙双方在修改合同时遇到了什么问题?

2. 合同草稿和定稿中的仲裁条款有什么不同?

3. 甲、乙双方协商过程顺利吗? 协商结果对哪一方更有利?

第十五课　追　账
Lesson 15　Demanding Payment of a Debt

一、追账委托

许天木：马先生，一家外国公司拖欠了我们一笔货款，我们多次催收，都无结果，只好请你们帮忙了。

马千里：我们是专业追账公司，十分乐意为你们提供服务。

许天木：希望你们能帮助我们尽快把这笔欠款收回来。

马千里：你们的焦急心情，我们能够理解。现在，国际贸易中拖欠货款的现象越来越普遍，越来越严重，我们公司每天都会接到债权人的讨债申请。

许天木：我们现在很困难，要是再过一两个月收不回这笔货款，我们公司就很难维持正常经营了。

马千里：我们会尽最大努力的。请说说情况吧！

许天木：我带来了我们双方签订的合同。

马千里：很好。我们首先需要知道债务人公司的

　　　　　名称、地址、电话、联系人等一些最基本的情况。

许天木：我们作过资信调查，这些情况都是真实的。

马千里：你们签订合同时是真实的，现在的情况就不一定
　　　　了。

许天木：马先生是说，这家公司现在倒闭了？

马千里：啊，我不是这个意思。我的意思是说，这个公司
　　　　现在的情况怎么样，是我们追账前必须调查的内
　　　　容。

许天木：我明白。我们有的公司吃过这个亏，追账时才发
　　　　现，不是债务人公司经营不好，无力偿还货款，就
　　　　是破产倒闭；不是恶意搬迁，就是销声匿迹。

马千里：这样的事经常发生，不足为奇！

许天木：马先生还需要我们提供什么情况？

马千里：有关证明债权成立的必要文件，除了合同外，比
　　　　如发票、信用证、提单、往来信函等。

许天木：好的，我随后就派人送来。

马千里：许先生，债务人欠你们多少货款？

许天木：400万美元。

马千里：啊，这可是一笔巨额货款！拖欠多久了？

许天木：快三年了。

马千里：快三年了？这么长的时间，你们没有采取有效的
　　　　追账行动？

许天木：我们做过各种努力，甚至迫使对方签署过《付款
　　　　备忘录》，可是债务人仍以种种理由拒绝付款。

马千里：这种备忘录，对跨国债务来说，往往是一纸空文。

许天木：说的也是，我们对跨国债务能有什么好办法呢？

马千里：你们在三年的时间里没有找过专业追账公司吗？

许天木：没有。

马千里：这就很遗憾了。现在全世界有 60% 的国际商务欠款是由专业追账公司处理的。

许天木：那些债权人是什么时候提出申请的呢？

马千里：一般来说，应收账款过期 60 天，债权人就应该进行追账前调查；超过 90 天，就应该立即请专业追账公司追账。

许天木：那么，我们现在申请是不是太晚了？

马千里：根据全球追账数据统计，一笔应收账款如果超过了 240 天，收回的机率就只有 50% 了。

许天木：那我们的损失就太惨重了！

马千里：许先生不要着急，我们立即采取行动，请你们密切配合！

许天木：一定！一定！

二、接触债务人

大　卫：汉斯先生，见到你真不容易！

汉　斯：啊，我很忙！听秘书说，你有重要事情要见我，什么事？

大　卫：我得先自我介绍一下，我叫大卫·格林。

汉　斯：我们在什么地方见过面吗？

大　卫：没有。我是受人之托来拜访你。

汉　斯：谁？

大　卫：中国的一家贸易公司，这是我的《授权证明书》。

汉　斯：噢，你是亚洲国际保理公司的追账主管。我不记得我与你的委托人有什么债务关系啊？

大　卫:哦？这可是 400 万美元的债务,汉斯先生忘了?

汉　斯:嗯……

大　卫:要不要我把合同、发票、你们的付款记录,给你看看?

汉　斯:噢,这样吧, 我让有关部门查一查,再给你一个答复,怎么样?

大　卫:什么时候给我答复?

汉　斯:尽快吧!

大　卫:汉斯先生,这笔账款已经拖欠近三年了,不能再拖了。

汉　斯:那是! 那是!

大　卫:我们希望能圆满了结这笔债务。欠债不还的后果,你是知道的。

汉　斯:当然。天天有人上门讨债,日子也不好过,是不是?

三、进展报告

马千里:许先生,我今天请你来,是要通报一下追账的进展情况。

许天木:有好消息了?

马千里:我们与债务人接触了几次,说明欠债不还可能带来的严重后果,给他巨大的信誉压力,劝说他清偿欠款。

许天木:有效果吗?

马千里:没有。随后,我们用电话、传真、欠资邮件和专业收款人员上门等多种方式,进行了"轰炸式"催讨,让他日夜不得安宁。

许天木：结果怎么样？

马千里：看来，我们是碰到一位"要钱没有，要命有一条"的角色了！

许天木：后来呢？

马千里：在采取持续不断催讨行动的同时，我们进行了大量周密调查，发现这家公司负债累累，已经临近宣告破产了。

许天木：在他们宣告破产之前，我们能上诉法院，取得债务人资产的处置权吗？

马千里：晚了。债务公司已经接到多家针对它的法院裁决，有两家债权人公司已经获得债务人公司所有资产的占有权。

许天木：我们的 400 万美元货款就收不回来了？

马千里：我想，我们已经完成对债务人的调查和分析。我们做了我们能做的一切。

许天木：你们不能再做点什么吗？

马千里：我们认为，任何进一步针对债务人的行动，都只能是浪费你们的资金。我们不得不遗憾地关闭这个案子。

许天木：我们太轻信对方了，现在自食苦果！

生词

1. 拖欠	tuōqiàn	default, be behind in payment
2. 催收	cuīshōu	press for payment of a debt
3. 尽快	jǐnkuài	as soon as possible

4.	焦急	jiāojí	anxious, anxiety
5.	债权人	zhàiquánrén	creditor
6.	讨债	tǎozhài	demand payment of a debt
7.	维持	wéichí	keep, maintain
8.	债务人	zhàiwùrén	debtor
9.	恶意	èyì	evil intentions, malicious
10.	搬迁	bānqiān	move
11.	销声匿迹	xiāoshēngnìjì	keep silent and lie low, disappear from the scene
12.	不足为奇	bùzúwéiqí	not at all surprising
13.	成立	chénglì	establish
14.	随后	suíhòu	subsequent
15.	行动	xíngdòng	action
16.	迫使	pòshǐ	force, compel
17.	签署	qiānshǔ	sign
18.	备忘录	bèiwànglù	memorandum
19.	理由	lǐyóu	reason
20.	跨国	kuàguó	transnational
21.	一纸空文	yīzhǐkōngwén	a mere scrap of paper
22.	欠款	qiànkuǎn	owe a debt, money that is owing, balance due
23.	统计	tǒngjì	statistics
24.	机率	jīlǜ	probability
25.	惨重	cǎnzhòng	heavy, disastrous
26.	配合	pèihé	cooperate
27.	拜访	bàifǎng	pay a visit, call on
28.	授权	shòuquán	authorize
29.	保理	bǎolǐ	agent, factor
30.	主管	zhǔguǎn	person in charge, executive

31.	答复	dáfù	reply
32.	了结	liǎojié	finish, settle
33.	后果	hòuguǒ	consequence, result
34.	进展	jìnzhǎn	progress
35.	通报	tōngbào	notify, report
36.	劝说	quànshuō	persuade
37.	清偿	qīngcháng	pay off, clear off
38.	邮件	yóujiàn	mail
39.	轰炸	hōngzhà	bombard
40.	安宁	ānníng	peace, tranquility
41.	角色	juésè	role
42.	周密	zhōumì	thorough, careful
43.	负债累累	fùzhàilěilěi	heavily in debt
44.	临近	línjìn	close to
45.	宣告	xuāngào	declare
46.	上诉	shàngsù	appeal
47.	法院	fǎyuàn	law court
48.	处置	chǔzhì	handle, manage
49.	裁决	cáijué	rule, verdict
50.	获得	huòdé	obtain
51.	占有	zhànyǒu	possess, occupy
52.	分析	fēnxī	analyze
53.	浪费	làngfèi	waste
54.	关闭	guānbì	close
55.	案子	ànzi	case
56.	轻信	qīngxìn	be credulous, believe readily
57.	自食苦果	zìshíkǔguǒ	eat one's own bitter fruit

专名

亚洲　　　　　　Yàzhōu　　　　　　Asia

练习

A

不是……就是……:

在这种"不是 A 就是 B"的格式中, A、B 为同类名词、动词、形容词, 也常常是小句, 表示两项中必有一项是事实。

In this pattern of "either A or B", A and B are of the same word category, they can be nouns, verbs or adjectives, or they may be clauses. It indicates that of the two items, one must be true.

一、熟读下列各句, 体会"不是……就是……"的意义和用法:

1. 不是你去就是我去。
2. 他们公司不是缺资金就是缺技术。
3. 皮包公司不是设计骗人, 就是赖账逃债。
4. 今天出席会议的不是政府要员就是大企业家。

二、用"不是……就是……"和下列词语造句:

1. 拒绝　　接受
2. 借钱还债　　财产抵押
3. 缺斤短两　　质量不合格
4. 前进　　后退

随后:

副词, 表示一件事情紧跟着另一件事情发生。

Adverb: It indicates that one thing happens immediately after another.

一、熟读下列各句,体会"随后"的意义和用法:

1. 你先去,我随后就到。
2. 会计先分析了公司的财务状况,经理随后作了补充。
3. 我开头还以为他在开玩笑,随后就知道他是认真的。
4. 他得到了银行贷款,随后就销声匿迹了。

二、用"随后"完成下列各句:

1. 他开车违反了交通规则,_____

_____。

2. 我公司先是资金周转不灵,_____

_____。

3. 我们经过几轮友好洽谈,已经达成一致协议,_____

_____。

4. 人们买东西往往先被新颖、独到的外包装吸引,_____

_____。

5. 饭店服务员热情地请客人坐下,_____

_____。

说的是:

认为对方说得对,表示同意对方的话。

It shows agreement, indicating that what the other party said was right.

一、熟读下列各句,体会"说的是"的意义和用法:

1. 说的是,我怎么早没想到找追账公司呢?

2．说的也是，我早该知足了！

3．你说的也是，我去找经理！

二、用"说的是"完成下列各句：

1．＿＿＿＿＿＿＿＿，让有关部门查一查，尽快给你一个答复。

2．＿＿＿＿＿＿＿，我们应该立即采取行动，请你们密切配合。

3．＿＿＿＿＿＿＿＿，天天有人上门讨债，日子也不好过。

4．＿＿＿＿＿＿＿＿，如果商品是一流质量，二流包装，三流

价格，在市场上就没有竞争力了。

B

一、熟读下列词语，解释其意义，然后各造一个句子：

1．一纸空文	4．负债累累	7．万事如意
2．自食其果	5．了如指掌	8．准确无误
3．销声匿迹	6．不足为奇	

二、用下列词语组词：

迫使	轻信	裁决	分析	清偿	处置
欠款	账款	破产	临近	损失	拖欠
催收	跨国	惨重	维持		

三、从上面选择适当的词语，完成下面的句子：

1．现在国际贸易中，＿＿＿＿＿＿＿＿＿＿＿＿＿＿＿＿＿。

2．如果这笔巨款不能＿＿＿＿＿＿＿＿＿＿＿＿＿＿＿＿＿。

3．现在我们公司资金周转不灵＿＿＿＿＿＿＿＿＿＿＿＿＿＿。

4．为了公司信誉，＿＿＿＿＿＿＿＿＿＿＿＿＿＿＿＿＿＿＿。

5. 我公司已完成对债权人的调查和分析_____

_____。

四、想一想,谈一谈:

1. 用你所学的词语,设计一个"追账"与"拒付欠款"的情景。
2. 请专业追账公司追账要提供哪些资料?
3. 为什么现在出现了专业追账公司?你知道什么叫"三角债"吗?
4. 中国有句俗话:"站着借钱,跪着要钱",意思是借钱容易要钱难,你能谈谈你的看法与体会吗?

五、阅读下面的短文,并回答问题:

躲过初一,躲不过十五

A公司是一家皮包公司,打一枪换一个地方。这天,A公司搬进一个新的办公室,电话线都还没有接通,秘书见王先生走进来,立即拿起电话。装模作样地说起来:"喂,张总吗?贵公司欠我们的300万货款,什么时候跟我们结清啊?什么,这一两天就可以?你这话可说过不只一次了,今天推明天,这月推下月,总得还吧?当然还?今天先付50万?不行!至少100万,我们现在有急用。人家也欠了你们的?那我们不管,实话告诉你吧,我们老板已经去你那儿了,你不付款,老板就吃住在你那儿了。"

啪!秘书放下电话,连忙笑着说:"啊,王总您来啦,快请坐,我给您倒茶去!""不用了,我是来要钱的,给了我就走。""哎呀,王总,您也听见了,我们也是一时周转不开,我正在催款呢!我们老板……""老板又不在公司是吧?我刚才在路上碰上他,他说钱已经准备好,就放在保险箱里,叫你给我。""你自己看吧,这屋里有没有保险箱!"王先生扫了一眼,屋子空荡荡的,除了秘书坐的这张桌子,别无一物。王先生正疑惑,又进来几个人,其中一个人问秘书:"我们是法院的,你们老板呢?""他不在。""去哪儿了?""不知道。他刚租了这间屋子,连电话都没有装,我也是他临时雇的。"王先生说:"可你刚才还在打电话?""那是老板教我这样做给催账人看的。"王先生一听,急了,对法院的人说:"同志,这怎么办?他跑了,还欠我50多万货款呢!""他不止拖欠你一家货款,法院早就作了判决,但他至今拒不执行,我们就是来强制执行的,没想到今天我们又扑了一个空。他躲过了初一,躲不过十五!"

1. 什么叫皮包公司?
2. 张总经理真的欠了A公司300万货款吗?
3. 什么叫强制执行?什么情况下法院才采取强制执行措施?
4. "躲过了初一,躲不过十五"是什么意思?

第十六课　索赔与仲裁
Lesson 16　Claim and Arbitration

一、质量不合格

史密斯：陈先生，我很遗憾地通知你，贵方这次出口的瓶装青岛啤酒有 10％质量不合格。我们不得不要求索赔。

陈其然：青岛啤酒是我国的名牌产品，在国际上有良好的声誉。我们在洽谈时，是按惯例、凭牌号商标成交，所以我们对商品质量是有信心的，你们对此也是信得过的，怎么会出现你说的问题呢？

玛　丽：我们已请商检部门仔细检验过了，确实有 10％的质量不合格，可能是更换包装瓶造成的。

陈其然：我们在合同中同意你方有商品复检权，但必须是我方认可的公证机构。请问，有他们出具的检验证书吗？

玛　丽：有的，这就是。

陈其然：好，我们拿回去研究一下，再给你们答复。

如果情况属实,我们理应赔偿。

二、货物短量

陈其然:史密斯先生,我们向贵方订购的化肥实际重量与合同不符,我们不能按合同付款。

史密斯:我们在合同的数量条款中,有溢短装幅度,货物重量短缺是允许的。

陈其然:但是,短缺数量远远超过了合同规定的 8% 的幅度。

玛　丽:怎么会? 不会是你们弄错了吧?

陈其然:没有。我国的商品检验局报告指明,贵方化肥包装有两种:一种每袋 100 公斤;一种每袋 120 公斤。数量短缺,可能是装运和计算失误造成的。

史密斯:好,请把贵国商检局出具的重量证明书给我看看。嗯,确实是我们出了差错。我对此深表遗憾,我方接受索赔。

陈其然:没关系,千里马也有失蹄的时候,史密斯先生不必介意。

三、商品损坏与灭失

史密斯:陈先生,我们向贵公司订购的瓷器,经检验,破损严重,我很遗憾,不得不向贵方提出索赔。

陈其然:史密斯先生,在查明破损原因以前,我方不能受理索赔,因为造成破损有多种原因。我们这笔生意,是按 F.O.B. 价格成交的,倘是交货装运前造成的,没有话说。如果是运输途中出的问题,按照合同中有关风险转移的规定,责任就不在我们了。

玛　丽:检验证明,破损原因确实是贵方造成的,请陈先生看看。

陈其然:好的。嗯,很遗憾,破损是因包装不善,装卸不慎造成的,责任的确在我方,我们接受索赔。不过,瓷器是易碎物品,按合同我们可有 1%～2% 的破损,索赔应考虑到这一点。

史密斯:陈先生的要求是合理的,我们可以接受。为了今后的业务关系,我方索赔也可作相应让步,所赔款项可用贵方产品冲销。

陈其然:好,谢谢。

四、争议的调解与仲裁

陈其然:史密斯先生,合同 453 号货款,已经拖延两个多月,无法议付,交涉多次,都无结果,看来,我们只能提交仲裁了。

史密斯:货款不能议付,责任不在我们。

陈其然:责任怎么不在你方? 是你们开立的信用证条款错误。

玛　丽:不。合同规定,凭样货,邯郸椒干,F.O.B. 天津新港,总价 75 万美元,每袋 20～25 公斤,信用证付款。我们按时开了信用证,并派船接货受载,我们是严格履行了合同的。

陈其然:史密斯先生不应该忘记,你方派来的船太小,船位容积不够,要求我们临时把每袋 20～25 公斤改为小包装,每袋 15 公斤。你方同时承诺修改信用证的有关条款。当时,我们双方达成了口头协议,但当货物装船启运后,你们却不履行诺言,所以才造成单证不符,无法议付。

史密斯:陈先生,你像是在开玩笑,这样大宗生意,怎么可以用口头协议成交?信用证是按合同开立的。我们要信守合同,怎么可以随便修改?

陈其然:我们说的都是事实,你方的承办人及船方都可作证,史密斯先生怎么可以出尔反尔呢?

史密斯:不是我出尔反尔,是陈先生出言无据。我以为,货款无法议付,根本原因是货物质量与样货不符,是你们没有信守合同。

陈其然:这不是事实。

玛　丽:破碎率大大超出合理的界限。

陈其然:是你方派的船太小,船方强行挤压进舱造成的,责任不在我方。

玛　丽:合同规定是邯郸椒干,但我们收到的货中有相当一部分是山西椒。

陈其然:哦,洽谈中,我们曾经说明,这次订货量大,交货期太短,我们难以组织足够货源按期交货,但你们反复请求我们满足你们的要求。史密斯先生不会忘记吧?

史密斯:是的,我们互相都很体谅对方的困难。

陈其然:所以我们为了顾全双方的合作关系与友谊,才提出用部分山西椒补足的方案。你们当时不仅同意,而且再三表示感谢。

史密斯:是的。但是合同中有约定吗?

陈其然:我们达成过口头协议。

史密斯:很遗憾,你们中国人重感情,我们西方人重理智,
　　　　我们只能按双方签字的合同办事。
陈其然:看来,我们双方无法协商一致,只好提交仲裁委
　　　　员会调解与仲裁了。
史密斯:我们同意。

生词

1.	仲裁	zhòngcái	arbitration
2.	合格	hégé	up to standard; qualified
3.	通知	tōngzhī	notify
4.	声誉	shēngyù	reputation
5.	品牌	pǐnpái	brand name
6.	信心	xìnxīn	confidence
7.	更换	gēnghuàn	change, replace
8.	必须	bìxū	must; necessary
9.	公证	gōngzhèng	notary public
10.	属实	shǔshí	be true
11.	短量	duǎnliàng	short weight
12.	溢短装	yìduǎnzhuāng	more or less (clause)
13.	失误	shīwù	slip-up
14.	差错	chācuò	mistake
15.	失蹄	shītí	slip
16.	不必	bùbì	need not
17.	介意	jièyì	take offence, mind
18.	灭失	mièshī	loss
19.	瓷器	cíqì	porcelain
20.	严重	yánzhòng	serious
21.	受理	shòulǐ	accept and hear a case

22. 倘是	tǎngshì	if, in case
23. 损坏	sǔnhuài	damage
24. 不慎	bùshèn	careless
25. 款项	kuǎnxiàng	a sum of money
26. 冲销	chōngxiāo	offset
27. 调解	tiáojiě	mediation
28. 拖延	tuōyán	delay
29. 交涉	jiāoshè	take up with, negotiate
30. 样货	yànghuò	sample
31. 椒干	jiāogān	dried chili
32. 临时	línshí	temporary, makeshift
33. 船位	chuánwèi	shipping space
34. 容积	róngjī	volume
35. 口头	kǒutóu	oral, verbal
36. 启运	qǐyùn	start shipment
37. 诺言	nuòyán	promise
38. 信守	xìnshǒu	abide by
39. 承办	chéngbàn	undertake
40. 作证	zuòzhèng	give evidence, bear wittness
41. 出尔反尔	chū'ěrfǎn'ěr	go back on one's promise
42. 出言无据	chūyánwújù	what one said is ungrounded
43. 界限	jièxiàn	limit
44. 强行	qiángxíng	force
45. 挤压	jǐyā	squeeze, press
46. 反复	fǎnfù	repeated
47. 体谅	tǐliàng	show understanding and sympathy for
48. 顾全	gùquán	show consideration for; for the sake of larger interest

49. 货源	huòyuán	supply of goods
50. 方案	fāng'àn	plan
51. 再三	zàisān	time and again
52. 理智	lǐzhì	reason, rationality
53. 委员会	wěiyuánhuì	committee, commission

练习

A

是……的：

用这个句式来强调已经发生的动作的时间、地点、方式、目的等；也可以强调一种东西的用途、来源。要强调的部分一般放在"是……的"中间，但如果动词有名词充当的宾语，"的"也可以放在宾语前，紧跟在动词后。

This pattern is used to emphasize the time, place, manner or purpose of an action that already happened. It can also stress the use or origin of a certain thing. The emphasized part is generally placed in between 是 and 的. But when the verb takes a noun as the object, 的 can also be placed before the object, immediately following the verb.

一、熟读下列各句，体会"是……的"的用法，并指出它所强调的是什么：

1. 我们对贵公司的产品质量是信得过的。
2. 出口商品都是经过贵国检验的，质量上有问题需由你方负责。
3. 我国出具的商品检验证明，是被世界承认的。
4. 货物短量如不超过溢短装幅度，我们是不能接受索赔的。

二、用"是……的"改写下列各句：

1. 销售不合格的商品有损贵公司信誉。
2. 这是我国过硬的名优产品，质量绝对有把握。
3. 合同条款上有明确规定，不执行不行。
4. 在查明破损原因以前，我们不能受理索赔。
5. 贵公司商品出口免检，来之不易。

信得过：

"信"是动词，"得"、"过"都是助词。"信得过"是动词带结果补语一类结构的词组，它的否定形式是"信不过"。类似的词组还有很多，如"对得起、对不起"，"做得成、做不成"，"睡得着、睡不着"，"回得来、回不来"等等。

In this expression, 信 is a verb, and both 得 and 过 are auxiliary words. 信得过（trust）is a phrase made up of a verb and its complement of result. Its negative form is 信不过（distrust）. There are quite a number of phrases similar to this one, such as 对得起, 对不起（not let somebody down; let somebody down）, 做得成, 做不成（can succeed; cannot succeed）, 睡得着, 睡不着（can go to sleep; cannot go to sleep）, 回得来, 回不来（can come back; cannot come back）, etc.

一、熟读下列各句，体会"信得过"、"信不过"的词义和用法：

1. 他这个人太滑头，叫人信不过。
2. 这家商店荣获"信得过商店"的称号。
3. 我们是老朋友了，你还信不过我吗？
4. 你要是信得过我，你就把这事交给我去办好了。

二、用"信得过"、"信不过"和下列短语造句：

1. 多年的贸易伙伴

2. 贵公司一向重信誉

3. 皮包公司

4. 贵国出具的商检证书

不必：

副词，表示事理上或情理上不是一定需要，不是非如此不可。

Adverb: need not; not have to. It means that there is no reason why a particular thing should happen, or why one should do it.

一、熟读下列词组，仔细体会每个词组的意义：

不必介意	不必降价	不必优惠	不必更换
不必赔偿	不必转运	不必修改	不必复检
不必索赔	不必答复	不必交涉	不必承诺

二、从上面选择五个词组各造一个句子：

难以：

是一种文言表达方式，意思是"不容易"。与"难于"相当。"以"、"于"都是介词。

Difficult to. It is an expression used in classical Chinese. It corresponds to 难于. Both 以 and 于 are prepositions, indicating where the difficulties lie.

一、熟读下列词组，仔细体会每个词组的意义和结构：

难以识别	难以相（置）信	难以把握	难以预料
难以猜测	难以查明	难以交货	难以仲裁
难以控制	难以突破	难以克服	难以许诺

二、从上述词组中选择适当的词组填空：

1. 真货、假货_____。

2. 去年成交额那么大,一般情况下_____。

3. 目前国际金融市场动荡不定,_____。

4. 这位老先生说话幽默,常常开玩笑,_____。

5. 世界能源危机在短期内_____。

6. 这个经济案件十分复杂,_____。

7. 你们的要求不符合互通有无、平等互利的原则,我们____

    _____。

8. 因为这批货物经过几次转船,货物灭失的原因,一时____

    _____。

9. 这笔生意订货量大,技术要求高,在短期内_____

    _____。

10. 俗话说:"天有不测风云",远洋运输途中会遇到什么风

    险,实在_____。

倘:

连词,也常用"倘若、倘使、倘或",它的意思和用法与"如果、假如"相同,不过表示的假设语气比较重。

This conjunction can also take the form of 倘若, 倘使, or 倘或(supposing; in case). Its meaning and use are the same as 如果 or 假如 (if), but with a stronger implication of supposition.

一、熟读下列各句,体会"倘"的意义和用法:

1. 倘若协商没有结果,只好提请仲裁了。
2. 倘若你不出面,这事就不好解决了。
3. 倘或听我一句劝告,也不至于这么糟糕!
4. 倘使没有市场,还有什么生意可做?

二、用"倘"和下列短语造句：

1. 重量与合同不符
2. 对方没有信守合同
3. 因包装不善破损
4. 货物质量与样货不符

B

一、用下列词语组词：

提交	冲销	调解	答复	拖延	严重
反复	仲裁	索赔	失误	强行	短缺
受理	幅度	商检	允许	启运	证明

二、从上面词语中选择适当词语，完成下列句子：

1. 这次商品复检结果，_____。

2. 货物数量，按合同规定_____。

3. 问题究竟出在哪里，等我们调查清楚后，_____

_____。

4. 考虑到我们多年的业务关系，我们同意_____

_____。

5. 我们要求赔偿，多次交涉，都没有结果，_____

_____。

三、熟读下列词组，并选择适当词组完成后面的句子：

深表同情	深表遗憾	深表不安	深表赞赏
深表关注	深表歉意	深表谢意	深表敬佩

1. 这次来访,受到贵方的热情接待,我们＿＿＿＿＿＿＿。

2. 贵国的经济体制改革取得了巨大效益,我们＿＿＿＿＿＿＿。

3. 你方提出的要求太高了,我们不能作出任何承诺,＿＿＿＿

＿＿＿＿＿＿＿＿＿＿＿＿＿＿＿＿＿＿＿＿＿＿＿＿。

4. 对贵公司没有严格履行合同,＿＿＿＿＿＿＿＿＿＿＿。

5. 对目前国际金融市场风云变幻、动荡不安的局面,

＿＿＿＿＿＿＿＿＿＿＿＿＿＿＿＿＿＿＿＿＿＿＿＿。

四、熟读下列词组,并选择适当的词组填空:

出言无据　　万无一失　　出尔反尔　　不言而喻
一无所知　　不必介意　　顾名思义　　名正言顺
至关重要　　尽力而为

1. 你说黄金行情看涨,我看你纯粹是＿＿＿＿＿＿＿＿。

2. 他一向说话有口无心,＿＿＿＿＿＿＿＿＿＿＿＿。

3. 这笔交易能不能成功,对我们双方都＿＿＿＿＿＿＿。

4. 一个业务推销员,如果对商品＿＿＿＿＿＿＿＿＿＿,

怎么向顾客推销呢?

5. 你是公司的经理,这事由你来决定,是＿＿＿＿＿＿＿

的。

6. 既然经商检局检验,供货与样货品质不符,＿＿＿＿＿

＿＿＿＿＿＿＿＿＿＿＿＿＿＿＿＿＿＿＿,应该退货。

7. 组织这批货源不论多么困难,我们都将＿＿＿＿＿＿＿。

8. 保险公司,＿＿＿＿＿＿＿＿＿＿＿＿＿,它的业务自然是办理

各类社会保险。

9. 洽谈中难免发生争议,大家都_____。

10. 天有不测风云,人有旦夕祸福,货物即使办理了保险,也

很难说就_____了。

五、想一想、谈一谈:

1. 在交易活动中,发生争端是不是常有的事? 一般怎么解
   决?
2. 一旦造成经济损失,怎样向对方索赔?
3. 出现了什么情况,才不得不提出仲裁?
4. 你有过索赔和涉及仲裁的经历吗? 谈谈具体情况。

六、阅读下面的短文,并回答问题:

哑巴吃黄连

我们工厂,委托一家外贸公司代理从国外进口一条化工生
产线。货到后,我们赶紧组织安装调试。在这个过程中,我们
发现设备质量、规格有许多与合同不符,根本无法投产。我们
请国家商检局来检验,证明确实是卖方没有履行合同,我们把
商检局出具的证明交给为我们代理进口的外贸公司,请向卖方
索赔。但卖方拒绝受理,答复说:"合同规定,应在货物到达目
的地后 60 天内商检,凭商检证书在 120 天内索赔,而你方没有
在规定期限内商检,设备质量出了问题,不能由我们负责。"我
们真是哑巴(yǎba)吃黄连,有口说不出啊!

1. 工厂有没有理由向卖方索赔?
2. 卖方是否有理由拒绝工厂索赔?
3. 依你看,应该是哪一方的责任?
4. 如果工厂把争议提交仲裁,哪一方可能败诉?

第十七课　代理协议
Lesson 17　Agency Agreement

一、要求独家代理

罗　斯：李先生，恕我开门见山。我这次来中国，是想跟先生商谈贵公司在美国的销售代理问题。

李　宁：欢迎啊，我们很乐意同罗斯先生讨论这个问题。

罗　斯：李先生知道，我们公司多年经销贵公司的产品，成绩显著。

李　宁：罗斯先生说得没错，我们非常感谢。

罗　斯：如果贵公司委托我在美国做产品经销的独家代理人，我相信，对我们双方都有利。

李　宁：哦，罗斯先生认为，目前的条件成熟吗？

罗　斯：我们公司已经具备了做独家代理的能力和条件。

李　宁：可是，根据我们在贵国做的市场调研，贵国对本公司产品的需求量很大，而你们公司以往的订货量却很有限。所以,我们不得不同贵国的多家客商建立贸易关系。

罗　斯:如果贵公司把产品的专营权交给我们,情形可能就大不一样了。

李　宁:为什么?

罗　斯:事实上,正因为贵公司在我国建立了多家代理关系,同业竞争十分激烈,所以我们过去主要经销别的公司的产品,经销贵公司产品,只是试探性的,订货量自然有限。

李　宁:你是不是说,今后你们打算中断同别的公司的业务关系,集中全部精力专营本公司的产品?

罗　斯:是的,就看贵公司给不给我们这个荣幸和机会了。

李　宁:我十分赞赏罗斯先生的气魄和才干! 罗斯先生能否给我们提供一些必要的资料呢? 比如贵公司经营的状况、网络、渠道、运作方式,以及作为独家代理的计划。

罗　斯:我们已经带来了!

李　宁:啊,你们是有备而来嘛! 那好,让我们研究研究吧!

二、权利与义务

李　宁:罗斯先生,我们经过研究,很高兴约请你作为本公司在贵国的独家代理人。

罗　斯:我感到十分荣幸!

李　宁:今天,我们就来谈谈具体细节吧!

罗　斯:好的。就请李先生先谈谈我的权利与义务。

李　宁：作为本公司的独家代理商，享有本公司产品在贵国的独家专营权。

罗　斯：这就是说，你们承诺，今后不在我国建立多家代理关系。

李　宁：是的。根据代理协议，你们还将得到应得的佣金和报酬。

罗　斯：这也是国际惯例。

李　宁：说到义务，我们也是遵循国际上一些通行的做法。

罗　斯：很好，我们今后可以少一些争议。

李　宁：作为我方的独家代理，你们不能在贵国经营其他国家同类和类似的产品，也不能把我们的产品再转口到贵国以外的地区去。

罗　斯：这是合理的限制，我们接受。

李　宁：你方还要按照我们双方商定的商品价格保证完成一定的年销售量和销售金额。

罗　斯：这是当然。但要有合理的销售定额和佣金，超过定额部份，要提高佣金比例。

李　宁：这可以商量。如果代而不理或不积极推销，完不成定额，也要扣付佣金，甚至取消代理资格。

罗　斯：这个条件也公平。

李　宁：你们作为有专营权的代理人，可以牵线搭桥，兜揽订单，以我们委托人的名义与客户签订买卖合同。不过，有一句丑话要说在头里。

罗　斯：请讲！

李　宁：你们要毫无保留地向我们提供一切真实情况，

在代理业务中,不得受贿,不得谋取私利,更不得串通第三者损害本公司的利益。

罗　斯：哦,这是代理人最起码的职业道德,不必叮嘱。

李　宁：为了有利于改进生产,我们还希望贵公司能够每半年给我们提供一次市场调研资料,把客户对我们产品的反应及时反馈给我们。对你们提供的此类信息,我们也将付给酬金。

罗　斯：好说,好说。既然你我双方同在一条船上,利害与共,本应互相通气,共商对策。

李　宁：那就让我们携手合作,同舟共济吧!

三、定额与佣金

李　宁：罗斯先生,我们今天协商销售定额与佣金问题。

罗　斯：李先生不妨先提出一个销售定额,供我们考虑。

李　宁：那也好。罗斯先生十分了解本公司产品在国际市场上的销售情况,不需要我作更多的说明,我就直截了当地说了。

罗　斯：我喜欢这种工作作风。

李　宁：你方作为本公司在贵国的独家代理,年销售量不能少于 2000 万美元。

罗　斯：2000 万? 这是不是太高了! 据我们对国内市场的预测,即使我们竭尽全力,充其量也只能完成1500 万的年销售量。

李　宁：本公司产品在贵国的年销售量,远远超过了2000 万美元。罗斯先生是不是太保守了!

罗　斯：可是市场有许多可变因素,难以预测。

李　宁：但是,罗斯先生成了本公司的独家代理后,没有

了竞争对手,也就控制了全部市场,还愁完不成
2000 万的年销售量?

罗　斯：好吧,2000 万就 2000 万,但佣金必须 5%。

李　宁：这个要价是不是有点儿离谱了。

罗　斯：不,一点儿也不离谱。李先生自然会算这笔账,
我们要完成这么大的年销售量,需要多大的开
支和投入。再说,你刚才就没给我留讨价还价
的余地,不是吗?

李　宁：好吧,我们也接受你的条件。我们这次商谈的
独家代理协议,有效期就短一点,三年,怎么样?

罗　斯：可以。

李　宁：三年期满后,如果我们双方都有继续合作的愿
望,可以再洽谈延期问题。

罗　斯：好,就请贵公司草拟一个文本,以便我们尽早签
字。

生词

1.	独家	dújiā	sole, exclusive
2.	开门见山	kāiménjiànshān	come straight to the point
3.	成绩	chéngjì	achievement, success
4.	显著	xiǎnzhù	notable, marked
5.	成熟	chéngshú	mature
6.	具备	jùbèi	possess, have
7.	调研	diàoyán	investigation and study
8.	以往	yǐwǎng	in the past
9.	有限	yǒuxiàn	limited
10.	专营	zhuānyíng	exclusive right of selling …

11. 情形	qíng xíng	situation, state of affairs
12. 同业	tóngyè	the same trade of business
13. 经销	jīngxiāo	sell on commission, distribute
14. 试探	shìtàn	feel out; trial
15. 中断	zhōngduàn	suspend, break off
16. 精力	jīnglì	energy, vigor
17. 赞赏	zànshǎng	appreciate, admire
18. 气魄	qìpò	breadth of spirit, imposing manner
19. 才干	cáigàn	ability, competence
20. 运作	yùnzuò	operation
21. 计划	jìhuà	plan
22. 有备而来	yǒubèi'érlái	come fully prepared
23. 约请	yuēqǐng	invite, ask
24. 享有	xiǎngyǒu	enjoy
25. 报酬	bàochóu	remuneration
26. 遵循	zūnxún	abide by
27. 转口	zhuǎnkǒu	re-export
28. 地区	dìqū	region, district
29. 定额	dìng'é	quota
30. 代而不理	dài'érbùlǐ	fail to perform the duty of an agent
31. 扣付	kòufù	deduct
32. 资格	zīgé	qualifications, status
33. 公平	gōngpíng	fair
34. 兜揽	dōulǎn	canvass, solicit
35. 名义	míngyì	name
36. 丑话	chǒuhuà	blunt words

37. 毫无	háowú	not in the least
38. 保留	bǎoliú	reservation
39. 贿赂	huìlù	bribe
40. 谋取	móuqǔ	seek, try to gain
41. 私利	sīlì	private gain
42. 串通	chuàntōng	gang up, collaborate
43. 职业	zhíyè	occupation
44. 叮嘱	dīngzhǔ	warn, exhort
45. 反应	fǎnyìng	response, reaction
46. 反馈	fǎnkuì	feedback
47. 酬金	chóujīn	monetary reward
48. 利害与共	lìhàiyǔgòng	have common interests
49. 通气	tōngqì	keep each other informed
50. 对策	duìcè	the way to deal with a situation
51. 携手	xiéshǒu	join hands
52. 同舟共济	tóngzhōugòngjì	cross a river in the same boat
53. 直截了当	zhíjiéliǎodàng	straightforward
54. 作风	zuòfēng	style
55. 预测	yùcè	predict
56. 竭尽全力	jiéjìnquánlì	spare no effort, do one's utmost
57. 充其量	chōngqíliàng	at most
58. 保守	bǎoshǒu	conservative
59. 控制	kòngzhì	control
60. 愁	chóu	worry
61. 离谱	lípǔ	be out of place, unreasonable
62. 开支	kāizhī	expenses
63. 投入	tóurù	put into

64. 余地	yúdì	leeway, room
65. 愿望	yuànwàng	wish
66. 延期	yánqī	extend, defer

练 习

A

大不一样：

"大"，是形容词，也是副词。作副词用时，表示程度的深浅。"大＋不＋形容词/动词"，表示程度深；"不＋大＋形容词/动词"，表示程度浅。

大 is both an adjective and an adverb. When it is used as an adverb, it indicates the degree of something. 大＋不＋adjective/verb means "to a great extent", while 不＋大＋adjective/verb means "not quite".

一、熟读下列各句，体会"大不一样"和"不大一样"的不同意义和用法：

1. 这两件事可大不一样。
   这两件事可不大一样。

2. 这两台电视的质量可大不一样。
   这两台电视的质量可不大一样。

二、选用"大不一样"、"不大一样"完成下列各句：

1. 独家代理和多家代理的权利和义务_____。

2. 在北京生活，自己能听会说和事事靠翻译_____。

3. 他的言谈举止，下海前和下海后_____。

4. 结婚后，他对母亲的态度_____。

5. 对不起,请问为什么你说的和你做的_____。

好说:

①客套话,在别人向自己致谢或恭维时,表示不敢当,②表示同意或好商量。

1) This polite formula is used to express modesty when someone extends thanks to you. 2) It is used to express agreement or that something can be settled through discussion.

一、熟读下列句子,体会"好说"的意义和用法:

1. 甲:这次能如期交货,多亏贵方大力协助。
   乙:好说,好说。我们是多年的贸易伙伴嘛。
2. 不就是订个舱位吗? 好说,好说,这事就包在我身上了。
3. 好说,好说。这样的事我们一定代劳,不用你操心。
4. 甲:这次谈判销售定额和佣金,承蒙贵公司关照,我们非常感谢。
   乙:好说,好说。来日方长,今后我们也有请贵方帮忙的时候。

二、请用"好说,好说"完成下列对话:

A. 我们要完成贵公司的定额恐怕有困难。
B. _____。
A. 5%的佣金可不低,能不能⋯⋯
B. _____。
A. 能否指定我们做贵公司产品的独家代理人问题,贵公司考虑得怎样了?
B. _____。
A. 关于独家代理的权利与责任,我们希望具体谈谈。
B. _____。
A. 我们双方的合作协议就要到期了,我们希望能在适当的时候洽谈延期的问题。

B. ＿＿＿＿＿＿＿＿＿＿＿＿＿＿＿＿＿＿＿＿＿＿。

充其量：

表示做最大限度的估计,有"满打满算它的数量也就是……"的意思。

It means making the estimation to the maximum (at most), that is, "as a maximum, its quantity is...".

一、熟读下列各句,体会"充其量"的词义和用法：

1. 他的资金不多,充其量一百来万。

2. 他不会去很久,充其量不过十来天。

3. 我们充其量加一天班,也就把这点事做完了。

二、用"充其量"和下列短语造句：

1. 代理商得到的佣金和报酬

2. 独家代理协议有效期

3. 你的签证延长时间

4. 他掌握的最新资料

就：

副词,用在两个相同的成分之间,表示容忍、消极的同意和不得已的让步。

Adverb: When it is placed between two identical elements, it expresses tolerance, passive agreement or reluctant concession.

一、熟读下列句子,指出句中"就"所表示的意义：

1. 这种商品的包装和装潢真好看,贵点就贵点吧。

2. 为了做成这笔交易,该让步就让步吧。

3. 广告费该花多少就花多少,这是不能省的。

4. 代销金额定为 15 万就 15 万,我们只好豁出去了。

二、模仿上面的例句,用下列短语造句:

说就说	走就走	拍卖就拍卖
处理就处理	扣付就扣付	调查就调查
签字就签字	赔钱就赔钱	限制就限制

B

一、用下列词语组词:

网络	反馈	信息	代理	销售
扣付	渠道	佣金	资格	经销

二、从上面选择适当的词语,完成下列句子:

1. 我们已经建立起一个＿＿＿＿＿＿＿＿＿＿＿＿＿＿＿＿。
2. 根据市场＿＿＿＿＿＿＿＿＿,我们可以增加一些订货量。
3. 我们为了改进产品质量,十分重视＿＿＿＿＿＿＿＿＿＿。
4. 作为独家代理商,＿＿＿＿＿＿＿＿＿,保证完成销售定额。
5. 为了证明你们的能力,请向我们提供＿＿＿＿＿＿＿＿。

三、熟读下列词语,然后选择适当的词语填空:

同舟共济	利害与共	讨价还价
直截了当	不妨一试	携手合作
信息反馈	开门见山	相互关照

1. 我公司非常重视＿＿＿＿＿＿＿,对你们提供资料,也可付
   适当佣金。

2. 我说话一向＿＿＿＿＿＿＿＿＿,不会转弯抹角,请你不
   要介意。

3. 我们既是贸易伙伴,就应该＿＿＿＿＿＿＿＿＿＿＿。

4. 今天讨论的问题很重要,需要马上决定,就请大家 _____,发表意见。

5. 这套管理方法,能大幅度提高经济效益,你们 ____ _____。

6. 既然是做买卖,都为了赚钱,_____,是正常 现象。

7. 你们俩都是第一次出外长途旅行,一路上要多多_____。

8. 他做什么事都觉得难为情,要什么,拒绝什么,从来不会 _____地说出来。

9. 我们热烈欢迎贵公司在我厂投资,希望我们今后 _____为了共同利益而积极进取。

10. 我们双方 _____,理应通力合作,同舟共济。

四、想一想、谈一谈:

1. 代理商与他所代理的公司或厂家是什么关系。
2. 代理商怎么开展自己的商贸活动?
3. 签订代理协议要注意哪些问题?
4. 你认为做独家代理商有风险吗?你有没有过这样的经验? 尝到过其中的酸甜苦辣吗?

五、阅读下面的短文,并回答问题:

精明的代理商

1986 年,7 万台菊花(júhuā)牌电扇首次出口欧洲,由于不 符合客商某种特殊质量要求,客商要求全部退货,并提出巨额索赔。在这困难的时候,侨居美国马里兰州的赵先生飞来中国,找到厂长,要求做菊花牌电扇在美国的销售代理人。厂长怕再遇风险,不敢贸然(màorán)答应。可赵先生是位精明干练的商人,他立即向厂长提供了大量信息。他说:"现在,北美、西欧、日本,电扇需求量日趋增长,仅美国的电扇年销售量就达2000万台左右。这对菊花牌电扇出口,是一个绝好的机会。"他把有关美国市场对电扇规格、质量、安全、色调等方面要求的资料,都给了厂长。菊花牌电扇厂的厂长被感动了,愉快地约请赵先生做代理商。不久,"菊花"厂与美国申士达公司签订了第一批60万台电扇的出口合同,并全部贴上美国的优质商标运往美国。

1. 赵先生是在什么样的情况下来中国的?

2. 赵先生是哪国人?他为什么主动要求做菊花牌电扇在美国的代理商?

3. 赵先生是怎样取得厂长的信任和承诺的?

4. 双方合作结果怎样?

第十八课　网上贸易
Lesson 18　E-Business

一、你有 E-mail 吗？

赵　林：麦克先生，这是我的名片！

麦　克：赵先生，你好！啊，你有 E-mail？

赵　林：怎么，麦克先生觉得很新鲜？

麦　克：我上一次来贵国，很多公司的老总给我
　　　　的名片都还没有 E-mail 嘛！

赵　林：现在可不同啰，两个人见面，常常会问
　　　　"你有 E-mail 吗？"

麦　克：没有中国朋友问我。

赵　林：当然不会问你，知道你有嘛。这是我们中
　　　　国眼下流行的时髦话！

麦　克：很有意思！

赵　林：现在差不多有名片的人，都有了电子信
　　　　箱。每天回家的第一件事，就是打开电
　　　　脑查看有没有电子邮件。

麦　克：没想到你们的信息产业也发展得这么
　　　　快！

赵　林：在这个信息时代，没有电子信箱，怎么

成?

麦　克：特别是我们这些商界从业人员，没有电子信箱，就等于没有眼睛，没有腿。

赵　林：麦克先生说得很对。现代信息技术的发展，不只是开拓和繁荣了信息产业本身，它影响最深的恐怕是人们的生活和传统的经济贸易形式。

麦　克：我国政府已经宣布，从 21 世纪开始，我国与各国的贸易将首先用电子数据交换进行，然后再处理文本单据。

赵　林：以网络技术为基础的电子商务，是全世界发展经济贸易的大趋势。网上交易、网上购物，已经成为一种消费时尚。以后，处理文本单据的传统方式，恐怕也要被抛弃了。

麦　克：是的，实现"无纸化贸易"，那才是真正意义上的电子商务！

赵　林：所以，生活在这样的时代，能没有 E-mail 吗？

二、虚拟市场

赵　林：麦克先生，你这次还得专程来中国，以后你就可以通过电子商务网络同我们做生意了。

麦　克：我当然希望这样。网上贸易的优势就是便捷、高效、交易成本低。

赵　林：我们的一些企业已经尝到了网上贸易的甜头。为了寻找货源，下午信息上网，第二天一大早，几十个供货商的 E-mail 就传来了。

麦　克：这是传统贸易方式不可比拟的。单是差旅费、通讯和商情查询费，就要节省一大笔开支，这自然也就降低了交易成本。

赵　林：过去我们常说，时间就是金钱，现在应该说，网络就是时间，网络就是金钱、就是效益！

麦　克：赵先生说得很对。现在，我想知道，我们之间是不是能顺利进行网上贸易？

赵　林：麦克先生的意思是……

麦　克：我的意思是，目前全世界有各种各样的电脑网络，有公用网，更多的是专用网，你们的网站建在哪里？

赵　林：当然是国际互联网！

麦　克：是 Internet 吗？

赵　林：就是因特互联网。

麦　克：Internet 目前是世界上最大的电脑互联网络，它几乎已经同全世界所有国家的国际性公用网络连接，估计用户已经超过 3 亿家。我们也是它的用户。

赵　林：我们国家与国际互联网连接的是中国电信，网名叫 Chinanet，对外贸易经济合作部在国际互联网上建立了官方站 MOFTEC，所以，我们之间的网上贸易没有障碍。

麦　克：现在已经投入使用了吗？

赵　林：当然。MOFTEC 网站上网的第一个月，访问客商就达 100 多万。

麦　克：是吗？我的信息太闭塞了！

赵　林：不仅如此，在 MOFTEC 站上，"中国商品市场"也已经正式开张，在这里汇集了成千上万个中国企业的产品,同时在外贸的各个环节上提供服务。

麦　克：这么说,我真的可以足不出户,就能同你们打交道了?

赵　林：是的。你可以在这个网上的"虚拟市场"捕捉商机,进入加密贸易洽谈室,做成你想做的生意。

麦　克：不过,在当今的电子商务潮中,违规操作乃至进行商业欺诈的事屡屡发生,网上交易的安全问题,一直是令商家们头痛的忧患。

赵　林：这确实是一个难题。我们可以通过跟踪系统对交易的各个环节进行监视,这就可以及时避免可能出现的风险。

麦　克：当然话又说回来,风险总是有的,传统贸易方式的风险其实更大。

赵　林：所以,贵国的许多大企业在网上都有虚拟的商业中心,交易额已经上千亿美元。

麦　克：是这样。总体来说,只有迟到者,没有失败者。

赵　林：我们对网上贸易也充满了信心。当然,我们的网络技术还不够发达,许多企业还只是"在线浏览,离线交易";我们……

麦　克：等等。什么叫"在线浏览,离线交易"?

赵　林：就是通过互联网寻找商机、发布信息、看货订货、讨价还价,其他商务环节,如转账、付款等,都还得按传统模式进行。

麦　克：我明白了。

赵　林：此外,我们的物流配送系统也还不够健全,在网上做生意,难免赔钱赚吆喝。

麦　克:降低库存,减少送货的费用,必须要有一个合理、完善的物流系统。

赵　林:啊,这个问题,涉及到技术、管理、营销、服务各个方面,解决起来难度很大。

麦　克:我们也经历过这个阶段,你们的信息产业发展这么快,不要多久,这种状况就会改变的。

赵　林:是的,真正意义上的电子商务离我们确实不远了!

麦　克:好,我们双方就从现在做起吧!

生词

1. 电子信箱　diànzǐ xìnxiāng　e-mail address
2. 查看　chákàn　check
3. 商界　shāngjiè　business circles
4. 开拓　kāituò　open up
5. 宣布　xuānbù　announce
6. 趋势　qūshì　trend
7. 时尚　shíshàng　fashion; in vogue
8. 抛弃　pāoqì　discard
9. 虚拟　xūnǐ　suppositional
10. 专程　zhuānchéng　special trip
11. 便捷　biànjié　convenient
12. 甜头　tiántou　sweet taste, good, benefit
13. 不可比拟　bùkěbǐnǐ　incomparable
14. 通讯　tōngxùn　communication
15. 商情　shāngqíng　market conditions

16.	查询	cháxún	inquire about
17.	节省	jiéshěng	economize, save, cut down on
18.	专用	zhuānyòng	for a special purpose
19.	网站	wǎngzhàn	web-site
20.	互联网	hùliánwǎng	Internet
21.	连接	liánjiē	connect
22.	障碍	zhàng'ài	barrier, obstacle
23.	闭塞	bìsè	ill-informed
24.	开张	kāizhāng	open a business
25.	汇集	huìjí	collect, come together
26.	成千上万	chéngqiān shàngwàn	thousands upon thousands
27.	足不出户	zúbùchūhù	without leaving home
28.	捕捉	bǔzhuō	catch
29.	商机	shāngjī	business opportunities
30.	加密	jiāmì	crypto-; coded
31.	违规	wéiguī	violate the rule
32.	操作	cāozuò	operation
33.	乃至	nǎizhì	and even
34.	屡屡	lǚlǚ	time and again
35.	忧患	yōuhuàn	suffering; hardship
36.	跟踪	gēnzōng	follow the tracks of, trace
37.	监视	jiānshì	monitor, keep watch on
38.	浏览	liúlǎn	browse
39.	发布	fābù	issue, release
40.	模式	móshì	mode
41.	物流	wùliú	flow of products
42.	配送	pèisòng	assortment and delivery
43.	健全	jiànquán	sound, perfect

44. 库存	kùcún	stock
45. 经历	jīnglì	undergo, go through
46. 阶段	jiēduàn	stage

练习

A

如此：

①指示代词,指上文提到的某种情况；②副词,表示强调或肯定,但有时可能表示嘲讽,这时就不是肯定而是否定了。

1）Demonstrative pronoun：It refers to the state of affairs mentioned previously in the text. 2）Adverb：It expresses emphasis or confirmation, but sometimes it expresses irony, and in such case it has a negative rather than a positive implication.

一、熟读下列各句,体会"如此"的词义和用法：

1．事情已经如此,我还能说什么？
2．你们如此不讲信誉,我们只好向消协投诉。
3．如此高见,我们算是领教了！
4．天天如此,年年如此,我们早就习惯了。

二、用"如此"和下列短语造句：

1．谋取私利
2．延期支付
3．竞争激烈
4．信息产业

乃至：

连词,用来连接两项以上性质相同或相近的事物或行为,表示事情所达到的最大范围或程度。多用于书面语。

It is a conjunction (meaning "and even") linking two or more matters or actions that are of the same or similar nature, indicating the maximum scope or extent of something. It is more often used in written Chinese.

一、熟读下列各句,体会"乃至"的用法:

1. 这个世纪乃至下个世纪,控制人口增长都是世界难题。
2. 20世纪末的金融危机对韩国、日本、东南亚各国乃至全世界的经济都产生了重大影响。
3. 现在,在商品市场、资本市场、人才市场乃至一切生活领域,都充满了竞争。

二、把"乃至"放在下列各句中适当的位置:

1. 现在,中国的商界从业人员、一些大学生都有BP机了。
2. 通过互联网寻找商机、发布信息、看货订货、讨价还价。
3. 他又结婚了,他的朋友、亲戚、父母都不知道。
4. 网上交易、网上购物、网上征婚,已经成为一种时尚。

屡:

副词,表示同样或同类行为多次反复。"屡屡"意思同"屡"相同,但"屡"修饰某些单音节动词,"屡屡"却不能修饰单音节动词。如说"屡遭失败",如用"屡屡",就要说成"屡屡遭到失败"。

This adverb expresses the repetition of the same action, or actions of the same type. 屡屡 has the same meaning as 屡, but 屡 modifies some monosyllabic verbs while 屡屡 cannot. For instance, 屡遭失败, or 屡屡遭到失败.

一、熟读下列各句,体会"屡"的词义和用法:

1. 他这一生是屡战屡败,屡败屡战。
2. 他这人是屡教不改,无可救药了。

3. 这家工厂屡屡发生劳资纠纷。

4. 由于不重视市场调研,董事会屡屡出现重大决策失误。

二、用"屡"、"屡屡"和下面的短语造句:

1. 设障碍

2. 工程事故

3. 花生霉烂

4. 资金短缺

时髦、时尚:

"时髦"是形容词,形容人的衣着或某种事物在一段时间里很流行,它在句子中作谓语时不能带宾语。"时尚",是一时受推崇、受追求的东西,一般作为名词。

时髦 is an adjective (meaning "fashionable"). It describes the fact that some garments or other things are very popular during a period of time. When used as the predicate, it does not take an object. 时尚 is a noun (meaning "fashion"), referring to things that people pursue or hold in esteem. It is generally used as a noun.

一、熟读下列各句,体会"时髦"、"时尚"的词义和用法:

1. 那个女孩特时髦。

2. 这种款式的衣服已经不时髦了。

3. 掌握和使用电脑已经成为一种时尚。

4. 结婚时大吃大喝已经不合时尚。

二、用"时髦"、"时尚"与下列短语造句:

1. 电子商务网络

2. 出国旅游、出国休假

3. 追求名牌

4. 人才投资

B

一、用下列词语组词：

查看	跟踪	闭塞	查询
电子信箱	信息	捕捉	商情
电子邮件	商机	汇集	网上

二、熟读下列词语，体会它们的意义和结构，然后各造一个句子：

不可比拟

成千上万

足不出户

尝到……甜头

赔钱赚吆喝

三、用括号中指定的词语完成下列句子：

1. _____已经成为一种消费时尚。（网上）

2. 现代信息技术的发展，_____。（开拓）

3. 以网络技术为基础的电子商务，_____。（趋势）

4. 网上贸易是传统贸易方式不可比拟的。_____。（降低）

5. 在当今的电子商务潮中，_____。（忧患）

四、想一想，谈一谈：

1. 电子商务对传统贸易方式有什么样的冲击？

2. 电子商务有没有风险和忧患，为什么？

3. 通过互联网可进行哪些商务活动？它能完全取代传统贸易方式吗？

4. 在网上做生意要具备哪些条件？

五、阅读下面的短文,并回答问题:

电 视 直 销

"儿子,你来量量,看长高一点儿没有。"母亲叫着。

"昨天刚量过了,还是没长!"儿子有点不耐烦地说。

母亲有些着急了。一天,她们全家看电视直销节目,节目中正在推销"见风长"牌增高机。节目主持人一边演示,一边绘声绘色地说:"只要每天坚持使用 15 分钟,三个月后就可以长高 1～15 厘米。"看了这个电视直销节目,母亲决定要为儿子买一台,儿子都 17 岁了,可身高只有 1.60 米。现在的姑娘,也不知怎么了,找对象非高个儿不要,什么 1.8 米正好,1.7 米凑合,1.6 米那是残废! 我儿子再不长个儿,那不就成残废了? 她为了儿子能娶上媳妇,多少钱也得买! 节目还没看完,母亲就拨通了订货电话。第二天,商家就把一台崭新的"见风长"增高机送来了,还十分认真地给儿子量了身高。量完,说:"好,三个月以后验证,如果未长 1 厘米,随时可以退货。"现在,已经 40 多天了,儿子每天按说明书要求使用 15 分钟,天天量,常常一天还量几次,可儿子那个头就是不见动静。

儿子终于烦透了,说死说活也不相信那"见风长"了。当娘的没辙,只好要求退货。不知打了多少电话,商家才派了个推销员来,又给儿子量了身高,果然还是 1.60 米。商家答应退货,但说,按公司规定每天要收取 0.02% 折旧费,使用 45 天,应该收折旧费 548.73 元!

1. 电视直销是一种什么推销方式? 它是怎么产生并流行起来的?

2. 电视直销的优点是什么? 缺点是什么?

3. 你读了上面的故事有什么感想? 退货时要付折旧费,合理吗？

4. 你有过通过电视直销购物的经历吗？请谈谈。

第十九课　在国外推销商品的多种形式

Lesson 19　Modes of Trade Promotion Abroad

一、推销形式

陈其然：乔治先生，我们公司将在贵国进一步开拓市场，希望能得到你的协助。

乔　治：我们是老朋友，我一定竭尽绵薄之力。不知我能为你做些什么？

陈其然：你知道，我们过去只习惯于同国外的进出口商、代理商、批发商打交道，甚至要通过五手、六手中间商才能进入国外的零售市场。

乔　治：这种经营方式，中间环节多，成本高，信息反馈慢，外汇风险也大。

陈其然：谁说不是呢？这种陈旧落后的经营方式，已经不能适应现在的国际贸易形势。

乔　治：电子商务的出现，已经对这种传统方式形成了巨大冲击。跨国公司的发展和全球经济一体化，也要求改变经营策略，提高经营水平。

陈其然：我们公司已经清醒地意识到了这一点。

乔　治：那么,你们准备怎么做呢?

陈其然：为了深度开发国外市场,我们首先要改变坐店经营的作风,上门推销!

乔　治：请继续讲!

陈其然：我们决定组织一个代表团到贵国去,争取供需双方直接见面。

乔　治：我可以为你们牵线搭桥。

陈其然：我们尤其希望同大型国际连锁企业集团建立联系,把我们的商品打入他们的采购系统。

乔　治：这是一个很高明的决策!

陈其然：一个大型的连锁企业可能有成百上千的分销店吧?

乔　治：是的。特别是大型国际连锁企业集团,它的分销店还可能遍布全世界。

陈其然：你想,我们的商品如果能打入--个连锁企业集团的采购系统,不就等于打入了成百上千的分销店?

乔　治：是这样。不过,打入连锁企业集团的采购系统,可不是轻而易举的事。

陈其然：我们知道,关键是看我们的商品是不是有很强的竞争力。

乔　治：还要消费者了解,要适销对路。

陈其然：你们是专业咨询公司,所以要请你们大力协助!

乔　治：我们可以提供有关情况。

陈其然：不只如此。

乔　治：你是说要我们为贵公司策划一次大型的公关活动？

陈其然：是，在你们国家大造一次舆论。

乔　治：引起强烈的轰动效应！

陈其然：是，把贵国的大型连锁企业吸引来，越多越好。

乔　治：然后，开展多种多样活动，让与会的企业家们了解你们公司，了解你们的产品。

陈其然：要力争他们成为我们的贸易伙伴，同我们建立起稳固的供销关系。

乔　治：好，我们义不容辞，一定把这次公关活动策划好！

二、展览会和博览会

陈其然：乔治先生，我们公司准备到国外去参加一些商品展览会和博览会，想向你咨询一些问题。

乔　治：很高兴能为你提供服务。

陈其然：你知道，参加贸易展览会，是经常使用的一种产品营销战略。

乔　治：是的，一次成功的参展，可以最大限度地提高企业和产品的知名度，随之而来的，可能是滚滚财源！

陈其然：不过，参展能不能成功，受许多因素的制约。

乔　治：首先是要进对门。

陈其然：这正是我要请你帮忙的。现在，世界各地有五花八门的展览会、展销会、博览会，有综合的，也有专业的，我们必须有所选择。

乔　治：应该选择最适合你们公司业务范围、又有很高知名度的参展。

陈其然：所以请你为我们公司提供一些资料,如展览会的性质、主办单位、参展单位、参观者来源、主办者的宣传工作。

乔　治：还有展览会的现场环境、配套服务和参展费用。

陈其然：对,这些都很重要。

乔　治：我们可以为你们提供一份详尽的资料。

陈其然：还有一个问题,就是展品的进出口手续。

乔　治：贵国是不是 ATA 单证册的缔约国?

陈其然：是。

乔　治：这就简单了。ATA 单证册是货物通关的护照。有出证商会担保的 ATA 单证册,既可以替代临时进出口通关报关单证,又可以作为向海关提供临时进口免税的担保。

陈其然：这太好了。这样,我们就有足够时间从容参展了。

三、展销会

陈其然：乔治先生,有关商品展览会的资料,我们已经收到了。

乔　治：还满意吗?

陈其然：太好了,谢谢你们!

乔　治：不用客气! 噢,我可以问一个问题吗?

陈其然：当然。

乔　治：你们怎么没有想到参加一个商品展销会呢? 甚至干脆独家举办一个商品展销会?

陈其然：当然想到过。不过,展销会比展览会的规模要大多了,我们必须运去足够的商品,供参观者选购,商品少了,参观者会失望的。

乔　治：难道你们的货源不充足?

陈其然：那倒不是,我们的商品丰富着呢! 只是办展销会手续更复杂,费用更大,我们对贵国市场行情也不甚了解。

乔　治：尽管这样,我还是建议你们在适当时候举办商品展销会。我了解我国人民对贵国产品的兴趣和需求。

陈其然：谢谢乔治先生,我们会认真考虑你的建议。

乔　治：展销会还可办成订货洽谈会,商品介绍和技术交流会。一举多得嘛!

陈其然：是的,除了参观选购外,也可以进行大宗生意洽谈,签订合同,举行专题商品介绍会和技术讲座,进行现场技术操作与示范。

乔　治：这样就可以吸引更多的人到展览馆,会造成轰动的。

生词

1. 形式	xíngshì	form
2. 绵薄	miánbó	humble effort
3. 批发	pīfā	wholesale
4. 零售	língshòu	retail
5. 陈旧	chénjiù	outmoded, obsolete
6. 落后	luòhòu	backward

7.	适应	shìyìng	suit, adapt
8.	形成	xíngchéng	form, take shape
9.	冲击	chōngjī	charge, pound
10.	一体化	yītǐhuà	integration
11.	改变	gǎibiàn	change
12.	清醒	qīngxǐng	sober
13.	集团	jítuán	group
14.	采购	cǎigòu	purchase
15.	高明	gāomíng	wise, clever
16.	决策	juécè	decision
17.	轻而易举	qīng'éryìjǔ	easy to do
18.	策划	cèhuà	plan
19.	舆论	yúlùn	public opinion
20.	强烈	qiángliè	strong
21.	轰动	hōngdòng	cause a sensation, make a stir
22.	效应	xiàoyìng	effect
23.	与会	yùhuì	participate in a conference
24.	力争	lìzhēng	work hard for, do all one can to
25.	稳固	wěngù	firm, stable
26.	义不容辞	yìbùróngcí	be duty-bound; have an un-shirkable duty
27.	营销	yíngxiāo	marketing
28.	战略	zhànlüè	strategy
29.	滚滚财源	gǔngǔncáiyuán	surging sources of revenue
30.	制约	zhìyuē	restrict
31.	五花八门	wǔhuābāmén	multifarious; of a wide variety

32.	主办	zhǔbàn	sponsor
33.	来源	láiyuán	source
34.	宣传	xuānchuán	publicity
35.	详尽	xiángjìn	detailed and complete
36.	缔约	dìyuē	sign a treaty
37.	商会	shānghuì	chamber of commerce
38.	替代	tìdài	substitute
39.	免税	miǎnshuì	exempt from taxes
40.	从容	cóngróng	unhurried, plentiful
41.	失望	shīwàng	disappoint
42.	不甚了解	bùshènliǎojiě	not know enough
43.	一举多得	yījǔduōdé	kill several birds with one stone
44.	专题	zhuāntí	special topic, special subject
45.	讲座	jiǎngzuò	lecture

练习

A

谁说不是呢：

"谁"，代词，可以指代一个人，也可以指不止一个人；可以指确定的人，也可以指不能肯定的人，或无须说出姓名的人；还可以指任何人。"谁说不是呢"句中的"谁"即是这种任指用法，意思是"没有人说不是"，"任何人都会说是"。

谁(who) is a pronoun which may be used to stand for a certain person, or persons, some definite person(s), or indefinite person(s), person(s) whose name there is no need to mention, or anyone. In 谁说不是呢(who would say no), 谁 is used for generic reference, implying that "nobody would say no", or "everyone would say yes".

一、熟读下列各句,体会"谁"的意义和用法:

1. 你们当中有谁参加过广交会?
2. 你知道他是谁吗?
3. 谁也不知道经理去哪儿了。
4. 这是我们公司的制度,不管是谁违反制度,都要受到处罚。

二、用"谁说不是呢"和下列短语造句:

1. 环境保护
2. 全球经济一体化
3. 网上贸易
4. 改变经营策略,提高经营水平

化:

后缀,加在其他成分后面,构成动词,表示转变成某种性质或状况。例如:工业化,农业化,现代化,具体化,多样化,绿化,美化,腐化,净化等等。

化 is a suffix(-ize, -ify) which is added to other elements to form verbs. It indicates a transformation into a certain nature or state. Examples include 工业化,农业化,现代化,具体化,多样化,绿化,美化,腐化,净化, etc.

一、熟读下列各句,体会用"化"作后缀构成动词表示的意义和用法:

1. 我们不能把事情简单化。
2. 世界经济一体化进程正在加快。
3. 中国正在深化改革外贸体制。
4. 我现在只有一个设想,还需要具体化。

二、用"化"和下列词语构成动词,然后造句:

1. 高档化   3. 男性化   5. 商品化
2. 复杂化   4. 美化

着呢:

    某些动词和形容词后带上"着呢":①表示对一种情况的肯定,并强调其程度深,往往有夸张的意味;②表示动作的持续,亦有强调的意思。

    It is used after certain verbs or adjectives. 1) It confirms a situation, emphasizing its high degree, often with a touch of exaggeration. 2) It is used to indicate and emphasize the continuous aspect of an action.

一、熟读下列句子,体会"着呢"的意义:

1. 现在,中国市场上的商品丰富着呢!
2. 推销商品的渠道和形式多着呢!
3. 外国朋友都说,在中国吃、住都经济实惠着呢!
4. 中国的丝绸、瓷器、茶叶,在世界上可受欢迎着呢。

二、用下面的词语加"着呢"造句:

落后   清醒   高明   强烈   详尽
稳固   从容   经济实惠   信息灵通

尽管:

    ①副词,表示动作行为不受条件限制或不考虑别的就可以进行;②连词,表示让步,用来连接复句,常与"可是"、"但是"、"然而"等相呼应。全句意思是承认甲事是事实,但乙事并不因此而改变。

    1) Adverb: Feel free to; not hesitate to. It says that the action or event is not restricted by any conditions, or one does not have to

consider anything if they do a certain thing. 2) Conjunction: Though; even though; in spite of.

It connects clauses, expressing concession. It often works in concert with 可是，但是，and 然而（yet, however, nevertheless）. The meaning of the whole sentence is that Thing A is a fact, but Thing B does not change because of it.

一、熟读下列各句,体会"尽管"的不同意义和用法：

1. 史密斯先生有什么意见,请尽管提出来,不必客气。
2. 您想买什么尽管说,我们尽量满足您的要求。
3. 尽管你来中国的时间不长,但你对中国的情况非常熟悉。
4. 尽管这次展销会是成功的,却也有不少地方需要改进。

二、用"尽管"改写下列各句：

1. 这个计划是保守了一点,但也不是容易实现的。
2. 你们放心好了,无论遇到什么困难,我们都会按期发货的。
3. 这届展销会商品琳琅满目,物美价廉,可仍然不能满足顾客的需要。
4. 这次参展的轻纺产品,价格是贵了点,可用料讲究,款式新颖,做工精细,还是深受顾客欢迎的。
5. 这些机器的性能非常可靠,你们就大胆使用吧,不要有什么顾虑。

B

一、用下列词语组词：

| 营销 | 战略 | 改变 | 规模 | 冲击 |
| 网络 | 策划 | 决策 | 形成 | 经营 |

二、熟读下列词语,体会它们的意义和结构,然后各造一
　　个句子:

　　竭尽绵薄之力　　　义不容辞　　　一举多得
　　轻而易举　　　　　不甚了解

三、用括号里的词完成句子:

　　1. 电子商务的出现,对传统的贸易方式形成了巨大的冲击。
　　　　_____。(改变)

　　2. 打入连锁企业集团的采购系统_____。(轻而易举)

　　3. 参加贸易展览会,_____。(战略)

　　4. 我们非常希望能成为你们的贸易伙伴,_____
　　　　_____。(稳固)

　　5. _____,
　　　　_____已经不适应现在的国际贸易形势。(陈旧)

　　6. 向国外推销商品要尽量减少中间环节,因为中间环节多,
　　　　_____。(成本)

　　7. 现在大型的国际连锁企业集团,_____。(遍布)

　　8. 某个商品能否打入一个连锁企业集团的采购系统,
　　　　_____。(关键)

　　9. 真高兴,这次在贵国举办的贸易展览会,在你们大力协助
　　　　下,_____。(轰动)

　　10. 我公司想深度开发国外市场,你们是专业咨询公司,____
　　　　_____。(提供)

四、想一想，谈一谈：

1. 在国外推销商品有哪些形式？你或你的朋友有过具体实践吗？请谈谈。
2. 为什么陈旧落后的经营方式已不能适应现在的国际贸易形势？
3. 要打入一个连锁企业集团的采购系统需具备哪些条件？
4. 一次成功的贸易展览会对参展者有深远的影响，为此举办者与参展者都要向对方提供哪些资料？做哪些事以保证成功？

五、阅读下面的短文，并回答问题：

各 具 特 色

现在各类博览会、展销会办得不少。不久前举办的全国轻工业博览会，津、粤(Yuè)、沪(Hù)三地的展览，给人留下了深刻的印象。

天津人实在，他们是用过硬的产品克服市场疲软的。上海人聪明，论吃的，口感好；论穿的，款式新；论用的，做工细，装潢美，变化快。很久以来，北京人就迷信上海货。广东人能干，在一个极小的展厅空间里，他们通过精心的布置和巧妙的推销，尽量展示自己产品的可爱可贵，使无数顾客驻(zhù)足不前。

1. 津、粤、沪三地的展览，各具什么特色？
2. 你参加过这三地的商品展销吗？有什么印象？
3. 你对北京的商品和经销方式有什么想法？

第二十课 广交会
Lesson 20 The Guangzhou Fair

一、会见总经理

宋　洁：卡特先生,热烈欢迎你来参加中国出口
　　　　商品交易会!

卡　特：谢谢总经理的盛情邀请,我感到十分荣
　　　　幸,这是我第一次来参加广交会,衷心祝
　　　　贺广交会胜利开幕!

宋　洁：谢谢! 许多朋友也是第一次来,我们的
　　　　广交会越办越兴旺了,你看,这座规模宏
　　　　大的广州对外贸易中心,已经显得不够
　　　　用了。

卡　特：我想,一是中国实施对外开放政策,搞活
　　　　了经济,繁荣了市场,增强了外贸能力,
　　　　所以招徕了五洲四海的客商;二是广州
　　　　是中国的南大门,比邻香港,也便利外国
　　　　客商往来。

宋　洁：卡特先生说得很对,我国从 1957 年起开
　　　　始在广州举办出口商品交易会,以后每
　　　　年举行春、秋两届,已经举办近百届了。

今年,得天时、地利、人和,广交会更是盛况空前。

乔　治:真令人鼓舞!

宋　洁:广交会上,集中了全国各进出口总公司和各有关企业、单位,组织了多类出口商品货源,平等互利,展卖结合,进出口结合,当面看样成交。买卖双方都感到省时、省力,既方便又实惠。

乔　治:这实在太好了,这样的贸易场所,高度集中,业务范围广,货源充足,选择性大,想做什么生意就可以做什么生意。

宋　洁:是的,广交会确实是独具中国特色的外贸形式。近几年,广交会又发生了很大变化,已经成了综合性多功能的对外经济贸易场所了。

卡　特:哦,看来,我这次是来对了,我不仅可以大饱眼福,而且可以成功凯旋。

二、参观展览厅

宋　洁:乔治先生,各层楼都有商品陈列馆和洽谈室,占地12万平方米,陈列着5万多种商品,我们一时无法都参观到,乔治先生最感兴趣的是哪些商品呢?

乔　治:我最感兴趣的是轻工、食品和工艺品。不过,我是第一次来参加广交会,想多看看。

宋　洁:那好啊,我们到处走走,凡是你感兴趣的展馆,就不妨多停留一会儿。

乔　治:这很好。

宋　洁:瞧,我们说着说着,就到了粮油食品交易团的陈列馆了。

卡　特：嗬，好丰富啊，真是五光十色，琳琅满目！

宋　洁：先生们，这里陈列的各类糖果糕点，食品罐头，大都品质上乘，风味独特，装潢美观，是送礼的佳品。

卡　特：嗯，我得选购几种带回去请朋友们品尝品尝！

宋　洁：乔治先生，我们到丝绸交易团的陈列馆了。有原料，半成品，也有深加工、精加工的高档产品，花色品种多样化，系列化，是全面了解中国丝绸的最好窗口。

乔　治：啊，好漂亮！真是花团锦簇，美不胜收！中国真不愧是丝绸之国！

宋　洁：乔治先生，我们现在到了高新技术和名优特新产品展区了。

乔　治：这个展区，我倒要好好看看。啊，这是海尔！这是长虹！这是春兰！嗯，还有小天鹅！

宋　洁：乔治先生很熟悉嘛。

乔　治：哦，这些都是国际知名品牌，我们国家各大市场都有出售。

宋　洁：是的，这些品牌已经远销世界各国。这届交易会在最重要的位置安排了摊位，展示这些品牌的新一代产品。

卡　特：这个展厅很大，都是高新技术产品吗？

宋　洁：是，都是高新技术、高附加值产品，除了家电产品，还有信息产品、音像视听产品、自动化办公产品、医疗器械等等。

卡　特：都是什么企业的产品？

宋　洁：国内有外贸自主经营权的生产企业和外商投资企业，是这个展区参展的主体。

卡　特：外商投资企业也来参展了，真新鲜！

宋　洁：最近几年，我国的三资企业发展很快，他们的外贸活动也日益活跃，他们出现在广交会上，一定会吸引更多的外商来华投资。

卡　特：是的，我也要认真研究研究这个问题。

宋　洁：欢迎你抓紧时机。机不可失，时不再来哟！

卡　特：一定，一定！

宋　洁：乔治先生，这届交易会正在举办几个大型国际研讨会，有没有兴趣去听听？

乔　治：讨论什么问题？

宋　洁："国际市场战略"、"利用电子贸易开拓全球多元化市场"、"成功进驻欧共体市场"等等。

乔　治：噢，都是很重要的问题。我们就去"国际市场战略"研讨会会场吧！

宋　洁：好的，我陪你去。这边请！

乔　治：谢谢你！我这次来广州，大开眼界，大饱眼福，真是不虚此行！

生词

1.	衷心	zhōngxīn	heartfelt, wholehearted
2.	祝贺	zhùhè	congratulate
3.	宏大	hóngdà	grand, great
4.	显得	xiǎnde	appear, seem

5.	胜利	shènglì	victory, triumph
6.	政策	zhèngcè	policy
7.	搞活	gǎohuó	enliven, vitalize
8.	增强	zēngqiáng	strengthen, enhance
9.	招徕	zhāolái	solicit, canvass
10.	比邻	bǐlín	neighbor, next to
11.	便利	biànlì	convenient
12.	届	jiè	session
13.	天时	tiānshí	Heaven's favorable weather
14.	地利	dìlì	Earth's advantageous terrain
15.	人和	rénhé	human unity
16.	盛况	shèngkuàng	a grand occasion, a spectacular event
17.	鼓舞	gǔwǔ	inspire
18.	结合	jiéhé	combine
19.	当面	dāngmiàn	to sb.'s face, in sb.'s presence
20.	看样	kànyàng	examine the samples
21.	高度	gāodù	a high degree
22.	大饱眼福	dàbǎoyǎnfú	feast one's eyes
23.	凯旋	kǎixuán	triumphant return
24.	陈列	chénliè	display, exhibit
25.	平方米	píngfāngmǐ	square meter
26.	轻工	qīnggōng	light industrial
27.	五光十色	wǔguāngshísè	multicolored;of great variety
28.	琳琅满目	línlángmǎnmù	a feast for the eyes, a superb collection of beautiful things
29.	停留	tíngliú	stay
30.	糖果	tángguǒ	confectionery, candy

31.	独特	dútè	unique, distinctive
32.	原料	yuánliào	material
33.	半成品	bànchéngpǐn	semi-finished products
34.	花团锦簇	huātuánjǐncù	bouquets of flowers and piles of silks; rich multicolored decorations
35.	美不胜收	měibùshèngshōu	so many beautiful things that one simply can't take them all in
36.	展区	zhǎnqū	exhibition area
37.	位置	wèizhì	position, location
38.	摊位	tānwèi	booth, stand
39.	一代	yīdài	generation
40.	医疗	yīliáo	medical treatment
41.	器械	qìxiè	instrument, apparatus
42.	主体	zhǔtǐ	main body
43.	日益	rìyì	increasingly, day by day
44.	机不可失	jībùkěshī	don't let slip an opportunity
45.	抓紧	zhuājǐn	grasp, seize
46.	研讨会	yántǎohuì	symposium, seminar
47.	会场	huìchǎng	meeting place, conference hall
48.	多元化	duōyuánhuà	pluralistic
49.	不虚此行	bùxūcǐxíng	the trip has been well worthwhile

专名

| 海尔 | Hǎi'ěr | Haier |

长虹	Chánghóng	Changhong
春兰	Chūnlán	Chunlan
小天鹅	Xiǎo Tiān'é	Little Swan
欧共体	Ōugòngtǐ	European Union

练习

A

真：

副词，表示事物性质、状态的程度，同时还表示说话人的感情，用在褒义词前表示赞许，在贬义词前表示厌恶。

Adverb: Really; truly; indeed. It is used to indicate the degree of a thing's quality or state. It also expresses the emotion of the speaker. With a commendatory term, it praises. With a derogatory term, it shows detest.

一、熟读下列句子，体会"真"的意义和用法：

1. 哎呀，真香！你的咖啡煮得真好。
2. 嗬，你穿上这身中式旗袍真漂亮。
3. 这种食品包装真够粗糙的。
4. 最近市场疲软，买卖十分萧条，真愁死人了。

二、用副词"真"改写下列句子：

1. 这座广州对外贸易中心，规模确实太宏大了。
2. 来参加广交会的海外客商实在多啊！
3. 参观完广交会的各个展厅，可是大饱了眼福。
4. 广交会集中了全国各地的名、优、特、尖、新产品，不愧是全面了解中国的窗口。

5. 这次,我来广交会晚了一步,没有完成订货计划,实在太遗憾了。

凡是:

副词,表示在某个范围内无一例外,意思是"只要是"。常用"就"、"都"、"便"、"一律"、"没有不"等词语同"凡是"相呼应。

Adverb: It says that within a certain scope there is no exception whatsoever. The meaning is "as long as it is (they are)...." It often works in concert with 就,都,便,一律,没有不, (every, any, all, without exception),etc.

一、熟读下列各句,体会"凡是"的意义和用法并说出句中"凡是"所指范围:

1. 凡是你感兴趣的展厅,都不妨多停留一会儿。
2. 凡是我们力所能及的,我们都会尽力去做。
3. 凡是我商店出售的商品质量不合格的,都可以退换。
4. 凡是投保了货物,一旦发生保险范围内的损失,我保险公司都负责赔偿。

二、完成下列句子:

1. 凡是孩子需要的,妈妈＿＿＿＿＿＿＿＿＿＿＿＿＿。

2. 凡是进出口商品,都要＿＿＿＿＿＿＿＿＿＿＿＿。

3. 凡是符合合同条款的,＿＿＿＿＿＿＿＿＿＿＿＿＿。

4. 凡是有利于发展双边贸易的建议,＿＿＿＿＿＿＿

＿＿＿＿＿＿＿＿＿＿＿＿＿＿＿＿＿＿＿＿＿。

5. 凡是参加过广交会的外国客商,无不＿＿＿＿＿＿

＿＿＿＿＿＿＿＿＿＿＿＿＿＿＿＿＿＿＿＿＿。

说着说着：

表示状态短暂持续后将发生或出现某种新的情况,表现状态持续的动词常是单音节动词。类似的格式有"走着走着"、"听着听着"等。

As we are speaking. It indicates that some new conditions will crop up after the present situation lasts for a short time. The verb for the continuing state of affairs is often monosyllabic. Similar expressions include 走着走着, 听着听着, etc.

一、熟读下列各句,仔细体会"×着×着"所表示的状态和它后面所出现的情况：

1. 他们谈着谈着,突然都陷入了沉思。
2. 他写着写着,竟不知为什么笑了起来。
3. 说着说着,他们到了丝绸交易团的陈列馆。
4. 在如此琳琅满目的商品面前,他看着看着,不禁连声赞叹起来。

二、用下列的短语,各造一个句子：

吃着吃着 · 说着说着 听着听着 谈着谈着
走着走着 想着想着 做着做着 洗着洗着
笑着笑着

日益：

副词,表示程度一天一天加深或提高,意思是"一天比一天更……",多用于书面语。

It is an adverb meaning "increasingly", or "day by day". It is more often used in written Chinese.

一、熟读下列句子,体会"日益"的意义和用法：

1. 中国人民的生活水平日益提高。

2. 中国的市场经济日益趋向成熟。

3. 全球的生态环境日益恶化。

4. 优化产品结构的成果日益显著。

二、用"日益"和下列短语造句：

1. 业务范围

2. 高新技术

3. 消费者权益

4. 售后服务

5. 商品包装、装潢

B

一、用下列词语组词：

抓紧	宏大	增强	空前	规模
时机	活跃	活力	盛况	日益

二、熟读下列词语，并选择适当词语填后面的空：

招徕顾客	风味独特	兴旺发达	大有可为
展卖结合	看样成交	市场繁荣	物美价廉
令人鼓舞	不虚此行	大饱眼福	美不胜收

1. 中国实施改革开放后，已经出现_____
_____的大好局面。

2. 各个商店为了_____把橱窗布置得花团锦簇，琳琅满目。

3. 今年的广州交易会_____，吸引了五洲四海的客商。

4．各地的糖果糕点，_____，大都是

_____。

5．最近几年，中外合资企业发展如此之快，真是_____

_____。

6．这是我第一次来参加广交会，真是大开眼界，_____

_____。

7．中国实行开放政策后，同世界各国的外贸业务往来____

_____。

8．中国的日用品、工艺品大都_____。

9．人们都说，广交会是了解中国的最好的窗口，真是____

_____。

10．广交会确实是独具中国特色的外贸形式。外商不仅可以

_____，还可以_____。

三、想一想、谈一谈：

1．你参加过广州交易会吗？谈谈你或你的朋友对广交会的
印象。

2．你品尝过中国的哪些风味食品？

3．你喜欢中国的工艺品吗？你在广交会上选购过它们作送
礼佳品吗？

4．你在参加广交会时遇到过什么有趣的事和麻烦？

四、阅读下面的短文，并回答问题：

津 交 会

中国天津出口商品交易会，是最近几年才出现的大型区域

性交易会。它是北京、天津等省市联合举办的,还包括西藏、新疆等少数民族地区。这个交易会,主要是积极组织出口成交,同时组织进口货单,洽谈合资合作以及承包工程,劳务输出,三来一补等多种业务。华北、西北地区是我国对外贸易的重要出口基地,具备发展国际贸易与技术合作的良好条件和巨大潜力。津交会充分发挥这两个地区的整体优势,加强区域联合,展示地区外向型经济发展的新面貌和对外贸易发展的新成就。展品丰富多彩,新颖独特,富有地方色彩,对外商有特殊的吸引力,港、澳、台以及美国、法国、日本、澳大利亚等世界各国和地区的客商纷纷涌向津门。

1. 天津出口商品交易会为什么叫区域性交易会?
2. 津交会与广交会有什么不同?
3. 你参加过津交会吗? 印象如何?

English Translation of the Texts

Lesson 1

ESTABLISHING RELATIONSHIP

(1) First Meeting

Li Ning:　　　Could you tell me which of you is Mr. Ross from New York City, USA?

Ross:　　　　I am Mr. Ross, and you are ...

Li Ning:　　　My name is Li Ning, representative from China Textiles Import and Export Corporation. The Corporation has sent me to meet your delegation.

Ross:　　　　Very pleased to meet you.

Li Ning:　　　Very pleased to meet you too. Did you have a good journey?

Ross:　　　　Yes, we were very lucky. The journey was a pleasant one.

Li Ning:　　　That's great. The coach is just outside. Please follow me this way.

Ross:　　　　O.K. After you. This is my first visit to China, and we count on your help, Mr. Li.

Li Ning:　　　It's my pleasure. Since you are our guest, we hope during your stay in China, you will have a pleasant experience both in your work and your living.

Ross:　　　　Many thanks.

Li Ning:	Mr. Ross, please allow me to introduce to you Mr. Wang from China National Textiles Import and Export Corporation. The corporation has entrusted him to have business negotiations with you.
Wang An:	Good morning, Mr. Ross. My name is Wang An. I am very glad to meet you. Welcome to China, and I expect a good cooperation between us.
Ross:	NI HAO, Mr. Wang. This is my card. Please allow me to introduce members of our delegation: my assistant Mr. Jackson, my secretary Miss Brown, and the rest are working personnel of the delegation. Miss Brown will be working closely with you. I believe that our cooperation will be successful as well as pleasant.

(2) Inquiring About How to Establish Business Relations

Ross:	General Manager Zhang, could you tell me what a foreign firm should do in order to establish business relations with China?
Zhang Xiang:	Mr. Ross, how did you yourself begin then?
Ross:	Through the introduction of a friend of mine, I got to know someone in a position of responsibility in Moftec. On his recommendation, I wrote a letter to the Foreign Trade Bureau of Tianjin Municipality enclosed with a catalogue of the goods we would like to purchase. The Foreign Trade Bureau of Tianjin sent me an invitation, and that's how I

came to China.

Zhang Xiang: You did the right thing in exploring the way. But actually, there is another way that is even simpler. You can simply approach Chinese commercial setups abroad, such as the official commercial offices, various corporations and their subsidiaries, or their residential agents, and ask for a copy of the introduction to China's various specialized corporations. You can then write to a certain corporation according to your needs, and they will get in contact with you.

Ross: What kind of information do I have to provide them with?

Zhang Xiang: Your business lines, together with the list of goods you either want to buy or to sell.

Ross: Oh, I see. This is really a much simpler way of establishing relationship.

(3) Channels of Establishing Business Relations

Ross: General Manager Zhang, what are the channels of establishing commercial relations with China?

Zhang Xiang: There are many channels indeed. Apart from what I talked about last time, there still exist such channels as various exhibitions and fairs held abroad, and the Guangzhou Export Commodities Fair and other local fairs held by various provinces and municipalities.

Ross: Did you say the Guangzhou Fair? I heard about it

	before. Is it held in Guangzhou?
Zhang Xiang:	That's right. It is a large-scale comprehensive trade fair. Trading corporations from all over China take an active part in it, and large numbers of clients from abroad also come to visit the Fair and hold business negotiations.
Jackson:	With the existence of the Guangzhou Fair, why is it still necessary for various provinces and municipalities to hold their own fairs?
Zhang Xiang	Each locality has its own advantages, and the local or regional fairs held by them have their special features.
Jackson:	That's true.
Zhang Xiang:	In recent years, we have frequently held large-scale fairs both at home and abroad for investment and trade, and this is a new channel.
Ross:	That's a very good channel, but how can we attend such fairs?
Zhang Xiang:	We can help you with the arrangements.
Ross:	That's superb. It is true that every road leads to Beijing. Thank you very much, General Manager Zhang, for your introduction.
Zhang Xiang:	It's my pleasure to give you some information about China. You are most welcome to do business in China.

Lesson 2

ENTERTAINING GUESTS

(1) Sending Invitations

Wang An: Mr. Ross, to welcome the delegation, General Manager Zhang of our corporation will give a dinner tomorrow evening at the Beijing Roast Duck Restaurant. I would like to know whether that would suit you or not.

Ross: Thank you. As the Chinese saying goes, the guests are at the host's disposal. And we will follow whatever General Manager Zhang has arranged for us.

Wang An: All right. That's settled then. Here are the invitations. You are all invited.

Ross: Thank you for your kind invitation. We feel greatly honored.

Wang An: The pleasure is ours to have your company. So, we will pick you up at half past six tomorrow evening. Will that be all right?

Ross: Thank you for all the trouble.

Wang An: Don't mention it. No trouble at all. See you tomorrow then.

Ross: See you tomorrow.

(2) At Dinner

Jackson: Welcome to all of you, Mr. Ross. Please take your

	seat.
Ross:	It's very kind of you, General Manager Zhang. Please accept our heartfelt thanks for your very kind invitation.
Jackson:	I hope we will spend a very pleasant evening together.
Ross:	No doubt about that. From the moment we set foot on Chinese soil, we have been receiving your warm and considerate hospitality. Every member of the delegation has been deeply moved.
Li Ning:	A Chinese saying goes that we should make our guests feel at home. We hope you will really feel at home while you are here.
Jackson:	That's well said. The Chinese people are always hospitable. I have also learned a Chinese saying, that is, a worthy host attracts many guests. And that is to say hospitable hosts always have guests from all directions.
Zhang Xiang:	Thank you for your kind words. We do hope to make friends with people coming from various countries. Oh, here comes the duck. Let's tuck in while it is still hot. First, please allow me to raise my glass to propose a toast to Mr. Ross and the delegation, and to our forthcoming friendly cooperation. Cheers!
Ross:	Cheers!

(3) After the Banquet

Zhang Xiang: Mr. Ross, please forgive us if there should be anything inappropriate at tonight's dinner. (Note: This is typical Chinese modesty.)

Ross: The dinner is superb. My friends and I are all feeling very happy because we have spent a most pleasant and unforgettable evening. I think we have tasted the best duck in Beijing.

Zhang Xiang: We are very glad to hear these kind words.

Ross: We are very glad too. I know a Chinese saying, which goes: "One is not a true man until he has been to the Great Wall." I would like to add that one has not been in Beijing until he has tasted Beijing duck. Only at General Manager Zhang's invitation, do I obtain the certificate of having been in Beijing tonight, that is, two days after I arrived in Beijing because I have eaten Beijing duck.

Li Ning: Mr. Ross has a good sense of humor. But since you have not been to the Great Wall, Mr. Ross, you can't be counted as a true man yet.

Ross: That's true. I must go to the Great Wall because I really want to become a true man.

Li Ning: Great. Mr. Ross, here is the program arranged for the delegation. Please read it over and let me know if you have any suggestions.

Ross: Thank you. Can the program be changed a little bit? We would like to visit the factory concerned and have a look at the production processes first because that way we can have some ideas before we enter into business negotiations.

Wang An:	That can be arranged.
Ross:	If time allows, can you arrange for us to visit a private owner of a small business? I would like to know something about what they have been doing after the adoption of the open policy in China, especially their management philosophy.
Wang An:	This can also be done. The private business owners are mainly engaged in the tertiary industry. They mainly run restaurants, tailor's shops, and hairdresser's. Mr. Ross, you can first be their customer and then their visitor.
Ross:	That's a good idea. "How can you catch tiger cubs without entering the tiger's lair?" General Manager Zhang, did I use this proverb correctly?
Zhang Xiang:	Mr. Ross deserves to be called a China hand. I hope you won't be eaten by the newborn Chinese tiger of private business owners.
Ross:	I surely won't. The program is settled then.
Wang An:	Good. Thank you again, Mr. Ross, for being able to come to the dinner. Wish you success, Mr. Ross. Good-bye.

Lesson 3
FIRST CONTACT

(1) Prelude to Communication

Zhang Xiang: Mr. Ross, I am very glad to see you again. Please

	be seated.
Ross:	Thank you. I am also very glad to meet you, General Manager Zhang, and your colleagues once again.
Zhang Xiang:	How were the visits during the last two days?
Ross:	We were deeply impressed. China is really a beautiful country.
Jackson:	We didn't expect the abundance of merchandise on the Chinese market. You can find whatever you can think of.
Ross:	What surprised me most were the markets of textiles and garments. Going into markets big or small, walking into streets and lanes wide or narrow, you can see vendors of garments. I seemed to have entered a kingdom of garments.
Li Ning:	Mr. Ross, what you said was absolutely right. As a matter of fact, China has become the biggest apparel exporting country in the world.
Ross:	The purpose of our present visit is to negotiate the import and export of garments. It looks that we have come to the right place.
Jackson:	We hope we can get energetic support from your company.
Zhang Xiang:	We'll do whatever we can to help. Although this is the first time for us to come into contact, I believe that we can soon become real friends.
Ross:	Real friends, fantastic. Let us trust, help and support each other.
Zhang Xiang:	This is the foreign trade policy that we have al-

ways adhered to, making friends extensively on the basis of equality and mutual benefit, and the exchange of needed goods.

(2) Inquiring About Each Other's Business Scope

Zhang Xiang: To be frank, Mr. Ross, we still do not know much about your company.

Ross: That's not surprising as ours is not a big firm and it is not widely known yet.

Jackson: But we have been doing well domestically and we will become a business partner that is of interest to you.

Zhang Xiang: What major items does your company deal in then?

Jackson: We mainly deal in textiles, including cotton, ramie, wool, silk, chemical fabrics, various yarns, cloths and products made of these materials.

Li Ning: These fall within our main business line too.

Ross: We hope to be able to import textiles from your country and also to export our textiles to your country.

Zhang Xiang: That's called reciprocity and the exchange of needed goods.

Ross: That's right. But this is just our first visit to China, and we need to do some study of the Chinese market so that we can know how things stand when we do our import and export business.

Zhang Xiang: It's not surprising that you would like to make

	those adjustments to the program as the main purpose of your present visit is to do market research.
Jackson:	That's correct. We have to know what goods are suitable for the market.
Li Ning:	That's really important. The company will go bankrupt if they can't sell their goods.
Ross:	Even after doing some research, it is better that we order some goods for trial sales. So we are prepared to make an order this time.
Zhang Xiang:	We can see that you are serious and conscientious in doing things. That makes one feel that you are trustworthy.
Ross:	Thank you for this impression of yours.
Zhang Xiang:	We have always held that there can be no true cooperation without trust.
Ross:	That's well said. We have already had a good beginning.
Jackson:	There is one more thing we'd like to bother you about.
Zhang Xiang:	Go ahead, please.
Jackson:	Entrusted by a friend, we would like to know something about your handicrafts, hardware and ready-made Chinese medicines.
Li Ning:	You know that these items do not belong to our scope of business, but we can act as a go-between for you.
Jackson:	Many thanks.
Zhang Xiang:	You are most welcome. Shall we take a rest now?
Ross:	That would be great. Let's go and have a cup of

coffee.

(3)Touching Upon Items of Interest

Zhang Xiang: Now we can sit down and continue with our discussion.

Jackson: Coffee is really a good thing, as it excites you.

Ross: Oh, but what makes us happier are our Chinese friends.

Zhang Xiang: Thanks. I think you must have brought with you an order list when you come to China, and you went to have a look at the Chinese market in the past couple of days. Have you formulated any plan already?

Ross: I think we have found needed goods that suit the market.

Jackson: We are particularly interested in your pure cotton goods and high-grade silk products.

Zhang Xiang: You have very good judgment. As a matter of fact, our pure cotton goods and high-grade silk products are very popular in all places of the world.

Ross: That we know. But please excuse my straightforwardness. In such matters as the technological level, design, color and variety, they still fall short of the expectations of the customers of our country.

Li Ning: We are clear about that and we have been working hard to increase the technological content and the value added of our products.

Ross:	We can cooperate in this respect. We can make investment to have a factory built in China.
Jackson:	We have advanced equipment, production process and the technology needed.
Zhang Xiang:	Yours is a good idea. We can make a feasibility study about it.
Ross:	That's great. I believe there will be a bright prospect of cooperation between us.

Lesson 4
INTENTION OF BUYING AND SELLING

(1) Discussion About the Products

Ross:	General Manager Zhang, this time we would like to order some textiles for trial sales. Could you show your designs and patterns to me?
Jackson:	It would be even better if you could provide us with some samples and catalogs.
Li Ning:	Oh, here are the catalogs. We can go to the sample room to have a look at the samples after our meeting.
Ross:	You know that we are most concerned about the quality of the products.
Zhang Xiang:	In recent years, China's textile industry has developed towards finer and deeper processing, turning out many new products, with the quality much improved as well.

Ross:	That's good news.
Li Ning:	They include high-grade pure cotton knitwear, high-grade pure silk products, highly dense down-proof cloths, fine count thin ramie fabrics, etc. We also produce series of high-grade cloths for interior decoration which are flame-proof, light-proof, heat-proof, thermally insulated, dirt-proof and static electricity proof.
Ross:	You have large varieties of designs and patterns indeed and we have seen some of them on the market, but the quality still falls short of expectations.
Jackson:	So far as I know, your products could only be sold at low prices and lacked competitiveness in the international market as the processing level was low and the quality not high enough.
Ross:	I have some figures here. For 127cm-wide silk piece goods, your products were sold at US $ 5.62 per meter, as against $ 65 for Spanish products, $ 37.13 for Belgian products, and $ 23.75 for French products. Even the cheapest Italian products were priced at $ 11.37 per meter. You really suffered great losses.
Zhang Xiang:	We have already paid attention to the situation you mentioned and have applied high-tech and new techniques to remold the production process of our textile industry, bringing about a fundamental change in the quality of our products.
Ross:	I have full confidence in the determination and ability of the Chinese people. Shall we go to have a

	look at the samples now?
Zhang Xiang:	Fine. Let's go.

(2) Talking About Prices

Ross:	General Manager Zhang, I am really surprised. The quality of your samples is extremely good.
Zhang Xiang:	What's your intention then?
Ross:	I have already indicated our intention to you, General Manager Zhang. We are thinking of ordering some high-grade silk and cotton products. But after reading your catalogs, we feel that the prices are too high to be acceptable.
Jackson:	I wonder whether you can quote us more preferential prices.
Zhang Xiang:	These products supplied by our corporation are of top quality with completely new designs. They have been well received since they were first introduced to the market. Actually they are among the best selling superior commodities of our corporation.
Ross:	But the prices are too high. Aren't you afraid that they will scare away new clients like us?
Zhang Xiang:	At the present prices, the customers are still scrambling to buy them and that shows the prices are quite reasonable. I believe that you will not run away.
Jackson:	Are the prices on the price list firm offers?
Li Ning:	No, they aren't, because many things remain to

	be discussed. The prices are subject to our final confirmation.
Jackson:	What are the factors that contribute to your final decision then?
Zhang Xiang:	It mainly depends on the quantity of your purchase. If the amount of your order is substantial, the price can be reduced.
Ross:	That will be difficult. As you know, the import and export of textiles is strictly controlled by quotas.
Zhang Xiang:	That we know of course, but you can still do your best.
Ross:	Even if we try our best, both the active and the passive quotas are limited.
Zhang Xiang:	To facilitate our offer, could you, Mr. Ross, give an indication of the approximate amount you would like to purchase?
Ross:	Could you give a minimum price on CIF San Francisco basis first? If your prices are favorable, our order will not be a small one.
Zhang Xiang:	Oh, this is just like playing chess. Someone must take the first move. If each is waiting for the other to begin, there will be a deadlock.
Ross:	I like your metaphor, General Manager Zhang. Well matched in this chess game of ours, I hope the game will end in a draw.

(3) Agency and Autonomous Management

Ross: Excuse me, General Manager Zhang, but we would like to go to see a couple of other companies.

Zhang Xiang: That's all right. It's understandable.

Ross: Then, can you introduce one or two companies to us?

Zhang Xiang: Yes, we can. In the past the import and export business was handled only by national trading corporations and there was only one specialized foreign trade corporation for the textiles business of the whole country —— our corporation.

Jackson: And we could only deal with you.

Zhang Xiang: That was true. But now the situation has changed. We have pushed forward the agency system in our foreign trade. Some productive enterprises entrust us with their import and export business, and even more productive enterprises and trading companies have obtained the right of autonomous management of their own foreign trade business.

Ross: That means that we can deal with more enterprises and companies from now on, is that right?

Zhang Xiang: That's right.

Jackson: Then can you introduce a couple more to us?

Ross: Especially those productive enterprises that can handle their own import and export business. Maybe they can meet some of our special requirements in product design, variety, and quality.

Zhang Xiang: O.K., we'll get in contact with them.

Lesson 5
TALKING ABOUT PRICE

(1) Inquiry and Offer

Smith: Mr. Chen, we plan to place an order of 50 tons of peanut kernels. Would you please briefly introduce your goods and prices?

Chen Qiran: O.K. We sell peanut kernels by samples. Mr. Smith, you can first have a look at our samples and the price list.

Smith: Well, these peanut kernels are plump, even, and fresh with a delicious taste. They really are of good quality. Can you guarantee that the goods supplied will be of the same quality as the samples?

Chen Qiran: You can rest assured about that because we always keep our business integrity and honor our contracts.

Smith: We have no doubt about that, but the price of US $ 485 per ton is too high to be acceptable.

Chen Qiran: That is our CIF price, which includes cost, insurance and freight. If we can make a deal, we can deliver the goods to Los Angeles by the end of next May.

Mary: But the price is too high for us to push the sale.

Chen Qiran: Our peanut kernels have for many years enjoyed a brisk market the world over. Even if the price is a bit higher, there won't be any problem in selling them.

Mary: But you know, Mr. Chen, there is fierce competition in the market. The price for Indian peanut kernels is much lower than yours.

Chen Qiran: I don't deny that. But just as the Chinese saying goes, the proof of the goods lies in the comparison. Mr. Smith, you are an expert in this line and I am sure you can make the distinction.

Smith: All right. I'll think about it.

(2) Counter-offer

Chen Qiran: Mr. Smith, what do you think of our offer yesterday?

Smith: Mr. Chen, after careful study, we still think that your offer is too high. If you do not see your way to lower the price, we cannot but give it up.

Chen Qiran: I don't think it is wise for you to do so. We can still negotiate. How about giving us a counter-offer?

Smith: We think that US $ 405 per ton is reasonable.

Chen Qiran: Mr. Smith, your counter-offer is much too low and it is too far away from our original offer. It seems it is really difficult for us to come to terms.

Smith: I believe in the sincerity of both sides. Can't we make a compromise with each other?

Chen Qiran: I agree to that. If you can increase the volume of

	your order, we can reduce our price by 5%.
Smith:	Mr. Chen, I am afraid that will be difficult. You know that the present international market is slack and bearish. What's more, peanut kernels deteriorate easily. We will be running big risks if we place too big an order. I hope you can understand.
Chen Qiran:	It is true that the present international situation is unstable and the market is a bit dull, but we are optimistic about the future.
Smith:	In this case, can you deliver the goods in several lots? If so, we can raise out price by 5%.
Chen Qiran:	This is still much too low. Let's make it US $ 450 per ton. That is the lowest we can go.
Smith:	The gap between us is still a big one. It seems both sides need more patience if we want to make a deal.

(3) Concession and Conclusion of Transaction

Chen Qiran:	Mr. Smith, what do you think of our price list?
Smith:	Mr. Chen, I have noticed that your prices this year are much higher than those of last year. Can you explain the reasons?
Chen Qiran:	In recent years, the prices of chemical fertilizer, water and electricity have all been raised, resulting in much higher costs for agricultural products. We have to make corresponding adjustments in our selling prices.
Smith:	This I can understand. But you must try to find

other methods to lower our production costs, and cannot simply transfer the increased prices of chemical fertilizer, water and electricity entirely onto the clients. If you do this, then your products will find no sale.

Chen Qiran: Mr. Smith, please note that the prices for the same kind of products in the international market have all gone up from last year's level, and by a bigger margin than ours too. Relatively speaking, the prices of our products are inexpensive. What's more, the exchange rate of your currency has been falling continuously. This we cannot neglect either.

Smith: That is true. But your offer is too harsh on us. Could you make some further concessions?

Chen Qiran: Mr. Smith, you mean to say that ...

Smith: We hope that you can reduce your price by another 5%.

Chen Qiran: You mean we have to cut a total of 10% from the original price quoted? That won't do. We can't do business at a loss, you know.

Smith: What about 8%?

Chen Q iran: If you could increase the quantity of your purchase by 20%, then we can agree to a further reduction of 3%. That's the lowest price we can quote.

Smith: O.K. Let's make a deal.

Lesson 6
DISCUSSION ON VARIETY AND QUANTITY

(1) Ordering Goods

Smith: Mr. Chen, I have an order list here for hardware. Please have a look and see whether you can guarantee supply.

Chen Qiran: Oh, they are all reputable famous brands.

Mary: That's right. Such goods as 808 brand drawer lock, Triangle brand stainless steel tableware, 555 brand nail clippers, Spear brand scissors all enjoy a ready market in our country. Every year our firm buys a large quantity but they are always sold out. So we hope you can satisfy our needs this time.

Chen Qiran: Hardware is among the daily necessities required by thousands of households but at the same time they are goods with a very small profit margin. In recent years, since the market has opened to competition, many factories have turned to producing profit-earning commodities, such as computers, high-grade video recorders, and multifunctional hi-fi systems. They are reluctant to produce hardware. There is an unprecedented shortage of supply, which cannot catch up with demand. Therefore, it is rather difficult for us to meet your requirements, Mr. Smith.

Smith: Mr. Chen, we are an old client of yours and you have to make allowance for us. As long as the quality is stable and the supply is guaranteed, we can assure you of our good prices too.

Chen Qiran: Well, if your prices are favorable, we'll approach the factories, asking them to produce famous-brand goods. We can guarantee that the quality will be first class and the assortment will include as many specifications and designs as possible. Mr. Smith, could you please give us an indication of your favorable conditions?

Smith: As for this, ... I think, first we will act in line with the international market situation, and secondly we will pay better prices for better quality goods. Can we first have a look at the samples? Anyway, we guarantee good prices for good quality products.

Chen Qiran: That sounds reasonable and we can agree to that. However, we have another request, which is that you have to guarantee an adequate minimum quantity for your order. If the minimum quantity is too small, then it will be very difficult for us to secure the supply of goods.

Smith: All right. We will definitely take that into consideration.

(2) Quantity of Order

Chen Qiran: Mr. Smith, I am sorry that because of a crop failure we can only supply 600 cases of the top grade *Maojian* tea, which you would like to purchase.

Smith:	Mr. Chen, the top grade *Maojian* tea that we bought from you last year sold well. This year, we would very much like to increase the quantity of our purchase. 600 cases can hardly meet our needs. Since we are a long-standing client of yours and the relationship between us has a long history, could you give us a special favor by increasing the quantity by 100 cases?
Chen Qiran:	We have done our best to ensure the supply of 600 cases. I am really sorry but we are unable to meet your request. I hope that we can satisfy you next time.
Smith:	If not 100 cases, how about 50 cases? This is the minimal quantity of our order.
Chen Qiran:	All right then. We'll add 50 cases. Mr. Smith, Fujian Oolong tea has had a good harvest this year and we hope you can buy some.
Mary:	I hope it is not a slow-selling item.
Chen Qiran:	You are joking, aren't you? Oolong tea is also famous Chinese tea. It is not only a drink, but also a nutritious tonic with special curing effects. Frequent drinking of Oolong tea is good to the health. It has won a warm welcome from our foreign friends.
Smith:	In that case, we can accept your suggestion. What is the minimum quantity of purchase then?
Chen Qiran:	Mr. Smith, since you are our long-standing client and we didn't meet your demand in the top grade *Maojian* tea, we would like to make up the differ-

ence with Oolong tea so that the total volume of transaction remains virtually unchanged.

Smith: Thank you for your kind consideration. That's settled then.

(3) Canceling the Order

Smith: Mr. Chen, because of the changes in the market situation, we would like to cancel the order we placed with you last week.

Chen Qiran: I don't think that is a proper thing for you to do. Both of us have always kept our business integrity and honored our contracts.

Smith: That is true. This time we really have no other alternative. I hope you can understand.

Chen Qiran: What is the real reason then? Can you give a reasonable explanation?

Smith: Mr. Chen, you know perfectly well that the international sugar market has been dull for a long period of time and the demand has been falling sharply. This week the price of sugar has fallen to the year's lowest level, registering a fall of US $3.60 per ton in one week. If we continue to take delivery according to our agreement reached last week, we'll have to suffer a great loss. Luckily we haven't signed the contract yet, so we can bring the matter up for adjustment.

Chen Qiran: This situation was already taken into consideration during out negotiations last week and the final

	price at which we concluded business was actually very favorable.
Smith:	That is true and we appreciate it very much. However, during the present week, the sugar market situation has become extremely grim and we cannot but take some corresponding measures.
Chen Qiran:	The market situation is undergoing a myriad of changes in the twinkling of an eye, and we believe it will turn for the better before long.
Smith:	Mr. Chen, as businessmen, we are practical as well as adventurous. I hope you can understand.
Chen Qiran:	All right then, we can agree to your request. However, we have some other goods in ample stock. Can you purchase some of those so as to sustain the total value of the transactions concluded?
Smith:	Fine. Courtesy demands reciprocity and it is impolite not to reciprocate. You can understand us and we can understand you. Let's go on to talk about another deal.

Lesson 7
DISCOUNT AND COMMISSION

(1) Asking for a Discount

Roden:	Mr. Li, after your consideration, what decision have you made concerning the question of dis-

	count?
Li Ning:	In principle, we do not give any discount.
Roden:	I am afraid that does not conform to the usual practice. The total volume of our purchase this time is substantial. According to convention, we are entitled to at least a 10% discount.
Li Ning:	The volume of your purchase this time is not small but they are all fast-selling goods. They can be sold quickly with a big profit margin. What's more, our price is most favorable and it actually amounts to a discount. Therefore we cannot give a further discount.
Roden:	I am sorry to hear that. It is most unfair to us.
Li Ning:	If you can further increase your volume of purchase, then we may consider allowing you a discount.
Roden:	All right then. We'll increase our order by 10%.

(2) Dispute on Discount

Roden:	Mr. Li, we have ordered 100,000 quartz clocks from you. How big a discount do you plan to allow us?
Li Ning:	2% from the net price.
Roden:	Isn't that too low? We can obtain a 10% discount from other countries when purchasing similar goods.
Li Ning:	I don't think you should forget, Mr. Roden, that our price is most favorable and we have taken the

discount into consideration. If you can, according to the contract stipulations, effect payment ahead of time, we can reduce the net price by another 2%.

Roden:
Mr. Li, our order this time is for new products that are for trial sale. That involves greater risks. In order to help open the market, will you please allow a bigger discount?

Li Ning:
We can consider this proposal. We'll go out of our way to allow you still another 2% discount. Thus the total discount is already more than 5%. To tell the truth, this is really exceptional treatment.

(3) Asking for Commission

Jones:
Mr. Zhang, this time we helped you in securing the deal. What commission are you planning to grant us?

Zhang Xiang:
I am sorry to say that according to our regulations, we do not allow any commission in principle.

Jones:
Mr. Zhang, I would like to call your attention to the fact that not to grant commission does not conform to the international trade practice.

Zhang Xiang:
Mr. Jones, we give remuneration only to middlemen and agents.

Jones:
That's exactly the case. You know perfectly well that we are but your agent.

Zhang Xiang:
O.K. then. We can, according to the trade value and the nature of the goods, pay you a fee for your

service.

Jones: No, I would rather be paid a commission that we are justifiably entitled to. You know, Mr. Zhang, ours is a firm that carries on commercial activities through obtaining reasonable commission.

(4) Dispute on Commission

Jones: Mr. Zhang, as sales agent for your products, we are concerned about our commission.

Zhang Xiang: That's perfectly understandable to us. But we have made our price most favorable to you, and therefore the commission should be reduced accordingly. What do you think if we make it 1%?

Jones: 1%? Are you kidding? Generally we get a 3% commission for each transaction. This time the trade volume is very large and so we deserve a commission that is higher than 3%. On the contrary you are only prepared to allow us a 1% commission. Isn't it unreasonable?

Zhang Xiang: We all know that commission is calculated as a proportion to the trade volume, and so, the larger the transaction, the more you will get for commission.

Jones: You cannot simply put it that way. In order to promote the sale of your products and secure the market share, we have to hire a few more salesmen, and spend more on advertising. Therefore, the larger our order, the higher the cost we'll have to pay. We are entitled to some corresponding compensation.

Zhang Xiang: You are compensated from your proportional commission.

Jones: But that is far from enough to compensate for our cost.

Zhang Xiang: I would make the following suggestion. If you can increase the volume of your order, we can consider allowing you another 1% commission.

Jones: We cannot accept the additional condition of yours. 1% commission is unprecedented in international trade, I am afraid.

Zhang Xiang: I don't think you can find another case for a price as low as we quoted either. If you insist on raising the commission, then we'll have to adjust our price somewhat. Mr. Jones, which way do you think is more reasonable?

Jones: It seems that we have very different ways of thinking and doing things and it is really regretful that it should be so difficult to bridge the gap.

Lesson 8
MODES OF PAYMENT

(1) Selecting the Currency for Payment

Li Ning: Mr. Ross, we would like to use Renminbi for the payment of our imports this time.

Ross: I am sorry to say that as a rule we use US dollars

to calculate the price, as it's more convenient.

Li Ning: As a matter of fact, to use Renminbi to effect payment is not inconvenient either. Many banks in Europe have accounting relations with the Bank of China, Beijing.

Ross: Since we are not familiar with this practice, it is easier to do it in US dollars.

Li Ning: Oh, the formalities are actually very simple. To negotiate payment, you just need to go to a bank in your country that has accounting relations with the Bank of China.

Ross: To be frank with you, we are worried that by using Renminbi for payment, our firm will suffer losses because of the fluctuations in the exchange rate.

Li Ning: Mr. Ross, you don't need to worry about that. The exchange rate of Renminbi is very stable and we can also negotiate a value-guaranteeing rate. Thus there can be no danger of things going wrong.

Ross: All right then. We'll try it once.

(2) Modes of Payment

Ross: Mr. Li, what modes of payment do you normally use?

Li Ning: Normally we accept payment by irrevocable letter of credit. You can effect payment against the shipping documents that you have received.

Jackson:	Do you accept D/A?

Jackson: Do you accept D/A?

Li Ning: I am sorry that we can't agree to that.

Jackson: Our firm has always been creditworthy in business. Once we receive the draft, we will accept it. And we will pay as soon as it is mature.

Li Ning: We do believe in what you say but we will be running great risks. An irrevocable letter of credit is much safer for our collection of foreign exchange. I hope you can understand, Mr. Ross.

Ross: Mr. Li, to open a letter of credit for such a large sum of money will involve a large expense, that is, we must pay a considerable sum of money as guarantee apart from the usual fee. This will undoubtedly raise the price of our imported goods and that will in turn affect the sale. I hope you can take all this into consideration.

Li Ning: I am sorry to say that just because the value of this transaction is very large and the present financial market is unstable, in order to ensure security, we cannot but use payment by letter of credit.

Jackson: What about D/P then?

Li Ning: Same as D/A, D/P doesn't provide a reliable guarantee from the bank. It is just that our risks are a bit smaller. I am sorry to say that we do not accept D/P either.

Ross: All right then. But you must also fulfill the terms as stipulated in the irrevocable letter of credit.

Li Ning: That goes without saying. We will effect shipment in time and try to advance it if possible. Will you please ensure that your letter of credit reaches us 30 days prior to the date of shipment so that we can make the necessary arrangements?

Ross: That can be done.

Li Ning: We have another requirement. Please see to it that the period of validity of your letter of credit is 15 days from the date of the signing of the bill of lading, and that the L/C is marked "valid in China" under "Place of Expiry".

Ross: All right. We'll see to that.

(3) Payment by Installments

Wang Jin: Mr. Green, the value of our imports this time is a large amount and we would like to use payment by installments. We hope we can have your cooperation in this respect.

Green: Mr. Wang, taking into consideration your actual difficulty and with a view to promoting our trade relations in the future, we agree to payment by installments this time. However, to give a long credit for such a large sum of money constitutes a heavy pressure on the turnover of our funds. We hope that you can pay a reasonably large proportion as down payment.

Wang Jin: That can be considered. After the official signing of the contract, we can pay half of the value as down payment, and the balance will be paid in two installments. Will that be all right?

Green:　　　　That's fine. Tomorrow we'll prepare a time draft for your acceptance. You can return it to me after it is countersigned by the Bank of China, Beijing to confirm your acceptance.

Wang Jin:　　All right. As long as you can make the delivery in time and see to it that the quality and specifications of the goods conform to the contract stipulations, we guarantee that the bank will effect payment when the draft accepted by us is mature.

Green:　　　　In order to clarify the contractual rights and responsibilities of both parties, we hope that the contract will clearly stipulate the quantity and date of each shipment and the details concerning payment.

Wang Jin:　　No problem about that. Our corporation has always abided by the stipulations of the contracts we enter into with foreign businessmen.

(4) Compensation Trade

Wang Jin:　　Mr. Green, we would like to adopt the mode of compensation trade for our import of the equipment for the open-cut coal-mine. Is that all right?

Green:　　　　The equipment under discussion this time is to develop your open-cut coal-mine. The coal produced by this mine will be high-grade coal for power generation, which has a low phosphorus and sulfur content, a medium ash content, and long flames. We will be pleased to sell this kind of coal in our country. Therefore, we do not have any objections in principle towards the adoption of compensation trade for this transaction.

Wang Jin: Good. Mr. Green, would you like direct compensation or comprehensive compensation?

Green: We would prefer direct compensation, simply because the energy crisis is an important factor affecting the economy of our country. Such good quality coal is not easy to obtain and we hope that you can pay for the total value of this transaction with the coal that will be produced with our equipment.

Wang Jin: Mr. Green, what you say is absolutely true. We also need the high quality coal produced by this mine, and therefore, we prefer comprehensive compensation.

Green: Do you plan to supply other clients with this coal? If that's the case, then we should be given priority.

Wang Jin: Even if we are planning multilateral trade, it is perfectly normal. However, at the moment, we have not talked with any other clients about exporting this product. I would like to reiterate that we do need this coal too. I hope you can understand, Mr. Green.

Green: O. K. then. Let's adopt comprehensive compensation. But we do hope that you can make the part for direct compensation as big as possible and reduce the part for indirect compensation.

Wang Jin: We can agree to this principle.

Lesson 9
DELIVERY AND SHIPMENT

(1) Date of Delivery

Ross: Mr. Li, how long does it normally take you to deliver the goods?

Li Ning: Generally we can get the goods ready for shipment 30 days after receiving the covering letter of credit.

Jackson: Can you expedite shipment in the case of seasonal goods?

Li Ning: It all depends. If the factory is heavily committed and alternative arrangements cannot be made, then it would be difficult to ship the goods ahead of time.

Ross: Timing is most important for seasonal goods. If they do not arrive in time for the selling season, even readily marketable goods will become unsalable, and they will have to be disposed of at reduced prices and we will suffer great losses.

Li Ning: I fully understand your point and we will guarantee delivery on schedule. As to whether we can make delivery ahead of time, we'll have to consult the producers. I reckon there will be some difficulties.

Jackson: Mr. Li, I hope you can give our case special

consideration.

Li Ning: We will do our best. But anyway we definitely cannot make delivery of the goods before September 15th because that is really beyond our ability.

(2) Date of Shipment

Li Ning: Mr. Ross, today we are going to discuss matters concerning shipment.

Ross: Fine. Would you please give your opinion first?

Li Ning: As this transaction is concluded on the basis of FOB terms, it goes without saying that the port of shipment is a Chinese port. Only if you send a vessel in time for the shipment, can we perform our contractual obligations to the full. If you fail to dispatch your vessel in due time, you will be held responsible for all the losses we thus incur.

Ross: We don't have any objection to this. The date of shipment stipulated in the contract is prior to May 30th next year. When can you get the goods ready for shipment then?

Li Ning: 30 days after we have received the covering letter of credit.

Jackson: Can't it be put forward a bit?

Li Ning: I am afraid that will be difficult. We need ample time to get the goods ready, make out all the necessary documents, and go through the customs formalities.

Ross: O.K. then. As soon as we get back, we'll arrange for a letter of credit to be opened. We hope that upon receipt of our letter of credit, you will inform us by fax without delay of the specific time of shipment so that we can dispatch a vessel for the loading of the goods.

Li Ning: We will see to that. We also hope that upon receipt of our shipping advice, you will inform us without delay of the time of the ship's arrival so as to facilitate our arrangement for the transportation and shipment of the goods.

Ross: No problem about that. I trust we will enjoy each other's full cooperation.

(3) Bill of Lading

Li Ning: Mr. Ross, shouldn't we have the matters fixed concerning the bill of lading as well?

Ross: This is exactly the question we are about to raise now. We hope that it can be stipulated in the letter of credit that the seller shall send one of the three original copies of the bill of lading direct to the buyer.

Li Ning: I am sorry that we cannot agree to this request about one third of the bill of lading.

Ross: Why not?

Li Ning: According to the international convention, the three original copies of the bill of lading are equally effective. In that case, you can take delivery without paying the bank to get the shipping

	documents, and we may not be able to collect payment for the goods, thus incurring losses of having neither the money nor the goods.
Ross:	You don't have the most fundamental trust in us.
Li Ning:	Please don't feel offended, Mr. Ross. We simply want to avoid unnecessary disputes concerning the bill of lading.
Ross:	O. K. We'll waive this request of ours. Then, what about demurrage and dispatch?
Li Ning:	I think we should indicate the daily quantity of loading and unloading in the additional terms of the contract.
Jackson:	There should be clear stipulations about the time of loading and unloading as well. According to our practice, the loading and unloading is carried out continuously for 24 hours a fine day, excluding holidays.
Li Ning:	I think it is better to make it clear in the contract that holidays are included if they are used, and excluded if they are not used. In this way, it is more flexible and disputes can be avoided in the subsequent calculation of demurrage and dispatch.
Ross:	Fine. I can agree to all these principles. Now let's get down to the discussion of details, shall we?

(4) Partial Shipment and Transshipment

Li Ning:	Mr. Ross, we have negotiated a big transaction involving large quantities. I hope we will be allowed

	to make partial shipments.
Ross:	I am afraid that won't do because they are all seasonal goods and we hope they will all arrive at the same time so that they can be sold in the selling season.
Li Ning:	We can guarantee that they will all arrive on schedule. However, as the goods are not produced by the same factory, we have to collect them in several Chinese ports for shipment.
Jackson:	How many partial shipments do you want to make then?
Li Ning:	Can we leave this open and just put " partial shipments allowed" in the contract?
Ross:	All right then. But I hope that you will reduce the number of partial shipments to the minimum, and guarantee that all the goods will arrive on schedule.
Li Ning:	Thank you, Mr. Ross, for your cooperation. There is another problem. This transaction was concluded on CIF basis, but our country does not have ocean-going vessels sailing direct to the destination designated by your firm. Therefore we'll have to arrange for transshipment en route.
Jackson:	Mr. Li, transshipment en route will prolong the time of transportation, increase the transshipment expenses and cause unnecessary damage. Mr. Li, I hope you can take all these adverse factors into consideration.
Li Ning:	We already have, but only transshipment will

enable the goods to arrive at the destination you designated unless you choose another destination that will suit both parties.

Ross: Well, let's study this suggestion of yours then, Mr. Li.

Lesson 10
PACKING

(1) Packing and Packaging

Chen Qiran: Mr. Smith, today we'll discuss matters about packing.

Smith: Fine. This is an important question that we need to discuss in detail.

Chen Qiran: We know that packing, as an important component of the goods, has at least three major functions, namely, to protect the goods, to facilitate storage and transportation and to communicate.

Smith: Whether it is the outer packing or the inner packaging, they need to have at least these three functions. Let's begin our discussion according to this principle, shall we?

Chen Qiran: In that case, shall we discuss the packaging or the outer packing first?

Smith: What about starting with the inner packaging, that is the packaging for the sale of the goods?

Chen Qiran: That's fine. You have examined our samples, and

	what is your impression of our packaging?
Smith:	In the present international market, there is fierce competition between similar products, and the packing and packaging play an important role in the successful promotion. I hope your firm can attach importance to this law of the market.
Chen Qiran:	Just as Buddha needs to be painted gold and humans need fine clothes, goods need good packaging. Well, Mr. Green, do you mean to say that you are not satisfied with our packaging?
Smith:	Please excuse my straightforwardness. If the goods are of first-rate quality but with second-rate packaging so that they can only be sold at third-rate prices, then the goods are not competitive in the market.
Chen Qiran:	We've had a profound lesson in neglecting the packaging in the past. It used to be heavy, cumbersome, coarse, ugly and unappealing, and was not convenient for storage or transportation so that every year we suffered great losses due to improper packaging.
Mary:	Packaging is also an important means in raising the value added to the goods. If the goods are of first-rate quality but with second-rate packaging, then they can only be sold at third-rate prices. This kind of latent economic loss is even more serious, I am afraid.
Chen Qiran:	That's right, and so we are now paying great attention to this question.

Mary: This is good news.

Chen Qiran: In recent years, great improvements have been made both in our packing and packaging. Just take our exported tea as an example. By changing the coarse and bulky packs to convenient and exquisite small packs, the price of Chinese tea on the international market has been raised by 10 to 50%.

Smith: Yes, we have noticed that in recent years the packaging of Chinese goods has become much lighter and finer. The pull-to-open cans for Coca Cola, the cans for Nescafe, and the packaging for foreign famous-brand soft drinks are all made in China and they have attained the quality level of similar products abroad.

Chen Qiran: Oh, Mr. Smith, it seems that you know about the Chinese packaging industry like the palm of your hand.

Smith: Oh, it won't do if I don't.

(2) Packing and Transportation

Chen Qiran: Mr. Smith, we have had quite a bit of discussion about packing. Do you still have any specific comments about it?

Smith: The tea bags we ordered this time are packed in high-grade filter paper free from toxin and odor, and they are healthy and easy to make. I am satisfied.

Chen Qiran: What about the canned tea?

Mary:	The canned tea is packed in finely processed cans that are air tight and easy to open.
Chen Qiran:	And the packaging?
Smith:	Generally speaking it is well designed, with Chinese national characteristics and in conformity with the psychology of the consumers in our country. They have an antique flavor and are extremely modern at the same time.
Chen Qiran:	It seems that there is something you are not satisfied with, Mr. Smith.
Smith:	The labeling is too simple. From the outside one can only see the name and origin of the product, but not some other important kinds of information such as the content of the ingredients, with or without artificial coloring, additives or antiseptics, the date of expiration, date of production, method of use, etc.
Chen Qiran:	The trademark and labeling of goods produced in China are all as simple as that.
Mary:	In our country, the customers won't take out their purse if they don't understand the goods. Thus you have given up a very good chance of advertising.
Chen Qiran:	Unfortunately, the rice has been cooked.
Mary:	You can cook another pot of rice to make perfect the packing materials, packaging design and printing, achieving the result of immediate attraction of the customers so that once they see the products they cannot tear themselves away until they have

	made the purchase.
Chen Qiran:	We'll do our best to persuade the manufacturers to do so. I believe that it is also their desire to have attractive packaging for their products, and that can add to the value of the goods as well.
Smith:	O.K. That's settled. Now we can talk about the outer packing, that is, the packing for transportation.
Chen Qiran:	Oh, Mr. Smith, you can rest assured about that. This batch will be packed in high quality secure plywood cases each lined with aluminum foil, and strengthened with two straps outside. Nothing can go wrong with it in ocean transport.
Smith:	That's good. With good inner packing, it will be waterproof, moisture proof, mildew inhibiting, odor proof and shockproof. I don't need to worry about ocean transportation of the goods now.
Chen Qiran:	The tea you ordered this time is not enough to fill one standard container, and I am afraid that it has to be shipped with other goods in the container.
Smith:	Please pay attention to the inner and outer measurements of the cases, as there can be quite a big difference between them for corrugated paper cartons. If it is not properly arranged, you may not be able to fit everything into one container, resulting in higher freight.
Chen Qiran:	We will certainly see to that.

Lesson 11
INSURANCE

(1) Risks and Scope of Insurance Coverage

Smith: Mr. Chen, from which company should we apply for marine insurance to cover an international transaction?

Chen Qiran: The People's Insurance Company of China unifiedly takes care of China's insurance business. PICC sees to the insurance of all import and export goods in China. Where the insured goods sustain loss or damage in transit, PICC undertakes to indemnify according to the risks insured.

Smith: That conforms to the nature of international insurance business.

Chen Qiran: That's correct. The insurance company is not liable for loss or damage caused by the intentional act or fault of the insured or by the failure to perform contractual responsibilities by the two parties, or those arising from normal losses in transit.

Smith: That is the same too. Could you tell me the main scope of coverage by your insurance company?

Chen Qiran: It mainly includes F.P.A., W.P.A. and all risks, three categories in all. At the request of the insured, general additional risks and special additional risks can also be covered.

Smith: What about the commencement and termination of cover?

| Chen Qiran: | Generally speaking, we adopt the usual warehouse to warehouse clause in international insurance. However, in the case of such special additional risk as war risk, the warehouse to warehouse clause does not apply, and there are additional provisions for transshipment. The details are highly complex. |
| Smith: | That being the case, I'll have to make a careful study of the insurance law of your country. |

(2) Scope of Cover

Smith:	Mr. Chen, could you give a brief account of the scope of cover for F.P.A. in your country?
Chen Qiran:	O.K. As the term implies, it guarantees that the goods arrive safely in sea or land transportation. To be more exact, it means that the insurance company will be liable for total loss of the insured goods caused in the course of transit by natural calamities or by accidents.
Mary:	Does it include particular average?
Chen Q iran:	Are you referring to the kind of losses that are not included in the general average—partial and deliberate sacrifice of the ship, freight, or goods undertaken for the common safety of the adventure in time of peril?
Mary:	That's correct.
Chen Qiran:	The original meaning of F.P.A. in English is free from particular average.

Mary:	Does your W.P.A. cover particular average then?
Chen Qiran:	It does. W.P.A. means with particular average in English. The coverage of W.P.A. includes partial losses caused in the course of transit by natural calamities apart from the entire scope of cover for F.P.A.
Mary:	It means that the coverage of W.P.A. is wider than that of F.P.A. then.
Chen Qiran:	That's right and it requires a higher premium too.
Smith:	Mr. Chen, since our order this time is placed on FOB basis, how should we arrange the insurance then?
Chen Qiran:	I suggest that you choose W.P.A.
Smith:	Can we also insure against war risk and S.R.C.C.?
Chen Qiran:	Sure you can, but those belong to the special additional risks.
Smith:	Now I understand, and we can proceed to the discussion of concrete terms for insurance.

(3) Premium and Indemnity

Smith:	Mr. Chen, we placed this order on FOB basis, and how are the liabilities to the risks divided between the two parties?
Chen Qiran:	FOB means free on board, that is to say, as soon as the goods are on board, the seller fulfills its task of delivery and the liabilities are transferred.
Smith:	Then, the risks are borne by you before the goods are on board, and they are borne by us as soon as

the goods are on board.

Chen Qiran: That is correct and it has been written into the contract.

Smith: Mr. Chen, as this batch of goods is vulnerable to breakage, can you insure against the risk of breakage for us?

Chen Qiran: That belongs to general additional risks. We can take the insurance for you but the extra premium will be at your expense.

Smith: Accepted.

Chen Qiran: O. K. As soon as the arrangement is made, we will send the insurance policy to you.

Mary: Thank you, Mr. Chen. Here is another question. In case shortage or breakage should be found upon arrival of the goods, how should we lodge claims?

Chen Qiran: The People's Insurance Company of China has settlement and inspection agent in your country. You can, against the contract, the insurance policy and certificates concerned, lodge claims right in your country.

Smith: Even so, we do hope that everything will be going well.

Chen Qiran: Let's hope so.

Lesson 12
CUSTOMS AND COMMODITY INSPECTION

(1) Customs and Commodity Inspection Practice

Chen Qiran: Mr. Smith, we can now begin our discussion on the clause concerning commodity inspection in our contract.

Smith: Mr. Chen, can you first brief us on the customs and commodity inspection practice of your country?

Chen Qiran: Sure. The customs must exercise supervision and control over the goods imported and exported, and that is an international convention. China is not excepted either.

Mary: Nevertheless, different countries may have different ways in exercising the supervision and control.

Chen Qiran: That is correct. The purpose of customs supervision and control is to safeguard the national interests and those of the trading partners. It is just natural that different countries may have different requirements of supervision and control.

Smith: It is exactly because of this that there may be quite big differences in the inspection requirements, especially when it involves safety, sanitation, environmental protection and the quarantine of animals and plants. Then, does your country have any special laws and regulations?

Chen Qiran: The laws and regulations in this respect are quite complicated, and I suggest that you have a close look at our "Commodity Inspection Law" and the detailed rules for its implementation.

Smith: Good. Tariff is another question that I am concerned with. Can you, Mr. Chen, give me a brief introduction?

Chen Qiran: Oh, here is good news. From 1992, our country has for several times lowered on its own the import tariff rate by a big margin, and the general level of import tariff has been reduced to 17% from the original 43.3%.

Smith: This is heartening news indeed.

Chen Qiran: The reduction involved 4874 tariff numbers, accounting for more than 73% of the scope covered by the tariff regulations.

Mary: Oh, I should acclaim loudly your country for its reduction of tariff barriers by such a big margin.

Chen Qiran: Thank you.

Mary: Mr. Chen, I have got another question.

Chen Qiran: Is it about the customs declaration formalities?

Mary: Yes, I hear that they are extremely complicated.

Chen Qiran: Oh, that was in the past. Now the declaration procedures have been much simplified. They are now both simple and fast.

Mary: Can you elaborate a little bit?

Chen Qiran: Now all customs have adopted the automatic clearance system. Declaration, examination of

	documents, tax collection, inspection and clearance are all computerized into a network.
Mary:	Ah, that is very advanced modern management.
Chen Qiran:	Yes, the person who is responsible for the declaration needs only to hand in the declaration form to the customs officer, wait at another window to get it back, and then he can bring his bill of lading or packing list to go to the supervision and control site for the inspection and clearance procedures.
Mary:	Oh, I now understand. The declaration is really fast and simple.

(2) Negotiation of Contract Terms

Chen Qiran:	Mr. Smith, we have reached agreement on many questions concerning commodity inspection.
Smith:	Yes, we don't have any disputes on the inspection standards of quality, specifications, packing and quantity.
Chen Qiran:	What do you think are the remaining questions then?
Smith:	We need some further consultation concerning which institution is to issue the inspection certificate, and the time and place of the inspection.
Chen Qiran:	I agree, as this has to do with the negotiation of payment, claim and its deadline.
Smith:	We would like to have the quality and weight upon arrival as final.
Chen Qiran:	Are you saying that the inspection is to be carried

out by the inspection authorities at the port of destination?

Smith: Yes, and their inspection certificate is to be taken as final for negotiation of payment and claim.

Chen Qiran: Mr. Smith, this is seldom adopted in international business now. You know that this is obviously unfavorable to the seller.

Smith: What are your suggestions then, Mr. Chen?

Chen Qiran: The certificate issued by the inspection authorities at the port of loading in our country be taken as the basis.

Smith: Ha ha, Mr. Chen, do you think it is fair to our side?

Chen Qiran: You retain the right of re-inspection upon arrival of the goods.

Smith: That's not too bad, and we can accept it.

Chen Qiran: But the institution for re-inspection should meet with our approval.

Smith: O.K.

Chen Qiran: And the deadline for re-inspection is within 30 days from the date of arrival.

Mary: From which date do we start the counting?

Chen Qiran: Of course from the date of arrival.

Mary: The port of destination for this batch of goods is extremely busy, and we can't finish unloading, unpacking and inspection within 30 days.

Chen Qiran: I know the situation of your port, and 30 days is ample time for re-inspection.

Mary: Are holidays included in the 30 days?

Chen Qiran:	Oh, only working days of course.
Smith:	O. K. then, that's settled.
Chen Qiran:	Mr. Smith, we need to fill out an application form for export inspection when going through the export formalities. We hope we can have your assistance.
Smith:	You mean. . .
Chen Qiran:	You know that we need to provide such documents as the contract, letter of credit, and letters exchanged.
Smith:	Oh, I understand. Mr. Chen is worried that we would not open the letter of credit in time and you can't effect customs declaration.
Chen Qiran:	Should the letter of credit not be in exact conformity with the contract, it does not only affect customs declaration, but also the subsequent negotiation of payment. Don't you agree?
Smith:	It is the most basic requirement to ensure that the contract and the documents are in conformity with each other, and we also hope that you will strictly perform this duty of yours.
Chen Qiran:	Sure. We will send you in due time such documents as the invoice, bill of lading, packing list, and other shipping documents. We guarantee that nothing should go wrong.
Smith:	Great! I hope we can take delivery safely without a hitch, and you can safely and smoothly collect payment for the goods.

Lesson 13
CREDIT RISK AND ITS MANAGEMENT

(1) Awareness of Credit Risk

Zhang Xiang: Xiao Wang, now that we have had some contacts with Mr. Ross, what is your impression of him?

Wang An: Very good.

Zhang Xiang: Oh, can you be more specific?

Wang An: According to Mr. Ross, their company is well funded, does big business and has good commercial reputation. In a word, theirs is a big client.

Zhang Xiang: And, what else?

Wang An: And...He is very sincere and frank.

Zhang Xiang: Then, you think we can set our mind at ease in dealing with them boldly?

Wang An: Oh, of course, this is up to you, my general manager.

Zhang Xiang: You little slicker! Please go and contact Ditao Commercial Credit Management Company and we will discuss a commission deal with them.

Wang An: General manager, you mean to entrust them with the credit survey? That is costly. Is it worthwhile?

Zhang Xiang: The survey cost is only several hundred dollars, and th business deal involves millions of dollars.

Wang An: But Mr. Ross says. . . .

Zhang Xiang: Oh, it is not reliable just listening to the client or depending on one's own impression.

Wang An:	I also know that in international trade, it is actually a kind of credit when you provide a foreign client with products or services before being paid and there exist credit risks. But....
Zhang Xiang:	We can't suspect our clients without reason, is that it?
Wang An:	Yes.
Zhang Xiang:	But we must be aware of the credit risk. There are quite a large number of frauds in international trade and all countries in the world have had lessons of this kind. Therefore they all pay great attention to the assessment and management of credit risks. Here are some materials which you should read attentively.

(2) Entrusting a Deal of Credit Survey

Davy:	Oh, welcome. Please take a seat.
Zhang Xiang:	Mr. Davy, we have come to entrust a credit survey to you.
Davy:	The secretary has given me your application form for that purpose.
Zhang Xiang:	We are engaged in a negotiation for an international deal of trade in goods and our partner is a new client. We know little about them apart from some exchange of letters and preliminary contacts.
Davy:	Credit management generally includes the three links of credit survey, credit monitoring and control, and demanding payment of overdue debts.

The credit survey should be the prerequisite for concluding a deal.

Zhang Xiang: That I understand. Not only with new clients, even old clients don't remain unchanged.

Davy: That's right. Old clients may have bad management, meet with difficulties in the flow of funds, or even go bankrupt or close down. Or there may be changes of personnel or important changes in their management strategies. All of these may bring about credit risks.

Zhang Xiang: So we have kept files of our clients from the beginning. But business is developing very fast, which involves large amounts of information, and we can only turn to professional credit consulting and management companies for assistance.

Davy: Now the professional companies of this kind have realized international networking and standardization for credit survey and they have complete databanks that can satisfy the various requirements of the clients.

Zhang Xiang: What kind of information can we obtain then?

Davy: The first is the actual existence of the company. For instance, whether the name, address, telephone number, fax number and web-site of the company supplied by the buyer are genuine, and whether it is a registered company at all.

Zhang Xiang: There have been cases like this. When you find that both your goods and money are lost and you want to take a legal action, you discover that the other party has left behind only an empty house. It turns out that the company you are dealing with simply does not exist.

Davy: Ha, that is the so-called briefcase company.

Zhang Xiang: After getting the money, they fled with the briefcase under their arm. Where can you find them?

Davy: Of course, even more important is that we check closely their payment records and other public records.

Zhang Xiang: That's right. What the seller is most concerned about is whether he can get payment for the goods safely without delay.

Davy: Some companies are solvent. They have the ability to pay for the goods in time and they did. Such records indicate their good commercial reputation.

Zhang Xiang: And we can set our mind more at ease when dealing with such companies.

Davy: Generally speaking, these companies would not delay or refuse to pay without reason.

Zhang Xiang: Are the public records you referred to legal records and pledge records?

Davy: Yes. Through these records, you can get to know whether the company has ever been prosecuted, for what reason, the verdict, whether the assets of the company are in pledge, and to whom.

Zhang Xiang: Mm, it is important to have such information, which can guard against potential risks.

Davy: Of course, official credit report also includes information about the company history, the

	shareholders, managers, performance, assets and debts, banking with whom, and the credit and financial situations.
Zhang Xiang:	That would be excellent. When can we have the report then?
Davy:	You want it ordinary or urgent?
Zhang Xiang:	As our guests do not stay in China for long and they hope to sign the contract soon, we'd better have the report within one week.
Davy:	That shouldn't be a problem. We need to sign a copy of "Trust Deed of Credit Survey of a Company".
Zhang Xiang:	What about the fees?
Davy:	It is included in the trust deed.
Zhang Xiang:	Fine. Please give me a copy of the trust deed.

Lesson 14
SIGNING THE CONTRACT

(1) Negotiating the Contract Terms

Chen Qiran:	Mr. Smith, after a few rounds of friendly negotiations, we have reached an agreement. Can we go down to the discussion of the text of the contract?
Smith:	Yes, on the basis of the previous rounds of negotiations, the wording of the contract will not be difficult. Neither of us is new in business, right?

Chen Qiran:	We've had the experience and know that Mr. Smith is an astute and experienced expert, a master in trade negotiation indeed.
Smith:	Oh, did I commit any breach of etiquette or make any offence in the negotiation?
Chen Qiran:	No, no, I really admire you, Mr. Smith.
Smith:	You flatter me, Mr. Chen.
Chen Qiran:	In order to facilitate the discussion, we have made a draft of the contract for your perusal, Mr. Smith.
Smith:	I don't think there should be any problem with the beginning and ending parts of the contract, but we need to have a good look at the contract proper and the appendices.
Chen Qiran:	Sure, sure. The contract is a deed that stipulates the rights and obligations of the two parties, and neither of us will take it as a trifling matter.
Smith:	You put it right. Both of us are honest and frank with each other. Neither of us will intentionally neglect or omit anything, as we don't want to leave any excuse for the subsequent non-performance of the contract.
Chen Qiran:	I appreciate very much this attitude of yours, Mr. Smith.
Smith:	Then I'll take it back and ponder over it carefully, and we'll discuss it tomorrow.

(2) Checking and Revising the Contract

Chen Qiran:	Mr. Smith, how do you like the contract? Is there anything that needs to be added or further clarified?
Smith:	I checked the articles of the contract one by one, and found that they are in exact conformity with our discussions, the terms are correctly used and the statements are clear and concise. On the whole I am satisfied.
Chen Qiran:	Things would be much simpler then.
Smith:	Yes, I fully agree to the clause about delivery and shipping marks and I have no objection to the quality inspection and penalty clause either.
Chen Qiran:	What about other clauses?
Smith:	I think that the following words should be added after the date of delivery for extra emphasis: "Should the seller fail to deliver the goods as scheduled, the buyer has the right to lodge a claim".
Chen Qiran:	All right. But since this transaction is done on FOB basis, shouldn't we also insert the following: "Should the buyer fail to dispatch a vessel for the delivery of the goods as scheduled, the losses thus incurred to the seller shall be borne by the buyer".
Smith:	O.K. that's fair. Put both of them in. Er, as for the quality of the goods, can we change FAQ to GMQ?
Chen Qiran:	Mr. Smith, we still think that FAQ is better. It stands for fair average quality, and the specifications have been clearly stated in the contract.

	GMQ stands for good merchantable quality and it has uncertain definitions that will easily lead to disputes. We suggest that such terms be avoided.
Smith:	All right, we'll agree to that, so we don't need to make any alterations here then. We'll inspect and accept the goods according to FAQ terms.
Chen Qiran:	Mr. Smith, if you don't have any more disagreements or additions to make concerning the contract and its appendices, we'll take it back to make the necessary alterations, getting ready for the signing tomorrow.
Smith:	I have no other suggestions. See you again at the signing of the contract tomorrow.

(3) Signing of the Contract

Chen Qiran:	Mr. Smith, we have prepared the contract with its appendices in duplicate, one written in Chinese and the other in English. Alterations and additions have been made concerning the questions we discussed yesterday. Will you please have a look? If there are no more questions, then we can put our signatures on it.
Smith:	All right, let me have a look. Er, this is a concrete, clear and perfect contract that has avoided all ambiguous and obscure phrases. I am very much satisfied with it. It has laid a good foundation for the smooth execution of the contract.
Chen Qiran:	It is also a good beginning for the friendly coopera-

tion between us. We hope that our cooperation will
continue.

Smith: Sure, a long-term cooperation.

Chen Qiran: Good. Let's sign then.

Lesson 15
DEMANDING PAYMENT OF A DEBT

(1) Entrusting the Recovery of a Debt

Xu Tianmu: Mr. Ma, a foreign company owes us a sum of
money and we have demanded the payment for
many times to no avail. Now we have to ask for
your assistance.

Ma Qianli: Ours is a debt collection agent and it is our great
pleasure to provide you with our service.

Xu Tianmu: We hope that you can help us get back this sum of
money as soon as possible.

Ma Qianli: We can understand your anxiety. Nowadays,
default has become a frequent phenomenon in international trade, which is getting more and more
serious. Our company receives applications for debt
recovery every day.

Xu Tianmu: We are in a very difficult situation. If we cannot
recover the money in one or two months, we can
hardly carry on.

Ma Qianli: We will do our best. Now please tell me your case.

Xu Tianmu: I have brought with me the contract.

Ma Qianli:	Good. First we need to know some basic information such as the name, address, telephone number, and the contact person of the debtor.
Xu Tianmu:	We did a credit survey and found that all the information you mentioned was genuine.
Ma Qianli:	It might be true when the contract was signed but it might be otherwise now.
Xu Tianmu:	You mean to say that company has gone bankrupt, Mr. Ma?
Ma Qianli:	Oh, I didn't exactly mean that. I was saying that the present situation of that company is something we must investigate before we go to demand the payment of the debt.
Xu Tianmu:	That I understand. Some of our companies suffered because it was not until they demanded payment that they found the debtor was either insolvent because of poor management or going bankrupt and closing down, or either had moved away maliciously or disappeared altogether.
Ma Qianli:	Such things happen too frequently and it is not at all surprising.
Xu Tianmu:	What else do we need to provide, Mr. Ma?
Ma Qianli:	Documents to prove your rights as a creditor, such as the invoice, letter of credit, bill of lading and letters exchanged, apart from the contract.
Xu Tianmu:	O.K. I will have them sent to you presently.
Ma Qianli:	Mr. Xu, how much does the debtor owe you?
Xu Tianmu:	Four million US dollars.
Ma Qianli:	Oh, that is a fortune. How long has it been out-

standing?

Xu Tianmu:	Nearly three years.
Ma Qianli:	Nearly three years? And you haven't taken any actions for the recovery of the money for such a long time?
Xu Tianmu:	We did all we could, and we even forced the other party to sign a "memorandum of payment". But the debtor still used all different reasons to defer payment.
Ma Qianli:	Such memorandum is a mere scrap of paper for an international debt.
Xu Tianmu:	That's true, but are there good ways for the recovery of such debts?
Ma Qianli:	During the past three years, didn't you ask for the help from a collection agent?
Xu Tianmu:	No, we didn't.
Ma Qianli:	That is regrettable. Now 60% of the debts in international trade are being pursued by collection agents.
Xu Tianmu:	When do the creditors normally put forward their application?
Ma Qianli:	Generally speaking, the creditor should start the investigation before the action of recovery when the account receivable is 60 days overdue. And they should entrust a collection agent to demand payment when it is 90 days overdue.
Xu Tianmu:	Then, is it too late for us to apply now?
Ma Qianli:	According to a global statistics for debt recovery, if a debt is overdue for longer than 240 days, the

probability of its recovery is no more than 50%.

Xu Tianmu: Then we will suffer a great loss.

Ma Qianli: Please don't worry too much, Mr. Xu. We will take immediate actions, and please give us your close cooperation.

Xu Tianmu: We surely will.

(2) Contact the Debtor

Davy: Mr. Hans, it is really not easy to meet with you.

Hans: Oh, I am very busy. My secretary told me that you had something important to see me about. What is it?

Davy: Let me introduce myself first. My name is David Green.

Hans: Did we meet somewhere?

Davy: No, I have been asked by somebody else to see you.

Hans: Who is it?

Davy: A trading company in China, and here is my letter of attorney.

Hans: Oh, you are the executive officer in charge of debt recovery from the Asian International Factoring Company. I don't remember owing your client any money.

Davy: Oh, this is a debt of 4 million US dollars. Have you forgotten, Mr. Hans?

Hans: Mm....

Davy: Do I have to show you the contract, invoice, and

	your record of payment?
Hans:	Oh, I would suggest letting the department concerned have a check before I give you a reply.
Davy:	When will you give me the reply then?
Hans:	As soon as possible.
Davy:	Mr. Hans, this debt has been outstanding for more than three years. It cannot be delayed any longer.
Hans:	Sure, sure.
Davy:	We hope that you can repay this debt satisfactorily and you know the consequence of not paying the debt.
Hans:	Sure. Life is not easy either if someone comes to the door to demand payment every day, is it?

(3) Progress Report

Ma Qianli:	Mr. Xu, the reason why I have invited you to come today is to report to you the progress of our debt collection.
Xu Tianmu:	You have good news?
Ma Qianli:	We contacted the debtor several times, and explained to him the severe consequence of non-payment so as to bring great reputation pressure to bear upon him to pay off the debt.
Xu Tianmu:	Was it effective?
Ma Qianli:	No. Later, we bombarded him with phone calls, faxes, and postage-due mail, and sent debt collectors to his doorway to press him for payment of the

	debt, which gave him no peace day or night.
Xu Tianmu:	What was the result?
Ma Qianli:	It looks that we have met with a person who holds "money I don't have, and life I have but one".
Xu Tianmu:	What happened later?
Ma Qianli:	While continuously pressing him for payment, we carried out a large amount of careful investigations and found that company was heavily in debt, already on the brink of going bankrupt.
Xu Tianmu:	Can we appeal to the court to obtain the creditor's lien before their declaration of bankruptcy?
Ma Qianli:	It's too late. The debtor company has received several verdicts from the court against it and two creditor companies have obtained the creditor's lien of its assets.
Xu Tianmu:	There is no way to get our 4 million US dollars back then?
Ma Qianli:	I think we have completed our investigation into and analysis of the debtor's situation. We have done all we can.
Xu Tianmu:	Is there nothing else that you can do?
Ma Qianli:	We believe that any further actions against the debtor are merely a waste of your money. We are sorry but we have to close this case.
Xu Tianmu:	We believed in the other party too readily and now we have to eat our own bitter fruit.

Lesson 16

CLAIM AND ARBITRATION

(1) Inferior Quality

Smith: Mr. Chen, I am very sorry to inform you that the quality of 10% of the bottled Qingdao Beer which you exported this time is not up to the standard set in the contract. We cannot but lodge a claim about it.

Chen Qiran: Qingdao Beer is our famous brand product that enjoys a good international reputation too. Though in our negotiation we agreed to conclude business according to our usual practice against the brand name and trademark, we are confident of the quality of the goods and you also take it as trustworthy. How come that such a problem should have occurred?

Mary: We have asked the commodities inspection department to examine the goods carefully and they found that 10% of the goods are not up to the standard. Maybe it has been caused by a change in the bottles.

Chen Qiran: In the contract we do agree to your right of reinspecting the goods but it must be carried out by a notary public approved by us. Have you got the inspection certificate issued by them?

Mary: Yes, here it is.

Chen Qiran: Fine. We'll look into the matter and then give you a reply. If the situation is just as you said, we will indemnify you.

(2) Short Weight

Chen Qiran: Mr. Smith, concerning the fertilizer we ordered from you, the actual weight received does not conform to the contract stipulations and therefore we cannot effect payment as stipulated in the contract.

Smith: We have included a more or less clause in the article concerning quantity. Short weight within the limits shown in that clause should be allowed.

Chen Qiran: But the short weight has far exceeded the 8% allowed in the contract.

Mary: How could that have happened? Are you sure you have not made a mistake?

Chen Qiran: No. The inspection certificate issued by our Commodities Inspection Bureau indicates that there are two different kinds of packing for this lot of fertilizer. One is 100kg bag and the other is 120kg bag. The short weight may have been caused by a miscalculation in shipment.

Smith: Oh, please show me the certificate issued by your Commodities Inspection Bureau. Er, we have made a mistake indeed. I am very sorry about it and we will settle the claim accordingly.

Chen Qiran: It's nothing serious. Even a winged steed may slip. Please don't take it too hard.

(3) Damage and Loss of Goods

Smith:　　　　　Mr. Chen, after inspection, we found that the porcelain ware we ordered from you suffered a heavy loss from breakage. I am very sorry about it and cannot but lodge a claim against you.

Chen Qiran:　　Mr. Smith, we cannot accept your claim before we find out the actual cause of damage because there may be many different reasons for the breakage. This transaction was done on FOB basis. If the damage occurred on or before the time of shipment, no doubt the responsibility is ours. But if it was caused in transit, according to the liability transfer clause in the contract, it is not our responsibility any more.

Mary:　　　　　Inspection shows that the breakage was actually your own fault. Mr. Chen, please have a look at this.

Chen Qiran:　　All right. Er, I regret to say that it is our responsibility because the damage was caused by improper packing and careless handling. We'll accept your claim. But because porcelain ware is easily breakable, the contract allows for 1-2% breakage. That should be taken into consideration when settling the claim.

Smith:　　　　　Mr. Chen, your request is a reasonable one, which we can accept. In view of our future business relations, we can make a concession concerning the indemnity, which can be offset by replacement of the damaged goods.

Chen Qiran: O. K. Many thanks.

(4) Mediation of Dispute and Arbitration

Chen Qiran: Mr. Smith, concerning Contract No. 453, its payment has been delayed for more than two months and the negotiation of payment has been rejected. No result has been achieved through repeated negotiations. We see no alternative but to refer the matter to arbitration.

Smith: The responsibility is not ours for the non-negotiation of payment.

Chen Qiran: Why isn't it yours? It is because of a mistake in the stipulations of your letter of credit.

Mary: That is not true. The contract stipulates that dried Handan chilies are sold against samples, FOB Xingang, Tianjin, total value being US $ 750,000, packed in 20-25 kilo bags, payment by letter of credit. We opened the covering L/C in due time and dispatched a vessel for the delivery of the goods. We have acted in exact accordance with the contract stipulations.

Chen Qiran: Please don't forget, Mr. Smith, the vessel dispatched by you was too small without enough shipping space and you made a temporary request for us to change the packing into smaller bags of 15 kilos each. You at the same time promised to amend the L/C terms accordingly. We entered into a verbal agreement at that time. However, after the goods were shipped, you failed to keep your promise and that caused the inconsistency between the documents and the L/C, which in turn resulted in the non-negotiation of payment.

Smith: Mr. Chen, you seem to be joking. How can a verbal agreement be counted on for such a big deal? The L/C was opened in exact accordance with the contract. We have to honor the contract. How can its stipulations be altered at will?

Chen Qiran: We have told the truth. Both your agent and the shipping company can evidence that. How can you go back on your promise, Mr. Smith?

Smith: We haven't. On the contrary, what you said is ungrounded, Mr. Chen. I believe that the fundamental reason for the non-negotiation of payment was that the goods supplied are not of the same quality as the samples. It is you who have not acted in exact accordance with the contract.

Chen Qiran: That is not true.

Mary: The breakage is much higher than what is allowed in the contract.

Chen Qiran: That is because the vessel you sent was too small and the goods were squeezed into the holds. The responsibility is not ours.

Mary: The contract stipulated for Handan chilies but the shipment included quite a large proportion of Shanxi chilies.

Chen Qiran: Oh, we did explain during our negotiation that this was a large order and the time allowed for delivery was too short for us to obtain enough supply of the stipulated goods in time. But you made repeated requests for us to meet your demand. Mr. Smith, you couldn't have forgotten, could you?

Smith: Yes, we both appreciated the difficulties of each other.

Chen Qiran: It was in view of our friendship and cooperation that we proposed to fill the order with some Shanxi chilies. Not only did you give your consent; you also expressed repeatedly your thanks to us.

Smith: Yes, but was it stipulated in the contract?

Chen Qiran: But we did reach a verbal agreement.

Smith: I am very sorry. You Chinese attach importance to sentiment and we Americans to reason. We can only act according to the contract signed.

Chen Qiran: It looks like we cannot come to an agreement. We'll have to refer the matter to arbitration.

Smith: We agree.

Lesson 17
AGENCY AGREEMENT

(1) Asking to Become the Sole Agent

Ross: Mr. Li, excuse me for coming straight to the point. The purpose of my coming to China this

	time is to talk with you about the question of your sales agency in the United States.
Li Ning:	You are most welcome. We are more than willing to discuss this question with you, Mr. Ross.
Ross:	You know, Mr. Li, that we have achieved marked success in distributing your products for many years.
Li Ning:	What you say is true, Mr. Ross, and we appreciate it very much.
Ross:	If you appoint us your sole agent in the United States of America, I believe that is beneficial to both parties.
Li Ning:	Oh, do you think the conditions are already mature at present for such appointment?
Ross:	We do have the ability and conditions to act as your sole agent.
Li Ning:	However, according to the market research we did in your country, there is a great demand for our products there, but the volume of your orders was rather limited. That's the reason why we have had to establish business relations with many other clients in your country.
Ross:	Things may be quite different if you give us the exclusive right of selling your products.
Li Ning:	Why?
Ross:	As a matter of fact, it was just because you established a number of agency relations in our country, which gave rise to fierce competition, and we mainly distributed products from other sources.

	Our sales of your products in the past few years were of a trial nature and naturally the volume of our orders was limited.
Li Ning:	Do you mean to say that you are going to cut off the business relations with other companies and concentrate all your efforts on the sale of our products?
Ross:	Yes, and that depends on whether you will give us this honor and opportunity.
Li Ning:	I do admire your talent and daring spirit, Mr. Ross. Can you provide us with some more detailed information such as about your business performance, network, channels and modes of marketing, and your plan as a sole agent.
Ross:	I have brought them with me.
Li Ning:	Ah, you have come fully prepared. Good, we'll have a discussion of the matter.

(2) Rights and Obligations

Li Ning:	Mr. Ross, after consideration, we are very glad to ask you to be our sole agent in your country.
Ross:	We feel highly honored.
Li Ning:	Today, let's discuss some details.
Ross:	Good. Will you please, Mr. Li, give us an idea about our rights and obligations?
Li Ning:	As our sole agent, you have the exclusive right of selling our products in your country.
Ross:	That means you promise not to establish other

	agency relations in our country, does it?
Li Ning:	Yes, and you will receive commission and remuneration which you are entitled to in accordance with the agency agreement.
Ross:	This is international convention as well.
Li Ning:	As for your obligations, we also abide by some common international practices.
Ross:	Good. That will minimize subsequent disputes.
Li Ning:	As our sole agent in your country, you are not supposed to deal in the same or similar products from other countries. Nor are you supposed to re-export our products to places outside your country.
Ross:	These are reasonable restrictions, which we can accept.
Li Ning:	You have also to guarantee a certain annual sales volume and value according to the price agreed upon by the two parties.
Ross:	That's natural, but the sales quota and the commission should be reasonable, and the commission should be increased for the extra sales on top of the quota.
Li Ning:	That can be discussed, but if you fail to perform or do not push the sale actively so that the quota is not fulfilled, the commission will have to be deducted accordingly, or the status as a sole agent may even be annulled.
Ross:	This is also fair.
Li Ning:	As an agent with exclusive rights, you may act as go-between, solicit orders, and sign business con-

tracts with clients as our agent. But one thing I must tell you bluntly beforehand.

Ross: Please go ahead.

Li Ning: You have to inform us of all factual conditions with no reservation. In the agency business, you shall not accept bribes, pursue private ends, or gang up with a third party to jeopardize our interests.

Ross: Oh, these belong to the minimum business ethics as an agent, and exhortation is not necessary.

Li Ning: In order to improve on our production, we hope that you will provide us semi-annually with market research information, advising us of the customer's reaction to our products without delay. Remuneration will also be paid for this kind of information.

Ross: There shouldn't be any problem about that. Since we are now in the same boat and have common interests, we should keep each other informed and consult with each other about measures to be taken.

Li Ning: Let's join hands and cross the river in the same boat.

(3) Quota and Commission

Li Ning: Mr. Ross, today we are going to negotiate the sales quota and commission.

Ross: Mr. Li, you might as well suggest a sales volume for our consideration.

Li Ning:	All right. As Mr. Ross knows extremely well about the sales situation of our products in the international market, there is no need for me to give further explanation. I would come straight to the point.
Ross:	I like this style of work.
Li Ning:	As the sole agent of our corporation in your country, your annual sales value should not be less than US $ 20 million.
Ross:	20 million? Isn't it too high? According to our prediction of our domestic market, even if we exert all our efforts, the best we can do is US $ 15 million for a year.
Li Ning:	The total sales value of our products in your country now has far exceeded US $ 20 million. Aren't you a bit too conservative, Mr. Ross?
Ross:	But there are many variable factors in the market, which are quite unpredictable.
Li Ning:	But when you become our sole agent, you will have no competition and therefore will have control over the entire market. You needn't worry a bit about accomplishing the quota of US $ 20 million.
Ross:	All right then. Let it be US $ 20 million. But the commission must be 5%.
Li Ning:	Isn't what you ask a bit unreasonable?
Ross:	Not at all. Mr. Li, you certainly know the accounts, that is, the expenses and efforts required in order to fulfil the annual sales quota. What's more, you didn't give me any room for negotiation

just now, did you?

Li Ning: All right. We'll accept your proposal as well. About the validity of this sole agency agreement, can we make it shorter this time, say three years?

Ross: That's fine by me.

Li Ning: When the period of three years is over, if both parties think that it is necessary to continue with this kind of cooperation, we can negotiate the extension problem then.

Ross: Good. Will you please prepare a draft agreement for our early signature?

Lesson 18
E-BUSINESS

(1) Do You Have E-Mail

Zhao Lin: Mr. Mike, here is my card.

Mike: Mr. Zhao, how do you do? Oh, you have got e-mail address on it.

ZhaoLin: Why? You find it strange, Mr. Mike?

Mike: When I was in your country last time, the business cards that I received from many CEOs did not have e-mail on them.

Zhao Lin: It's different now. When two people meet, they often ask: "Do you have e-mail?"

Mike: No Chinese friends have asked me that.

Zhao Lin: Of course not, because they know that you have.

	To ask that is in vogue in China now.
Mike:	That's very interesting.
Zhao Lin:	Now almost all those who have business cards have e-mail and the first thing when they get home is to switch on the computer and check the e-mail.
Mike:	I didn't realize that your IT industry developed so fast.
Zhao Lin:	At this information age, how can one manage without e-mail?
Mike:	Especially for people like us working in business. Not having e-mail is just like not having eyes or legs.
Zhao Lin:	You put it well, Mr. Mike. The development of modern information technology has not only got the IT industry opened up and flourishing, but its most profound influence may well be in the area of people's life and traditional modes of economy and trade.
Mike:	Our government has announced that from the 21st century onwards, our trade with other countries will first be conducted through EDI, and paper documents will only be treated afterwards.
Zhao Lin:	E-business based on computer network technology is a great trend in the development of the world's economy and trade. Trading and purchasing on the net is becoming a fashion of consumption. The traditional way of handling paper documents will eventually be discarded, I am afraid.
Mike:	Yes, when all trade is done through EDI (without

the use of paper), that will be e-business in its true sense.

Zhao Lin: So, living in such times, will it do without e-mail?

(2) Virtual Market

Zhao Lin: Mr. Mike, you have made a special trip to China this time, but you can do business with us through the e-business network in the future.

Mike: I certainly hope so. The advantages of e-business are convenience, efficiency, and low cost.

Zhao Lin: Some of our enterprises have come to know the good of e-business. In order to look for supply of goods, they put the information on the net in the afternoon, and received e-mail from scores of suppliers early the next morning.

Mike: This is incomparable by the traditional mode of trading. It reduces substantially the expenses for travel, communication and market survey. This of course lowers the cost of trading.

Zhao Lin: In the past we often said: "Time is money". Now we should say: "Network is time, is money, and is benefit".

Mike: You put it right, Mr. Zhao. Now I would like to know whether our two parties could carry on trade on the net smoothly.

Zhao Lin: Mr. Mike, you mean. . . .

Mike: What I mean is this. There are all sorts of computer network in the world. Some are public and even more are specialized. Where is your web-site?

Zhao Lin: Of course with the Internet.

Mike: Did you say the Internet?

Zhao Lin: Yes.

Mike: The Internet is now the biggest computer network in the world. It is connected with almost all the public computer networks in all countries of the world. It is estimated that it has more than 300 million users. We are one of them.

Zhao Lin: In our country, it is China Telecom that connects the Internet. It is called Chinanet. The Ministry of Foreign Trade and Economic Cooperation has established on the Internet an official web-site called MOFTEC. Therefore, we don't have any barriers in carrying out e-business between us.

Mike: Has it been put to use?

Zhao Lin: Of course. During the first month after it started operation, it was visited by more than 1 million people.

Mike: Really. I am too ill informed.

Zhao Lin: Not only that, on the MOFTEC web-site, the "Chinese Commodities Market" has officially started operation. It has gathered products from tens of thousands of Chinese enterprises, and provided service in all the sectors of foreign trade.

Mike: In that case, I can really deal with you without stepping out of my own room, can't I?

Zhao Lin: Yes. You can catch business opportunities in this "virtual market" on the net, and do business as you wish by entering the crypt-negotiation room.

Mike: However, in the tide of e-business today, illegal operations and frauds are not infrequent. The problem of safety in e-business has always been a headache for the businessmen.

Zhao Lin: That is really a hard nut to crack. But we can use the tracing system to monitor all the links of the transaction and thus avoid the possible risks in due time.

Mike: But on the other hand, there have always been risks. As a matter of fact, the risks hidden in the traditional modes of trade were even greater.

Zhao Lin: Therefore, many big enterprises in your country have established virtual commercial centers on the net and the trade volume has almost reached 100 billion US dollars.

Mike: That is true. Generally speaking, there are only latecomers and no losers.

Zhao Lin: We have full confidence in e-business as well. But of course our computer networking technology is not fully developed yet and many enterprises are still at the stage of "to browse on line, but to conclude deals off line". We....

Mike: One moment. What is meant by "to browse on line, but to conclude deals off line"?

Zhao Lin: That is to seek business opportunities, issue information, look at samples, place orders, and negotiate the price through the Internet. But other business links such as transferring accounts and effecting payments are still carried out in the traditional modes.

Mike: I now understand.

Zhao Lin: Besides, our product flow system for assortment and delivery is not yet perfect. If we do business on the net now, it is hard to avoid losing money just to make a loud cry.

Mike: A rational and perfect product flow system is necessary in order to reduce stock and lower the cost of delivery.

Zhao Lin: Oh, this problem involves various aspects such as technology, management, marketing, and service, and it is very difficult to solve.

Mike: We have undergone this stage as well. Your information industry has been developing very fast and the situation will change before long.

Zhao Lin: Yes, the e-business in its true sense is not far off.

Mike: Good. Let's get started from now.

Lesson 19
MODES OF TRADE PROMOTION ABROAD

(1) Modes of Promotion

Chen Qiran: Mr. George, our corporation will further open up market in your country and we hope that we can

	have your cooperation.
George:	We are old friends and I will do my utmost. But how can I be of help?
Chen Qiran:	You know that in the past we were accustomed to dealing with foreign importers, exporters, agents, and wholesalers. In this way we sometimes had to go through five or six middlemen before we could enter the retail market in a foreign country.
George:	This mode of operation had too many intermediate links, resulting in high cost, slow feedback and high foreign exchange risks.
Chen Qiran:	No one would disagree with you. This outdated and backward mode of operation can no longer suit the present situation of international trade.
George:	The emergence of e-business has formed a tremendous charge against this traditional mode. The development of transnational corporations and the globalization of the world's economy also require that the management strategy be changed and the management level be raised.
Chen Qiran:	Our corporation has come to a sober understanding of this point.
George:	What is your plan then?
Chen Qiran:	In order to develop foreign markets in a deep-going manner, we will first of all change the operation style of waiting in the shop to promotion by visiting the clients.
George:	Please go ahead.
Chen Qiran:	We have decided to organize a delegation to visit

your country so that the parties of supply and demand can meet face to face.

George: I can act as go-between.

Chen Qiran: We particularly wish to establish relations with large-scale international chain stores so that our products can enter their purchase system.

George: That is a wise decision.

Chen Qiran: A large-scale chain store may have hundreds or even thousands of outlets, is that so?

George: Yes, especially those large-scale international chain stores. They may have outlets all over the world.

Chen Qiran: Just imagine. If our products could enter the purchase system of such a chain store, wouldn't it be the same as entering hundreds or even thousands of outlets.

George: That's true, but it is no easy matter trying to enter the purchase system of these chain stores.

Chen Qiran: We know. The key lies in whether our goods have strong competitive power.

George: And they should be known by the consumers, salable and in good demand.

Chen Qiran: Yours is a professional advisory firm and that's the reason why we invite your vigorous help.

George: We can provide relevant information.

Chen Qiran: Not only that.

George: You want us to plan a large-scale activity to promote public relations for your company, is that right?

Chen Qiran: Yes, we'd like to whip up opinion in your country.

George:	To cause a strong sensation.
Chen Qiran:	Yes, to attract large chain stores in your country. The more, the better.
George:	Then, you will carry on various activities to let the participating entrepreneurs know your company and your products.
Chen Qiran:	To do all we can to make them our trading partners, and establish with us stable supply and marketing relations.
George:	Good, we are duty-bound to plan well this activity of public relations.

(2) Exhibitions and Fairs

Chen Qiran:	Mr. George, our company has planned to attend some commodity exhibitions and fairs, and I'd like to ask your advice on several questions.
George:	It is my pleasure to be of help to you.
Chen Qiran:	You know that joining trade fairs is a marketing strategy that is frequently used.
George:	Yes, successful participation in one exhibition may increase the popularity of the enterprise and its products to the maximum, which may result in surging sources of revenue.
Chen Qiran:	But the success of joining an exhibition is restricted by many factors.
George:	First and foremost, it is to choose the right door to enter.
ChenQiran:	That's exactly where I need your help. Now there

are all kinds of exhibitions, commodities fairs, international fairs, both professional and specialized. We must make our own choice.

George: You must select the best-known ones that suit your business scope.

ChenQiran: And so we ask you to provide us with some information such as the nature of the shows, sponsors, participants, sources of visitors, and the publicity campaign by the sponsors.

George: And the environment of the exhibition venue, auxiliary services, and the fees for joining.

Chen Qiran: Yes, they are all important.

George: We can provide you with a copy of detailed information.

Chen Qiran: I have another question about the import and export procedures for the exhibits.

George: Is your country a member of the ATA documentary book?

Chen Qiran: Yes.

George: That makes things simple. ATA documentary book is like the passport for the clearance of goods. ATA documentary book guaranteed by the issuing chamber of commerce can both be substituted as provisional documents for the clearance of goods, and used as guarantee for the exemption of duties on temporary importation.

Chen Qiran: That's terrific. In this way, we'll have enough time to join the exhibition in an unhurried manner.

(3) A Commodities Fair

Chen Qiran:　　Mr. George, we have received your materials about the exhibition.

George:　　Are you satisfied?

Chen Qiran:　　Fantastic. Many thanks.

George:　　You are welcome. Oh, may I ask a question?

Chen Qiran:　　Sure you can.

George:　　Why didn't you think of joining a commodities fair? Or even hold one by yourself.

Chen Qiran:　　Of course we did. But it is of a much larger scale. We must ship enough commodities for visitors to choose and purchase. They will be disappointed if there are not enough commodities.

George:　　Don't you have enough supply of the goods?

Chen Qiran:　　It is not that. But it involves more complicated formalities and higher expenses. And we don't know enough about the market situation in your country yet.

George:　　Even so, I still suggest that you hold a commodities fair at an appropriate time. I know the interest in and demand for you goods by the people of my country.

Chen Qiran:　　Thank you, Mr. George. We will take your suggestion into serious consideration.

George:　　A commodities fair can be run as one for the negotiation of orders, for the introduction of commodities and for technological interchange, killing several birds with one stone.

Chen Qiran: Yes, apart from visiting and choosing from a variety of goods, negotiations can be conducted for large orders, contracts can be signed; seminars and lectures can be given to introduce commodities and new technology, and operations and demonstrations can be carried out on site.

George: In this way many more visitors can be attracted to the exhibition hall and a sensation can be created.

Lesson 20
THE GUANGZHOU FAIR

(1) Meeting the General Manager

Song Jie: Mr. Carter, you are warmly welcome to attend the Chinese Export Commodities Fair.

Carter: Thank you for your kind invitation, General Manager, and I am greatly honored. This is the first time for me to attend the Fair. Please accept my sincere congratulations on the opening of the Fair.

Song Jie: Thank you. There are many other friends who have come for the first time too. Our Guangzhou Fair is becoming more and more prosperous. You see that this huge Chinese Foreign Trade Center does not seem to provide adequate space now.

Carter: I think that the reasons are: firstly, China's implementation of the policy of opening up to the rest of the world has enlivened its economy, prospered the market and increased its foreign trade capability so that clients from all over the world are attracted, and secondly, Guangzhou is China's south gate near to Hong Kong, which facilitates the coming and going of foreign businessmen.

Song Jie: You are absolutely right, Mr. Carter. China started to hold its Export Commodities Fair in Guangzhou in 1957. Two Fairs, one in spring and the other in autumn, have been held each year ever since then. Now scores of sessions have been held. This year, because of the favorable conditions in the climate, the geographical position, and the support of the people, the attendance at the Fair is unprecedented.

George: It is really inspiring.

Song Jie: The Fair has assembled all the national import and export corporations and various categories of export commodities. On the basis of equality and mutual benefit, the Fair combines import with export, and exhibition with transaction. Deals are concluded after examining the samples on the spot. Both the sellers and the buyers feel that the Fair, saving both time and energy, is convenient as well as practical.

George: That's very good indeed. In such an arena of trade, which is highly concentrated, including a wide range of business and allowing a high level of selectivity, one can do all kinds of business accord-

	ing to one's own choice.
Song Jie:	That's true. The Guangzhou Fair is a form of foreign trade which indeed has unique Chinese characteristics. In recent years, the Guangzhou Fair has also undergone great changes. It has become a comprehensive, multifunctional venue for foreign economic relations and trade.
Carter:	Oh, it seems that coming here has indeed been the right thing to do. I not only can feast my eyes but will go back with many successes too.

(2) Visiting the Exhibition Halls

Song Jie:	Mr. George, the Fair building occupies an area of 120,000 square meters, with more than 50 thousand exhibits on display. There are exhibition rooms and negotiation rooms on each floor. We cannot see all of them at one go. What are the goods that you are most interested in, Mr. George?
George:	I am particularly interested in light industrial goods, foodstuffs and handicrafts. But since this is my first visit here, I would like to see as much as I can.
Song Jie:	All right, let's have a look round. We will have a longer stay in those halls that you are interested in.
George:	That's fine.
Song Jie:	Look, without noticing, we are already in the ex-

hibition hall for the Cereals, Oils and Foodstuffs Trading Delegation.

Carter: Oh there are so many things on display. The great variety of exhibits is really a feast for the eyes.

Song Jie: Dear gentlemen, most of the confectionery, cakes and canned foods on display here are of top quality, with special flavor and fine packing. They are extremely good as gifts.

Carter: Er, I should take some of these back so that my friends may have a taste of them.

Song Jie: Mr. George, this is the hall for the Silks Trading Delegation. The exhibits include materials, semi-finished products, and deep-processed high grade finished products, with designs and varieties which are diversified and seriated. It is the best window to a comprehensive understanding of Chinese silks.

George: Oh, they are really beautifully, so many piles of silk as beautiful as flowers that I simply cannot take them all in. China deserves the name of "the country of silks".

Song Jie: Mr. George, we are now in the exhibition area for high-tech, famous brand, top quality and special products.

George: I'd like to have a close look at this area. Oh, this is Haier, this is Changhong, that is Chunlan and we have Little Swan as well.

Song Jie: You are very familiar with them, Mr. George.

George: Oh, these are all internationally famous brands and they are sold in big stores in our country.

Song Jie:	Yes, these brands have been sold far and wide to various countries in the world. This session of the Fair has allocated the most prominent position for the display of the new-generation products of these brands.
Carter:	This hall is big. Are they all high-tech products?
Song Jie:	Yes, they are all high-tech products with high value added. Apart from household appliances, there are IT products, audiovisual products, office automation products and medical instruments.
Carter:	What kind of enterprises are they produced by?
Song Jie:	They mainly come from production enterprises that handle their foreing trade business independently, and those enterprises with foreign investment.
Carter:	Enterprises with foreign investment also take part in the show. That's really something new.
Song Jie:	Enterprises with foreign investment have been developing very fast in recent years and they are more and more active in foreign trade. Their presence at the Guangzhou Fair will surely attract more foreign businessmen to come and invest in China.
Carter:	Yes, we'll have to study this matter earnestly as well.
Song Jie:	You are most welcome to seize the opportunity. Don't let it slip as it may never come again.
Carter:	Sure, sure.
Song Jie:	Mr. George, the Fair is holding several large-scale international symposia. Would you like to go and listen to them?

George:	What are the topics under discussion?
Song Jie:	"Strategy for the International Market", "The Use of E-Business to Open Up the Global Pluralistic Market", "The Successful Entering into the EU Market", etc.
Georgge:	Oh, they are all important issues. Let's go to the symposium on "Strategy for the International Market".
Song Jie:	All right. I'll accompany you there. This way, please.
George:	Thank you. This trip to the Guangzhou Fair is a real eye-opener to me, and a feast for the eyes. It has been a worthwhile journey indeed.

生词总表
Vocabulary List

G

W

责任编辑：龙燕俐

封面设计：安洪民

经贸中级汉语口语

上册

黄为之　编著

*

ⓒ华语教学出版社

华语教学出版社出版

（中国北京百万庄路 24 号）

邮政编码 100037

电话：86-010-68326333／68996153

传真：86-010-68994599

电子信箱：sinolingua@ihw.com.cn

北京外文印刷厂印刷

中国国际图书贸易总公司海外发行

（中国北京车公庄西路 35 号）

北京邮政信箱第 399 号　邮政编码 100044

新华书店国内发行

2001 年（大 32 开）第一版

（汉英）

ISBN 7-80052-538-4／H·870（外）

02600

9-CE-3359PA